CW01368632

The English Town

The English Town

A History

Jeremy Black

First published in Great Britain in 2025 by
Pen & Sword History
An imprint of Pen & Sword Books Limited
Yorkshire – Philadelphia

Copyright © Jeremy Black 2025

ISBN 978 1 03612 379 6

The right of Jeremy Black to be identified as
Author of this Work has been asserted by him in accordance
with the Copyright, Designs and Patents Act 1988.

A CIP catalogue record for this book is
available from the British Library.

All rights reserved. No part of this book may be reproduced, transmitted, downloaded, decompiled or reverse engineered in any form or by any means, electronic or mechanical including photocopying, recording or by any information storage and retrieval system, without permission from the Publisher in writing. NO AI TRAINING: Without in any way limiting the Author's and Publisher's exclusive rights under copyright, any use of this publication to "train" generative artificial intelligence (AI) technologies to generate text is expressly prohibited. The Author and Publisher reserve all rights to license uses of this work for generative AI training and development of machine learning language models.

Typeset by Mac Style
Printed in the UK by CPI Group (UK) Ltd, Croydon, CR0 4YY.

The Publisher's authorised representative in the EU for product safety is Authorised Rep Compliance Ltd., Ground Floor, 71 Lower Baggot Street, Dublin D02 P593, Ireland.
www.arccompliance.com

For a complete list of Pen & Sword titles please contact

PEN & SWORD BOOKS LIMITED
47 Church Street, Barnsley, South Yorkshire, S70 2AS, England
E-mail: enquiries@pen-and-sword.co.uk
Website: www.pen-and-sword.co.uk
or
PEN AND SWORD BOOKS
1950 Lawrence Road, Havertown, PA 19083, USA
E-mail: uspen-and-sword@casematepublishers.com
Website: www.penandswordbooks.com

For Carmel Black

Contents

Preface		viii
Introduction: The Urban Setting		xii
Chapter 1	From the Outset to 1500	1
Chapter 2	Tudor Towns	30
Chapter 3	Stuart Towns	43
Chapter 4	1700–1750	64
Chapter 5	1750–1800	89
Chapter 6	1800–1850	110
Chapter 7	1850–1900	125
Chapter 8	1900–1950	144
Chapter 9	1950–2000	159
Chapter 10	Towns Today	173
List of Abbreviations		187
Notes		188
Index		206

Preface

'Dingy back-to-back houses crowded into courts and alleys of incredible ugliness with a complete disregard for light and air; noisy, smoky and odorous factories scattered at random among the residential parts of the town – all lay under a perpetual pall of smoke from the maze of chimney-pots. Desperate and expensive efforts were being made to rectify faults of fifty years' standing, and the twentieth-century pendulum had swung to the other extreme with a vengeance… Narrow streets which were death-traps to modern traffic were being widened at a fantastic cost.'

Fiction, in this case Barhaven, a manufacturing town, described by W. Stanley Sykes (1894–1961), a West Yorkshire doctor, in his much-reprinted *The Missing Money-Lender* (1931), captures a reality, of both imagination and background experience, for writer and reader alike. Towns are the worked environment, reflecting past and present, their social experiences, economic opportunities, political shocks, cultural aspirations, and much else. Towns are also centres, both stages and subjects, for the collective imagination and, as such, settings for most of our lives as well as counterpoints to each other and to the countryside.

There is an accumulative process to most English towns, at once constructive and destructive. Even the quieter country towns have seen a changing urban lifestyle and fabric. This was a process captured by novelists and honoured in sepia-tinged photographs, but otherwise often lost with the memories of the dying. Again reflecting the extent to which detective novels have to present what appears 'real' as a background to their often improbable plots, Patricia Wentworth, in *Anna, Where Are You?* (1953), wrote of a fictional town with its 'new by pass,' the latter a feature of recent decades:

'Ledlington has a good many points in common with other county towns. Some of it is old and picturesque, and some of it is not. In the years between the two world wars [1918–39] its approaches have been cluttered up with small houses of every type and shape. When these have been passed there are the tall ugly houses of the late Victorian period[1] with their basements, their attics, their dismal outlook upon the shrubberies which screen them from the road. Still farther on a beautiful Georgian house or two, or older still, the mellow red brick and hooded porch of Queen Anne's time [1702–14] – comfortable houses in their day, converted now for the most part to offices and flats. Here the road narrows to the High Street, winding among houses which were built in Elizabethan days. New fronts have been added to some, incongruous plate-glass windows front the street. A turning on one side, very competently blocked by the quite hideous monument erected under William IV [1830–7] to a former mayor, leads to the [railway] station. Nothing more inconvenient could possibly have been devised, but the answer of course is that nobody devised it. Like nearly anything else in England it just happened that way. Every few years some iconoclast on the council proposes that the monument should be removed, but nothing is ever done about it.'

The history of English towns is a political, social, economic, and cultural history, the last in part illustrated here by means of extensive quotations from contemporary literature. This is highly significant as towns and urban living took on meaning in large part due to their presentation.

The nature of non-fictional urban sources is perforce skewed toward the overlapping categories of government, the Church, the educated (who tend to write the newspapers), and the wealthy. Yet, there is plentiful other material, and it provides very instructive commentary, both in its own right and with reference to what it says of other sources. Thus, the records left by a Devizes baker offer much for the late eighteenth century.[2]

So also with the light thrown by the interest in urban history, although this has in recent centuries not been as central as fiction. Thus, it is significant that urban history enjoyed prominence in the early-modern period (sixteenth and seventeenth centuries), in large part as an aspect of urban identity at a time of specific political disputes over town interests.[3] The latter, however, was not the context in the recent period of concern with urban history, as that concern has very much been academic in its forms and content.

From the Roman period, towns were vital spheres of national life and important forcing houses for modernisation and modernity. Towns constituted the living space of the most articulate and best-informed members of society, indeed of the urbane. Furthermore, they were one of the principal products of human activity, the section of the environment most amenable to action, and of society most open to regulation.

Indeed, town planning, whether achieved or only an aspiration, revealed concern with air and light, public hygiene and open spaces. Yet in the past, as in the present, the creation of a regulated environment is not simply functional in its rationale, for example seeking to improve transport. This creation also reflects an intellectual plan based upon moral vision, an attempt to create harmony upon Earth, a spirit of change. Indeed, Daniel Defoe captured this in terms of divine intentions, writing, in his *A Tour Thro' the Whole Island of Great Britain* (1724–7), of Ipswich:

> 'I cannot think but that Providence, which made nothing in vain, cannot have reserved so useful, so convenient a port to lie vacant in the world, but that the time will some time or other come (especially considering the improving temper of the present age) when some peculiar beneficial business may be found out, to make the port of Ipswich as useful to the world, and the town as flourishing, as Nature has made it proper and capable to be.'

The specific manifestations of the spirit of change ranged from new drains and larger police forces to religious renewal, but the need for conscious direction and improvements to the urban environment was widely accepted. Much action derived from the scale of the resulting issues facing urban communities as well as central government, from disorder and crime, to poverty and pollution. The desire for improvement repeatedly created issues, as did the inherent situation.

It is impossible to tell national history without understanding the urban experience. For each town, their particular position and relative ranking, their environmental impact, physical structure, economic significance, social experience, and cultural standing and contribution, are all important factors; and in aggregate these are significant as part of the themes of nationhood.

Most of us in England live in towns, settlements larger than villages. The same is true of Britain as a whole, and Europe, indeed the world, but the history of English towns is that of the first major modern country that urbanised, and with urbanisation a key part of its national history. This then is town history and national history.

A personal note. Born in London (however much Wikipedia once gave me a Cambridge birth), I lived there until 1975, and then, after a brief period in rural Scotland, in Cambridge (1975–8), Oxford (1978–80), Durham (1980–3), Newcastle (1983–96), and Exeter (1996–). During my London years, I saw relatively little of the towns elsewhere in the country until I began youth hostelling. Subsequently, academic research took me across the urban landscape as record offices are invariably in towns and usually in county capitals.

So also with lecturing and examining in other universities. Indeed, Higher Education is as one with much of modern English life in being located in towns. Even the campuses built outside towns, for example those of East Anglia (Norwich), Essex (Colchester), Lancaster, Sussex (Brighton), Warwick, and York, are both relatively small towns in their own right and part of the wider local and regional urban community. Yet, as so often with towns, they are also a product not only of national networks but also of international ones.

Revisiting towns during thinking about the writing of this book has proved pleasant and instructive despite repeated rail strikes, although Ian Cook's determination on a cold day to make me appreciate Poundbury, in the face of my reluctance, was overly bracing. When he asked three young women whether they enjoyed living there, I told them they needed to watch that sort of approach from elderly men.

I have benefited from the advice of Jonathan Barry, John Blair, Grayson Ditchfield, Perry Gauci, Bill Gibson, Martin Pitts, Nigel Ramsay, George Robb, Mark Stoyle, and Henry Summerson on earlier drafts of all or part of the book. They are not responsible for any remaining errors. The book is dedicated, with much affection, to my niece Carmel, a committed Londoner.

Introduction

The Urban Setting

'[The] infamous borough of Mitchell, a paultry village consisting of about 20 poor thatched cottages ... the chief support of the place is election for burgesses, at which time they make no scruple of selling their votes to the highest bidder, and afterwards inform against their benefactors if the adverse party will bribe them to it.'

John Evelyn, Cornwall, 1702. Mitchell, a 'rotten borough', returned two MPs from 1547 to 1832. In 1831, there were seven voters.[1]

This was not the famous writer of that name.

'HE MAY BE IN *YOUR* Town.' The caption in the fictional *Daily Flicker*, in Agatha Christie's novel *The ABC Murders* (1936), captured the identification of people and place that once made towns so much more important. Ever since the 1851 census, Britain has had an urban majority, defined then in terms of settlements of over 2,000 inhabitants, a definition, moreover, that did not capture the extent to which there were also short-term visitors from the surrounding hinterland for work and/or leisure. Towns, large or small, have been the settings for an experience that is not defined by the touchstones, timetables, and pressures of rural life.

Town life has also alarmed many. Turning back to 1763, Lieutenant-General Joseph Yorke, son of a Lord Chancellor, an MP and diplomat, was in no doubt about the problem posed by London:

'Don't you think that the overgrown size of our metropolis is one great cause of the frivolousness, idleness and debauchery of the times? I have often wondered that the Legislature has not long since laboured to put bounds to its increase, for it is really too big for the good observance of the Law of the Gospel ... a weak Police can lay but little restraint upon such multitudes.'[2]

The capital, as it clearly was from the eleventh century, and large towns, more generally, have greatly influenced notions of urban life. Discussion of London, always the largest town over the last millennium, and indeed for nearly two millennia in so far as estimates are possible for the first post-Roman centuries, has had a disproportionate impact on the account of English urban history, indeed on English history as a whole. It had exceptional features due to scale and function, but in addition, in practice, much that was seen in the capital (Westminster, the centre of government, was a separate entity, but part of the same urban area) was a matter of quantitative rather than qualitative difference, being also found elsewhere.

Towns, for example, were the central points in the overlapping worlds of crime: they provided a concentration of victims and a recruiting ground of and for criminals.[3] In this way, crime both affected urban living, as with the development of home security, and was affected by it, as in the opportunities and challenges posed.

Moreover, crime helped focus and fire the images and anxieties of urban life.[4] Thus, the playwright Thomas Dekker (c.1572–1622) depicted urban swindlers, as in *The Belman of London* (1608), as organising themselves as if a shadow economy, part of an overlap between criminality and the non-criminal world. This overlap was taken further in themes of a similar organisational structure and ethos for criminal and non-criminal networks,[5] themes that were also to be seen in the early eighteenth century, with John Gay's *The Beggar's Opera* (1728). London as the capital of the state was a parallel to London as the capital of crime. Towns were also the key markets for stolen goods, and the places where there were established networks dealing in new or second-hand goods that could be used by criminals, part of the interplay of makeshift economies and criminality.[6] This situation continues to the present, towns today being the central places for drug-dealing and the sale of contraband cigarettes. The so-called 'county lines' in drug-dealing originate in towns.

As prisons were usually in towns, it is worth remembering that part of the urban population was those detained, whether their offences were urban or rural in their location. Thus, in early 1678, the County House of Correction at Stafford, established in 1649, held ten prisoners: three men for being pilferers and two for being idle and leading a bad course of life; one woman for pilfering, two for being idle and disorderly, one for being very disorderly, and one for having bastards, the last a cause of extra cost for the Poor Rate.[7]

Prostitution was part of urban life. In his novel *Moll Flanders* (1722), Defoe described this as of considerable scale in London and bringing the risk of venereal disease: 'sowing the contagion in the life-blood of his posterity … when he is, as it were, drunk in the ecstasies of his wicked pleasure, her hands are in his pockets,' supplementing her income through theft. In his *Life of Gladstone* (1903), John Morley was to use 'the great sin of great cities' as his euphemism for prostitution.

Similarly, with the staging in towns of what historians termed the 'moral economy' of the crowd, it was commonplace to see action being undertaken to ensure appropriate conduct, an instance of which was reported by *Berrow's Worcester Journal* in its issue of 25 September 1766:

'Yesterday there was a great disturbance here, occasioned by the market people asking 8d and some 9d a pound for butter, and refusing to take 6d, whereupon the populace seized several baskets, and sold out the butter at 6 pence per pound.'

Such activism was also seen in rural areas but was more present in towns, or, at least, much more likely to be reported there. This activism, which could be seen in response to both prices and wages, could rest on desperation, as noted in the Durham report in the (London) *Daily Post* of 30 January 1731:

'Great numbers of the wives and children of the coal-pit men are begging about in all the neighbouring towns, by reason their husbands have not their usual work, and are forced to draw coals about for small pay, to prevent starving. We are in great dread of them.'

A sense of popular life as out of control linked moralists across the ages, although they were inclined to downplay the extent to which there were still 'rules', in the sense of conventions, in such activity. In his *Tour*, Defoe was harsh in his account of Charlton Horn Fair, a scene of popular festivities, held at Cuckold's Point on the Thames east of London until, in 1872, it was closed because of its disorder:

> '...the yearly collected rabble of mad-people, at Horn-Fair; the rudeness of which I cannot but think, is such as ought to be suppressed, and indeed in a civilised well-governed nation, it may well be said to be unsufferable. The mob indeed at that time takes all kinds of liberties, and the women are especially imprudent for that day; as if it was a day that justified the giving themselves a loose to all manner of indecency and immodesty, without any reproach, or without suffering the censure which such behaviour would deserve at another time... I recommend it to the public justice to be suppressed, as a nuisance and offence to all sober people.'

This was less serious, however, than the real and potential political aspect of disorder. Thus, during the 1722 elections, John, Lord Perceval, a Whig, reported of the Tory opposition, 'The mob which is generally High Church have where they are strongest been insufferably rude as at Westminster, Reading, Stafford etc.'[8] In turn, writing from York in 1721 to an opposition political ally, Philip, 1st Duke of Wharton provided evidence of the impact, however short-lived, of the bursting of the fraudulent financial speculation of the South Sea Bubble on that town, as well as illustrating the ambiguous nature of contemporary evidence:

> 'The city itself is but poor, the trade being very low and the last stroke to our credit has completed their misery. On the other hand everything is excessive cheap which in some degree makes amends for the scarcity.'[9]

York, however, was not conspicuous in the 1720s as an example of civic decline. There was extensive building in the city, a new Mansion House testified to civic pride and wealth, and York sustained an active local press. Wharton's letter, indeed, can be seen as an unreliable source, one written for political purposes, his description of York intended to be repeated to others as proof of the deleterious impact of the fiscal situation. On the other hand, in 1722, a Tory was one of the two MPs elected, unlike in the general elections of 1715 and 1727 and the by-election of 1725. Thus, there was an electoral revolution in 1722, with the Tory top of the poll and it is possible that this owed something to short-term economic difficulties.[10] More generally, the prosperity of the period should not detract from the severity of short-term problems. How far the same point can be made for other instances repays consideration.

Differently, in 1773, George III reflected on the contrasts in urban opinion when he left London, where criticism of him and his governments was vociferous, and had been so since 1761, to visit Portsmouth. This was reflected in London-based visual satires, as well as newspapers and pamphlets. In contrast to the usual situation with ports being particular centres of illegality due to the prevalence of smuggling and the evasion of customs duty, the presence in Portsmouth of the leading naval base resulted in an attitude of loyalty, one that was to be repeated when George visited again in 1778 and 1794. On the 1773 visit, the painter Joshua Reynolds observed:

> 'The King is exceeding delighted with his reception at Portsmouth. He said to a person about that he was convinced he was not so unpopular as the newspapers would represent him to be. The acclamations of the people were indeed prodigious. On his return all the country assembled in the towns where he changed horses. At Godalming every man had a branch of a tree in his hand and every woman a nosegay which they had presented to the King (the horses moving as slow as possible) till he was up to the knees in flowers, and they were all singing in a tumultuous manner, God Save the King. The King was so affected that he could not refrain shedding abundance of tears, and even joined in the chorus.'[11]

There are, moreover, problems involved in assessing the evidence of trends, as well as the perceptions of contemporaries, as with the observation that 'towns are forever declining from some golden age in the distant and undefined past.'[12] There is also in any discussion of urban politics, the vexed question of how far policy and, separately, change are to be explained by élite wishes and how far popular agency played a role.[13]

There is an attempt in this book to offer the long-term perspective that captures the reality of the reworking of towns and neighbourhoods to reflect changing needs and opportunities.[14] The emphasis is more particularly on the recent centuries for it is then that the country became increasingly urban in lifestyle and attitudes.

This was far from an unproblematic or uncontentious process, and there is a danger that a general account can smooth out these elements. On 25 May 1924, the *Times* noted: 'The life of England becomes every day more urban and yet the people never cared more about the country.'

Moreover, alongside growth, permanence and durability, can come decline and crisis, either for towns as a whole or for sections of both towns and their population. This is an aspect of the complexity that is central for town life and urban prosperity. They require reasons for sustaining prosperity, not least in order to provide for the resources and services they receive, a process only more recently provided in part by redistributive taxation and the consequent funding of social welfare. Indeed, from the outset, towns required reasons to exist and grow. Nothing was inevitable.

The problematic nature of urban history extends to the sources used. Urban maps are a key element, although the mapping of smaller towns was limited prior to the nineteenth century, unless they were dominated by one large landowner, as with Woburn and the Dukes of Bedford. In the past and to this day, urban maps are generally organised in terms of streets, such as the *London A-Z*. In the 'A-Z'-ing of life, habitations emerge as the spaces between streets. Differences within a town, for example of wealth, or of environmental or housing quality, are ignored. The perceptions that create and reflect senses of urban space, often rival, contested and atavistic, are neglected, in favour of a bland uniform background that is described, and thus explained, insofar as there is any explanation, in terms of roads. This is not a world of neighbourhoods, of upwardly or downwardly socially mobile quarters, of areas largely inhabited by families or by singles. Such blandness is necessary in order to highlight the roads, although the roads are not depicted in proportion to their traffic density. Furthermore, town maps today are very much ground level, with little, if any, suggestion of the vertical, although the Tudor mapmaker John Speed tried to convey verticality in his maps with castles, churches and walls, as with the map of

Exeter.[15] Today, focused on the roads, the town is a space to be traversed, a region to be manipulated, or overcome, in the individual's search for a given destination, and not an area composed of neighbourhoods, one to be lived in and through.[16] There are clues to environmental quality in maps in terms of the presence of parkland and the distance between streets, but no guidance to pollution, and nothing that matches the awareness of detailed variations known by political canvassers, police officers, or estate agents. For them, the town is a geography of zones and boundaries, a geography more particularly of detail.

There can also be a comparable weakness in historical atlases of towns. Thus, *Mapping the Past – Wolverhampton 1577–1986*, which was published by the Wolverhampton Library and Information Services Division in 1993, included, as its last map, a section of the Ordnance Survey map for the city centre. This showed the new ring road and the accompanying text referred to the clearance of 'sub-standard housing'; but there was no reference to the destruction or dislocation of neighbourhoods that were involved. The reader had to infer them, but that was clearly not the intention.

Rather like social groups,[17] towns are not easy to define or classify, not least in contrast to other settlements. From an archaeological point of view, definitions of site status can be derived from the evidence of consumption,[18] but other factors are pertinent. Thus, Cadbury, a large hill-fort, where a noble warrior, possibly the prototype of King Arthur, lived, was a pre- and post-Roman military 'town', a fort as town rather than town as fort. This is indicated by its name, Cadbury, meaning Cada's fort, the word 'burg' found in the names of many early towns meaning fortress.

The conceptual issue of towns in a non-urban world poses anthropological questions, with ritual and symbolic activity as a cause, rather than an outcome, of political and economic activity, and of town formation accordingly. Hence, the significance of religious sites, and of minsters in the generation of a large number of Anglo-Saxon towns, notably small ones that were not seaports.[19] Alternatively, consumption as a factor in the definition of towns, and with consumption far from restricted to material goods, can be less helpful for periods in which wealth may be more concentrated outside towns, albeit sometimes in suburban or 'ex-urban' neighbourhoods: the 'ex-urbs' is an

American term not used in England, one that reflects the need to distinguish between types of suburbia.

Separately, legal definitions of urban status in the past or present, for example as boroughs, are of limited value, a point captured by the use of the term 'rotten boroughs' to refer to boroughs with few inhabitants, for example Old Sarum near Salisbury. Even those with more inhabitants could be under a degree of control or, at least, very considerable influence. Yet, scepticism about the degree of influence could also be expressed over more populous boroughs where the representation was in part controlled. The Courtenays, Earls of Devon, were Lords of the Manor of Honiton where they appointed the Returning Officer as well as officials, and members of the family won elections there, as in 1734 and 1754. There are further complications. Medieval Durham, for example, was divided into five 'boroughs', ensuring no single town hall, as well as scant general communal activity.[20]

The idea of legal status as determining a town focused on charters which agreed privileges and rights. London gained one, the first, in 1067, Bristol in 1155, and so on; with the establishment of local courts considered as crucial, and thus providing a legal freedom from the personal and communal duties of being under a lord. Elected officials were also important.

Yet such criteria were particular to a period, and did not exist for other settlements that were clearly towns, notably earlier Anglo-Saxon ones. The *Domesday Book* of 1086, by when only London clearly had a charter, reveals that over 30 towns probably had over 1,000 people, with 17 of these having over 2,000,[21] and some towns, notably London and Lincoln, having considerably more. Legal definitions across Europe paid only limited attention to size or function. Thus, in the eighteenth century, in Poland towns were legally incorporated institutions, irrespective of size or function. Settlements without owners were defined as towns in Russia and all subject to the same laws and regulations, and contrasted legally with settlements that were the property of an individual or an institution. Manchester was not incorporated until 1835.

City status in the past, as well as today, is also open to much debate. There is no fixed definition of a city in Britain, and, in practice, it has been a matter of royal pleasure exercised through governmental decision, as with Southend in 2022. The traditional practice of a cathedral town having city status, a practice that excluded many leading towns, was seen when Henry VIII made the six towns to which he gave cathedral status, cities, but was not automatic. Rochester, which has a cathedral, lost its city status in 1998 as a result of local governmental changes. It was only in 1974 that a royal charter affirmed city status for Ely, and Guildford has a cathedral but was turned down for city status in 2002.

There has been the often reluctant concession that major urban centres, such as Birmingham, should gain city status. In 1907, a minimum threshold for city status of 300,000 people was proposed, but not followed; and the results over the years in defining city status have been episodic and inconsistent.[22] This remains the case today, and discussion over the towns that attain city status are apt to underplay or ignore completely the political factors involved, political both in the partisan context, but also in the wider sense of appropriate social indicators and cultural assumptions. Cambridge was not a city, officially, until 1951. More recent creations include Brighton and Hove (2000), Derby (1977), Preston (2002), and Wolverhampton (2000).

Moreover, classification, parameters, and measures of urban status and activity change across time, one seen in particular when status is changed by government action. The disappearance of towns in part reflects the expansion of others, as with Bromley, a medieval market town eventually swallowed up by London. Parliamentary redistribution of seats returning MPs was another aspect of governmental change.

A number of medieval boroughs failed altogether.[23] By then definitions linked to size of population made clear sense but, earlier, notably for Anglo-Saxon England before 1000, it is somewhat unclear that later definitions of big and small towns are of great help.

In his *Tour*, Defoe, who was very concerned with the positive advantages of commerce, ranked towns in large part with reference to how far they helped the nation's commercial interests, rather than employing historic designations as cathedral sees or county centres. For Defoe, Liverpool, which was neither, was more consequential than, respectively, St David's or Oakham:

'My business is not the situation or a mere geographical description of it; I have nothing to do with the longitude of places, the antiquities of towns, corporation buildings, charters etc. but to give you a view of the whole in its present state, as also of the commerce, curiosities and customs.'

These problems were scarcely limited to England, and the same is true of the use of modern definitions, for example that of the town as a creator of 'effective space', a nexus whose most crucial export was control and the locus of a characteristic urban lifestyle. This approach ignores the large number of small settlements, classified as towns, who only in part matched this definition.

In general, a functional definition of town is adopted here, one that indeed did alter in its measures but was of importance in order to distinguish towns from countryside. These differences were varied, but significant, and of importance to attitudes and cultural stereotypes as well as to functional factors. Whatever the criteria, the town as a whole may be of only limited value as the unit for attention. Neighbourhoods within which kin lived, poor relief was sought, worship was conducted, and sociability occurred, were more significant than towns as a whole.[24] That element continues to the present, with many identifying with primarily local concerns and occupational affiliations and caring little about nearby neighbourhoods of different social background, such as Blackbird Leys, a poor part of Oxford.

The 'small people of the town', to use a phrase of Thomas Usk, a late fourteenth-century London scrivener, were, and remain, those for whom the sources are most fragmentary, unless they record the unwelcome attention of the law. Such people overlapped with marginal groups, such as prostitutes, vagrants, lepers, migrants from within the British Isles as well as beyond, those who were marginalised, in part by their actions, in part simply by being, but to a large degree in the response of the authorities. An urban history that takes full account of these groups is not one that is easy to attempt, but this dimension needs to be borne in mind.[25] A good source are workhouse admissions registers, not least because they reflect the social strains of much urban life, especially family breakdown linked to economic crises, dearth, death and desertion.[26] They are often the only means of identifying the otherwise anonymous urban poor individually by name.

It is important to strike a balance. Defoe counterpointed a sense of aggregate national improvement with the much more varied fortunes of particular communities, observing in the *Tour*:

'since the increase of shipping and trade, bigger ships being brought into use, than were formerly built, and the harbour at Minehead being fairer and much deeper, than those at Watchet and Porlock, and therefore able to secure those greater ships, which the others were not, the merchants removed to it.'

Separately, the proclamation of Charles III as king in 2022 was very much an urban activity, and necessarily so for it is in towns that the institutions of government, secular and religious, such as county council headquarters and cathedrals, are situated. So also across the centuries. Thus, on 30 December 1718, the *St James's Evening Post* reported from Malling in Kent:

'This afternoon the bailiff of this town, attended by a number of loyal gentlemen, mounted on horseback with their swords drawn, read His Majesty's declaration of war against Spain, and afterwards proceeded to the Crown Tavern, where a noble bowl of punch was provided to His Majesty's health, success to the war and the present ministers.'

Alongside the emphasis on towns or, more specifically, individual towns, it is important to underline the extent to which the history of towns is inseparable from that of the country as a whole. Towns were dependent on the state being able to provide security against external and internal threats, and on the strength and development of the economy. Thus, the rise in domestic agricultural production was important to the ability of towns to grow, as was the increased use of coal, as opposed to bulkier wood which was harder to transport and gave less calorific value by volume. In the seventeenth and eighteenth centuries, this opened up major contrasts with Continental Europe.[27] The growth of English towns depended on a dynamic national market economy with no internal tariff boundaries.

These contrasts enable us to look at the issue of English exceptionalism anew. The constitutional-political route to this is not initially very helpful, as medieval and early-modern English towns were scarcely 'ahead' in terms of liberty and freedoms when compared with many of their Continental counterparts, notably in (modern) Germany, Italy, and the Netherlands; although, as far as more united states were concerned, especially France and Spain, English towns did emerge as 'ahead.' In part, this was due to the chartered liberties of individual towns, a situation matched on the Continent; but, more generally, this advantage was a result of the parliamentary system and practice.

This was even more the case because boroughs were over-valued in the House of Commons, in comparison to the electorate of the county seats. There were far more borough than county seats, however much the prestige of the latter. Conversely, there was no representation of towns in the House of Lords. However, peers might act as patrons of towns, and speak up for them and try to maintain their interests.

As the power of the House of Lords declined, in large part due to its lack of tax-raising abilities, so that of the Commons rose in relative terms. Moreover, a key theme of longstanding political contention was resolved, during the 'Revolution Settlement' after the 'Glorious Revolution' of 1688–9, in favour of Parliament meeting every year. This was accompanied by frequent elections, and considerable parliamentary powers over taxation, albeit without Parliament gaining any executive power. This left England as a polity in which the towns were crucial politically, a situation that was not challenged by subsequent Parliamentary union with Scotland and Ireland, nor by imperial expansion and wealth and the opportunities it could bring for the state, for example enabling Portuguese rulers not to call the Cortes. In England, as elsewhere, urban history is very much part of total history.

Chapter 1

From the Outset to 1500

The skeletons offer a bleak account of urban life. In 1987, 436 were removed when the churchyard of St Margaret's Fyebridge in Norwich was excavated. In use from about 1200 to 1486, the cemetery yielded evidence of privation, pain and limited physical capacity. It was a part of the town that was poor, and others were not.[1] Nevertheless, the evidence from these skeletons could have been repeated right across the urban landscape, as shown by the analysis of the over 10,000 skeletons from the graveyard of St Mary Spital in London buried in the mid-thirteenth century, probably as a result of famine.[2] The wealthy also suffered much from the hazards as well as general nature of life, even if one of their standard characteristics was greater weight; and this absence of malnutrition did have significant health advantages, mental as well as physical.

With the Bronze Age in England, which began in about 2500–2000 BCE, and lasted until about 800 BCE, there was a clear shift from nomadism to settlement and farming, although this development has also been put earlier, in the Neolithic Age.[3] The increased permanence of larger settlements was linked to the development of trading routes, for example along the middle Thames, and related commercial networks. As a different but related process, there is increased evidence of fortifications, notably of defended hill-top settlements, although there is considerable debate as to whether these were permanent settlements. The lack of water on many hilltops suggests otherwise; although, encouraging higher settlement, some riverbanks would have been threatened by seasonal flooding. Defensive enclosures were not all on hilltops. Thus, there was an Iron Age one at Abingdon.

During the succeeding Iron Age, which began in about 800 BCE, the population rose and agriculture improved. In a related process, by the time of the first Roman attacks in 55 and 54 BCE, proto-towns (larger and more complex settlements), tribal 'states' with chieftain patterns of tribal organisation, and populations of tens of thousands, and coins (with the first written words), came to exist in southern England.

There were Iron Age proto-towns, known to the Romans as *oppida*, but Iron Age England had not developed an urban civilisation; although there are the problems posed by the nature and interpretation of the archaeological record as well as by the need to rely for literary sources on Roman material,[4] relating to Julius Caesar's invasions of 55 and 54 BCE or to the permanent conquest that began in 43 CE. Late Iron Age *oppida* that were to become the sites of Roman cities and that had urban characteristics, notably as political centres, included Chichester, Silchester, Colchester and, possibly, Canterbury and St Albans – to use their later names.[5] These would have been different, at least to a degree, to the 'imposed' towns established by the Romans at locations that had previously not been *oppida*. Focusing on these imposed towns, rather than on towns as emerging as markets for rural hinterlands, Roman towns in England served political and military purposes, indeed on a pattern that was more significant for urban history, English and non-English, than is sometimes allowed.[6]

In contrast to the situation in southern England, relatively low population levels and a poorly-developed agricultural base in northern England, as in Wales, Scotland and Ireland, ensured that there was only a small surplus of wealth to support urban life. Yet, in northern as much as in southern England, the Romans very much brought a new intensity in urban activity, one highlighted by the limited development of towns in northern Europe outside the Roman world – although the later histories of towns such as Aberdeen (a Scottish town later, but not during the Roman period) scarcely suggest that Roman conquest was necessary for subsequent prominence.

Roman forts proved the basis for a number of towns, such as Carlisle, Chester, Exeter, Lincoln and York, as well as less successful towns such as Great Casterton, while Colchester, Lincoln and Gloucester developed as *coloniae*, towns for veterans. The military basis, or at least context, for early Roman urban settlement was clear in 60 CE, when the Iceni rose under their ruler, Boudicca, and destroyed the major settlements, which were then Colchester, St Albans and London, only to be totally defeated soon after. Yet the military origins could be very short-term, for towns that were legionary fortresses could swiftly lose this function, for example Exeter, although it nevertheless remained a town of consequence.

The administrative hierarchy and military system were not unchanging during the Roman period which lasted until 409. The major towns remained significant, however, albeit with differing emphases. Rectilinear grid street plans, centred on forums and basilicas, developed in these towns and the surviving engineering is impressive. In York, which became the capital of the province of *Britannia Inferior* (northern Roman Britain), the Roman sewer in Church Street was made of huge millstone grit blocks and was used to serve the legionary bath buildings nearby. Ironically, perhaps, Emperor Septimius Severus died of disease at York in 211 after invading Scotland.

Some towns, usually now with 'chester' in their name, emerged alongside fortresses, but others developed apparently as a result of initiatives by native élites that were keen to adopt Roman culture and material life. Writing of the 70s and 80s, the Roman historian Tacitus noted that the Britons 'spoke of such novelties as "civilisation", when really they were only a feature of enslavement.'[7] Whatever their origin, towns were centres of authority, trade, consumptions and Roman culture, including, eventually, Christianity. The last succeeded the Olympian cults, that of Mithras, and local cults, for example at Bath, in many urban locations.

Towns were in practice arranged in networks of government and economics. Thus, in the rural hinterland of London, supplies for it were organised by the smaller towns of the region such as Brentford, Ewell and Staines. For these and other purposes, roads linked towns. Thus, from London, Watling Street went to Chester and Dover, Ermine Street to York, and Stane Street to Chichester. At the same time, Chester, Gloucester, Lincoln, London and York were also river ports, while the Roman presence was ultimately dependent on maritime links to the Continent, links that were important to the development of London, and the Kent ports of Dover and Richborough from which the first stage of Watling Street ran to London.

London was established by the Romans at a strategic location on the north bank of the Thames, which, as in the case of most rivers, was much wider than today, remaining so until embankments were built from the mid-nineteenth century onwards when major rivers were in effect canalised. Moreover, the river was tidal to where the Romans built London. The low gravel banks of the north bank provided well-drained firmness for construction, and also a good site for the first bridge across the Thames. This communication node therefore linked a maritime route to the rest of the Roman Empire with roads within Roman Britain, notably Ermine Street and Watling Street – roads that are the basis for modern routes, respectively the A10 and A5. The first stage of the latter beyond London is the Edgware Road.

After Boudicca's revolt was decisively crushed in 60 CE, London was speedily rebuilt and repopulated, a testimony to the dynamism of Roman Britain, the economic possibilities of London, and the Roman determination to hold on to Britain at all costs, although it could not have made a return on the expenditure on its huge army. The town quickly attracted not only foreign settlers but also the indigenous population. New buildings in the late first century CE included public baths and a wooden amphitheatre. Not a legionary (leading military) base, for these were in or near frontier zones, London, nevertheless, developed as the key port. This made it more suitable as a city and governmental centre than the original official Roman capital, Colchester. This state of affairs prefigured the relationship between London and Winchester in the eleventh century.

Different to the other major centres in Roman Britain in being a major port, London nonetheless was not one of the leading provincial towns of the Empire, like Lyons or Trier. In part, this was because Britain's economic and demographic weight in the Empire was less than that of France or Spain. Nevertheless, as a town of considerable scale, London had large buildings, as well as a very large forum, considerably more extensive than Trafalgar Square; thanks to its commerce and role within the Empire, the town also had a highly cosmopolitan community. Roman London was the key point for the imperial coloniser, and trade and governance were organised accordingly.

Aside from the large suburb on the south bank, the standard Roman rectilinear grid street-plan in the main town, centred on forum and basilica, was an attempt to give shape to a more complex reality in which there were variations in land-use by function and fashion, commerce and manufacturing. Indeed, differentiation by purpose and area has been a lasting characteristic of London (as other towns), the purposes frequently dependant on external links, but also linked to the possibilities of the site.

Alongside buildings in stone, much was more cheaply built out of timber, which was readily available locally, and mud brick. This was a way to respond to the large number of settlers, although most lived in small, crowded houses, and thus in a dirty and noisy town. As in other periods of London life, there was a tension between town life and quality of life, one that was particularly acute in periods when numbers rose. Thus, the drains of Roman London could not readily cope with the need for sanitation, a recurrent problem.

London remained important, being the capital of Roman Britain in the fourth century, and with the sole mint and thus being the centre of liquidity; but the archaeological record from that century is sketchy and coinage finds lower than in the previous two centuries. At the same time, finds of coins minted in Roman London are quite common, testifying to its relatively high profile within the Empire and the extent to which its economy was integrated with the rest of the Empire.

Functions frequently overlapped but there was a contrast between 'public towns', which had governmental functions, and 'small towns', which lacked this role. Yet, alongside this classification, which itself downplayed overlaps,[8] each category was subject to change, indeed crisis. Indeed, it has been argued that there was a degree of irrelevance to towns in the fourth century, with much of the native population treating them as marginal.[9] This analysis suggests that it was not the 'Barbarian' invasions alone that put paid to Roman towns. Instead, the collapse of the Roman tax state in part involved the unravelling of relations between towns and a countryside that had scant need for them.

The end of the Roman Empire in Britain in 409–10 CE did not initially mean the end of Roman Britain. St Germanus, Bishop of Auxerre, who visited in 429, noted the survival of towns, but that their defence was in local hands, rather than those of Roman troops. A major cause of the fifth-century instability was probably that inhabitants of the more upland areas, which were less Romanised in the civil sense, retained much more idea of fighting and using weapons in their own traditional ways, and therefore found the Romanised lowlanders very easy victims once imperial power was withdrawn. These lowlanders may have been identified as separate peoples, and organised as polities, on the basis of late-Roman town-territories and dioceses; or the process of identification and organisation may have involved less continuation and indeed less need for civic structure, municipal organisation, and an urban system.[10]

Whatever the extent of earlier dissolution, the 'Barbarian' conquests of the fifth, sixth and seventh centuries, nevertheless brought change. Continuity of site use (although probably not of urban institutions) at some of the major towns, for example Canterbury, has been suggested by archaeological work. Urban building continued into the sixth century at Wroxeter.

However, a reliance on wood ensures that there are few remains of buildings from the fifth, sixth and seventh centuries, and the problems of excavating ephemeral timber structures were particularly serious before new archaeological techniques were developed in the 1930s. In addition, the remains in cities were affected by later building work and by the destruction of material in centuries of cellaring. The large-scale funding of rescue archaeology by developers in London from 1973 onwards greatly improved prospects. The excavations at No. 1 Poultry provided evidence of numerous Roman buildings and thousands of artefacts, including tools. In 2006, during restoration work at St Martin-in-the-Fields, archaeologists discovered a massive late-Roman sarcophagus complete with human skeleton, which appears to have been buried according to Christian practice. Excavations in Covent Garden in the 2000s produced finds from the early Saxon period, of the late sixth or seventh century. It is probable that more work will produce additional valuable finds, perhaps reducing still more the timespan of London's apparent abandonment, with comparable results for other towns.

The substance as well as structures of urban life changed, leaving plenty of evidence in the shape of negative evidence, including in the form of the nature and extent of animal and plant remains, both of which had been part of urban life. Thus, in contrast to the Roman period, gardens and orchards for subsequent centuries left less evidence, while ceramics came to be locally-produced and of lower quality, and stone was no longer quarried, but simply removed from existing buildings.[11]

Cross-sections of the archaeological record in towns such as Exeter and London provide clear evidence of discontinuity in settlement. Anglo-Saxon rulers initially did not live within the Roman town walls, trade was of limited importance, and there was a focus on subsistence agriculture. The relevance of towns and town life in this period was limited, and the extent to which

England was inevitably going to follow a pattern of urban significance comparable to France is unclear. Certainly, there is far less evidence for urban activity in fifth and sixth century England than for France.[12]

Little, significantly, is known of London in the fifth or sixth century, and the contradictions between written sources and archaeological evidence, both fragmentary, are also telling. The Roman town seems to have been substantially deserted, in part because, alongside its decline, the centre of remaining settlement moved west, along the banks of the Thames and also inland: towards the Strand and Covent Garden, the new Saxon settlement of Lundenwic to the west of the old walled city, a settlement that was close to the countryside of which it was very much part.

In turn, providing an example of how expansion could follow contraction (as was very differently to be shown in the sixteenth century with recovery from the long-term impact of the Black Death), a revival in both Christianity and the volume of trade brought an increase in activity in Lundenwic in the seventh century. This increase drew on the energy and wealth of the East Anglian and Kentish royal dynasties, and also on the developing importance of renewed links with the Continent. At the beginning of the seventh century, a church dedicated to St Paul was established in London as the seat of the bishop for the East Saxons, who dominated Essex and Middlesex. Like many other early Saxon churches, the first St Paul's was sited within the former Roman town, in this instance on top of Ludgate Hill, the height of which is easy to overlook today in a different topographic context. Small and built of timber, it burned down in 675 before being rebuilt, again in timber which was plentiful in the region.

London was not a key political centre. Anglo-Saxon England developed into a number of major kingdoms, but none of them was centred on London, which limited control over the town whose population apparently proved adept at playing off the different kingdoms, although perhaps none of the competing kings was strong enough to take and hold it. As the centre of a bishopric, London was one of a number of such towns. It was more important thanks to its role as a port, however, and thus remained a key focus of both land and water routes. Settlement, which grew significantly from about 670, continued to centre not on the area of the old Roman town but to the west of the river Fleet, around the Strand. Near Charing Cross, there was a reinforced embankment upon which ships were beached so that they could be unloaded. In the 730s, Bede described London as 'a mart of many peoples'. Wool from the Cotswolds, or woollen cloth, was probably exported from London to France and the Low Countries, thus ensuring revenue for whoever could control the trade. Although Norwich was also an important commercial centre, Canterbury lacked London's commercial role and was affected anyway by the decline of the Kentish kingdom. Moreover, whatever the political consequences, including vulnerability to attack, London's role as a frontier town on the borders of several kingdoms and sub-kingdoms provided an opportunity for inter-state trade.

Christianity helped revive urban purpose[13] since the need for diocesan centres, for the Church very much followed a town-based organisation. These centres included Canterbury, Rochester, London, Winchester, Sherborne, Hereford, Worcester, Lichfield, York, Hexham, Dunwich, Caistor and Leicester. Pope Gregory had intended two archepiscopal sees, at London and York, each with twelve bishoprics, which was probably a legacy from the Roman Empire, but this did not match political realities. It was as a result of the influence of Aethelbert, king of Kent (r. *c.*583–616), in supporting the conversion mission of St Augustine, that Canterbury, his capital, was the see of the Archbishop, but Aethelbert also backed Augustine in establishing bishoprics at London and Rochester. This served a religious purpose but also helped bind these towns to his kingdom.

In turn, York, the centre of the kingdom of Northumbria, gained archepiscopal status in 735, while king Offa of Mercia (r. 757–96) sought to have the Mercian see, Lichfield, given archepiscopal equality with Canterbury and York, although without lasting effect. Aside from bishoprics, there were also minsters, such as Leominster, Southwell and Stratford-on-Avon, ecclesiastical centres, in part mission centres, that became the basis for important towns.[14]

Individual religious foundations reflected the topography of towns and in turn helped define their townscapes.[15] As in Winchester, the location of churches within towns was the result of particular topographies. Urban layout was of significance for the structural stability of buildings, for the continuity of neighbourhoods, for drainage, for defence, and also for the more general value of the town as a setting for power and governance. Urban design, including the possibilities for ceremonial entries and passages, affected the street grid and the layout of buildings.[16]

The coalescence of smaller kingdoms into larger ones also provided a need for capitals, a hierarchy among towns, a basis in the royal and governmental presence for political protection for towns. Protection could only go so far however: work on a fossilised human stool discovered in 1972 has indicated the unhealthy nature of life in York in about 950,[17] with a limited diet and evidence of a large number of intestinal worms.

A small number of leading ports – Ipswich, London, Sandwich, Southampton and York – developed spectacularly in the eighth century, as overseas and coastal trade became more regular; although the extent of a distinctive urban governance is less clear. Southampton, which may have been planned by King Ine of Wessex (r. 688–726), who also built Taunton,[18] is estimated to have covered 111 acres, and was a major centre of trade and minting. These emporia made sense in terms of trade networks that included Continental trading towns notably Dorestad, Quentovic and Ribe.[19] The pre-Viking settlement at Ipswich, a new settlement, eventually covered around 50 hectares. Here, the river Orwell combined with the North Sea, more specifically the southern part of the North Sea, to provide important links. The earlier foundation of Ipswich, probably in the early seventh century, may well have been intended to provide resources for the East Anglian dynasty, as well as encouraging commercial links with the Continent. At the same time, the really helpful character of archaeological finds, understandably does not always explain the reasons for change. Hence in Ipswich the causes and stages of urban settlement invite discussion that by its nature is far from conclusive.[20]

As a major instance of the significance of economic developments for urban growth, a significance that raises the question of what otherwise might have occurred, the expansion was linked with expanded trade with the Low Countries and the Rhineland; there was also a silver economy, with the silver coming from the Harz mountains in Germany. Particular wealth came from the scale and importance of English wool exports. Extensive metal-detector finds from the 1990s revealed that the volume of coinage in the early eighth century was very high in eastern and southern England, reflecting these exports and, in turn, encouraging trade, including local commerce. The southern North Sea was a unifier that contributed to the wealth of eastern England and the development of its towns.[21] There were major mints in Canterbury, Ipswich and London and a smaller one in Rochester. This reflected the monetarisation and commercial strength of East Anglia and Kent, even if they lacked political power, as they increasingly did, being subsumed into larger kingdoms.[22]

The situation was different in western England, where there was less monetarisation, for example in the North-West Midlands. As a result, the ability of Offa to gain control over London was important to the economics and finances of Mercia and provided a tax basis for his policies, notably his determination to dominate his neighbours, as well as being significant for the emergence of the town. There were also fortified Mercian towns, for example Hereford and Tamworth.[23]

The Viking invasions of the late ninth century led to much devastation with the attackers concentrating on towns and monasteries, storming Canterbury in 851 (when Sandwich was also attacked), and York in 866, and taking many other settlements. Church activity was much disrupted, some bishoprics, such as those of Hexham, Caistor and Dunwich, disappearing; while episcopal seats were moved, for example from Leicester to Dorchester-on-Thames, and from coastal Lindisfarne, via Chester-le-Street, to Durham. The situation, however, was different to that of the fall of Roman Britain, in that urban life and institutions were more ephemeral, in many respects far more ephemeral, than had then been the case. Perhaps not being tied into a single overarching system of government allowed them flexibility and adaptability.

By the tenth century, however, a more extensive urban network was in place. Numerous *burhs*, earth and timber fortified positions, were founded, not only as military bases against the Vikings, blocking routes, covering river crossings and anchoring a frontier,[24] but also as towns that both secured royal authority and forwarded economic activity. It used to be argued that many were founded by Alfred, king of Wessex (r. 871–99), but it is now generally accepted by specialists that the fortified places were mostly established before Alfred, whereas true urbanisation came later and for different causes.[25] It is increasingly possible that Offa was much more important than Alfred in the construction of *burhs*.[26]

Some settlements, such as Bath, Chichester, Exeter and Winchester, were re-foundations of Roman towns and/or of post-Roman settlements. Thus, Hereford, the seat of a bishopric by 680, had early eighth-century fortifications, but was reconstituted as a *burh* in 893, being followed by Shrewsbury. Hereford, Tamworth and Winchcombe indicate rampart sections respectively from the Mercian and West Saxon eras of control.[27] Some *burhs*, such as Bridport, were newly-created places. So also with Viking settlements. Some had refurbished Roman fortifications, as at York, while others were newly fortified, notably in the East Midlands, as with Nottingham and Derby.

The location and growth of *burhs* were also related to developments in the transport system, with that at Oxford linked to the construction of a bridge across the Thames which facilitated movement to and from the port at Southampton.[28] Similarly, Stamford, a Viking settlement on the River Welland, became more significant than nearby Great Casterton on the more minor River Gwash.

Wessex became dominant, although finds in the late 2010s in Oxfordshire and Herefordshire of coins minted in London and produced jointly in the names of Alfred and his Mercian contemporary Ceolwulf II (r. 874-c.879) indicate that Mercia continued to be an influence. With the Vikings pushed back, London, nevertheless, passed from Mercian to West Saxon rule.

Edward the Elder, Alfred's successor, built a number of *burhs*, including Manchester in 919, established in order to limit the danger of Viking invasion of the north-west Midlands from the Irish Sea. The driving back of the Vikings also focused on the capture of towns, notably the Five Boroughs (Derby, Leicester, Lincoln, Nottingham, Stamford), each the fortified *burh* of a Danish army ruled as a Danish *jarldom*. The capture of York, Northampton and Bedford was also significant. York was a key place in dispute, stormed by the Vikings in 866, captured by Athelstan of Wessex (r. 924–39) in 927, regained by the Vikings after Athelstan's death, and finally falling to the House of Wessex in 954. It was the token and reality of control of the North, or, at least, of Yorkshire, which helps explain the significance of the Viking attempt in 1066 to seize and hold it anew, an attempt that led to two battles that year, at Fulford and Stamford Bridge.

In the tenth century, Viking-fortified positions became part of the governmental structure of the English state that was created from the

House of Wessex. This was not a state that required or was constrained by precise ethnic, tribal or geographical borders. Instead, towns and their governmental purpose and means played a major role, not least in terms of a system of public courts and governance, although the intensive lordship shown by the Crown in Wessex and south Mercia, and the related urban network, was not matched further north, in Northumbria beyond the River Tees, which increased the significance of control over York.

Under Athelstan, the role of towns was demonstrated anew by the improvement of the coinage, a process secured by re-minting. During the tenth century, minting became very nearly a royal monopoly. As a sign of their significance, Canterbury, London and Winchester were allocated eight moneyers each, while most towns only had one. In addition, the Church continued to focus on towns and was a major aspect of their jurisdictional complexity, as with 'Liberties', or quasi-autonomous areas of exempt jurisdiction, for example the Liberty of St Peter of York.

After a successful renewed Viking assault, King Cnut of Denmark and his sons (Harold Harefoot and Harthacnut) ruled from 1016 until 1042. Cnut also ruled Denmark and Norway, and therefore a governmental centre on the east coast of England was more suitable than Winchester, the capital of Wessex. Without his predecessors' cultural, religious and historical ties to Winchester and all that it represented, Cnut and his successors made London their military and governmental centre. This was a classic instance of the importance to London of broader political developments. It benefited from the resulting commercial links, but also suffered from the Danish removal of bullion from the country. Harthacnut, Cnut's surviving son, died in 1042 at the wedding feast in Lambeth of a prominent *thegn*. The dynasty of Wessex then returned in the person of Edward the Confessor (r. 1042–66), who became king in part by popular acclamation in London.[29]

Meanwhile, London benefited from the commercial growth of England and from the expansion of foreign trade. German, French, Flemish and Scandinavian merchants are all documented as present in the early eleventh century. The wealth earned from wool exports proved the basis for an effective silver currency, which in turn supported specialist crafts and assisted the process of government. This wealth also made possible the huge sums raised for *Danegeld* in the years on either side of 1000, sums that explain finds of English coin in Scandinavia.

By 1100, London had a population of between 10,000 and 20,000. Growth, including in Southwark south of the Thames, involved infilling and the development of new streets lined with timber houses. Property boundaries were fixed. Archaeological work in the 1990s at the eastern end of Cheapside has shown that the Poultry was built up with a row of buildings from the tenth century, followed by new streets, and then with the surviving open spaces filled in by 1200 with large stone properties in what was now a mercantile area.

Part of the growing wealth was spent on the Church: on parish churches, monasteries, nunneries and hospitals. Much of the land surrounding London was indeed granted to the Church in late Saxon times. Edward the Confessor rebuilt St Peter's monastery, or the West Minster, as a larger structure and also constructed the first royal palace on the site at Thorney Island where the river Tyburn entered the Thames. The first large Romanesque building in England, Westminster Abbey's new church, was consecrated in 1065 and Edward was buried there in 1066. Winchester, the capital of Wessex, had in part been replaced, although it was still the site of the Treasury and Exchequer into the 1150s, being moved to Westminster under Henry II.

The overall significance of urban activity increased, as towns were seen as useful and indeed were developed to be useful. By 1066, as a result of migration from rural areas, migration that was spontaneous and not government-directed, about (this was a pre-census age) 10 per cent of the population lived in towns. This section of the population was more clearly under royal government than rural areas. Linked to this, both towns and royal power were most present in the South where again they were more significant for the economy.

With the Normans, who, under William I (r. 1066–87), 'the Conqueror', seized power in 1066 following victory near Hastings, towns were brought under a new ruling group which had very few links to its predecessors. The consequences very much varied by town. The particular role of new local lords was important, as was that of the Crown,[30] although evidence is patchy.[31] Thus, the location (and resulting disruption) of many of the castles built by the Normans centred on towns.

There were a number of factors, including local resources and politics, as well as military imperatives, but the control of towns and the routes focused on them was important. For example, the first castles in Lincolnshire were at Lincoln and Stamford, the latter a key position on the route to the north, the lowest crossing place, by ford or bridge, on the River Welland. There was no national 'master plan' implementing strategic considerations, but William maintained castles in the shire towns, such as Exeter, Nottingham and Oxford, as part of the framework of royal government. London, where the White Tower was to be the centre of the Tower of London, was crucial to this process, and the monarchy settled down at Westminster with buildings there that satisfied its residential, administrative and religious needs. Many castles, for example at Cambridge, Chester and Wallingford, were built over existing towns, devastating their townscapes. This was an aspect of the destruction brought by the Norman Conquest.

The first castle at Norwich was a 'motte and bailey' structure, a wooden stockade atop an earth mound. Consolidation led to more imposing and permanent structures. By 1125 Norwich's mound was crowned by a strong, square stone keep. In addition, the Norman presence in northern England was anchored with the building of castles, particularly in Durham (1072), Newcastle (1080), and Carlisle (1092). When William II occupied Cumbria in 1092, he both created a town, with peasants rounded up and transported there to man it, and built a castle. The city wall around Carlisle was begun in 1122. Newcastle's earliest murage grant, the right to take tolls to raise money for building or repairing walls, was in 1265, but it is possible that there was an earlier ring of earthworks.[32]

The resources devoted to castle building had a serious impact on society. So also with Norman civil wars, notably that under Stephen (r. 1135–54). Control over both Lincoln and, in particular, London proved especially important to the course of that conflict, as also to the civil war at the close of John's reign and the beginning of that of Henry III.

Stone-built cathedrals and churches also took many resources over many years and expressed power, as when the great Northumbrian holy man St Cuthbert was disinterred, removed and reburied in the bold new cathedral at Durham in 1104.[33] Dioceses and abbeys were taken over by Norman appointees, the first in St Peter's Abbey, Gloucester, being Serlo, in 1072.

The reorganisation of the diocesan system included the transfer of sees to more major urban centres, for example from Crediton to Exeter, Sherborne to Salisbury, North Elmham to Norwich, and Dorchester-on-Thames to Lincoln, and the foundation of new bishoprics at Ely and Carlisle. There were new monastic foundations too, but the key Anglo-Saxon urban ones, including Bury St Edmunds and St Albans, continued, and furthered their economic and spiritual value to their towns by encouraging pilgrimages.[34] Both of these towns were named from saints. The cult of relics was also crucial in Canterbury. The presence of Coventry Priory greatly encouraged the growth of the town, a process also seen in, for example, Gloucester. Coventry Priory had rights in at least 75 per cent of the properties in Coventry, but in 1355 lost its control of much of the town. Part of Coventry had the Earls of Chester (a royal appanage from 1254) as its lords. Church control could be unwelcome, as in Abingdon, where a riot in 1327 against the Abbey's control of the market led to the destruction of many records. There was also serious trouble at Bury St Edmunds.

The Church's role in medieval towns, itself a role divided by particular institutions, contributed greatly to their polyfocal character for it sat alongside royal government, local aristocratic influence, and the activism of the citizens themselves. The latter was activism both of the community and of particular groups. The occupationally-linked guilds were important to the latter, and were generally linked also to particular churches and localities.[35] The Conquest was followed by settlement from the Continent, with distinctive areas within towns formed accordingly, as in Hereford, Norwich and Nottingham.

This polyfocal character had consequences in the physicality of the townscape, in competing jurisdictions jealously guarding their privileges and independence, and in the economic and social character of neighbourhoods, as well as in their politics, culture, ideology, collectivist institutions and philanthropic activism. Solidarity was divided and fractured as well as operating for shared goals.[36] Relations between towns and their patron owners, both clerical and secular, could be poor, but there was also the possibility of a closer relationship, not least if the owners took note of the interests and, even more, self-assertion of their towns.[37] The polyfocal character of towns was dynamic, notably due to political contention, judicial decisions, royal favour, land purchase and building, with developments such as the role of royal government prompting responses.[38]

The development of London's government brought to the fore many processes seen elsewhere, and notably the growth of a sense of urban identity.[39] In a society that was referential to the past and reverential of it, this process was based heavily upon precedent and the perceptions of history. Edward the Confessor had issued a writ confirming the laws and jurisdiction of the London guild of *cnihtas*, probably founded in the reign of Edgar (957–75); and this writ was placed on the altar of the priory of Holy Trinity, Aldgate, in 1125 as confirmation of the guild's gift of land and rights. A link can be drawn thence to the 1191 commune, which advanced claims for London's interests and, in turn, brought together Londoners of both English and Norse ancestry. A key and lasting element of the town's identity was that it took precedence over differences in ancestry and lineage and instead brought otherwise distinct groups into a commonality of shared identity and interest: by 1191, in consequence, the distinction between Anglo-Saxons and post-1066 settlers was more or less obsolete. Pride in London's history, and a strong sense of its distinctive identity and importance, played a role in this assertiveness, and was also expressed in the laws and customs known today as the London Collection that was assembled during the period of opposition to King John in the early thirteenth century.

In a parallel process, in London and elsewhere, various mercantile and craft guilds emerged, defined their roles, and, in multiple directions, asserted their economic and political interests, controlling local production and trade in a process involving regulation, lobbying, litigation and a certain amount of violence. In London, these guilds, which were linked to the dense and varied texture of ecclesiastical foundations and activity, were to become the City Livery Companies. They were important to the creation in the Middle Ages of the distinctive features of government that provided the context for London's later development, with parallels elsewhere. These included a depth of governance that shared, and thus grounded, authority and responsibility. Accountability was to a degree eased by the relative population stability of the fifteenth century. Moreover, this accountability related to the lack of direct rule by the monarchy, although the king could, and did, intervene when he saw fit, and impose direct rule. This was usually only for short periods, but the possibility probably made for a degree of volatility, as some factions welcomed this and others did not.

The use of writing became more common, first with civic government in the second half of the thirteenth century, on the evidence of letter books and coroners' rolls, and, in the same period, with the increase in the use of written documents by merchants and artisans. The use of seals proliferated, and these were largely made to be attached to documents.

Citizenship became an earned right, acquired through membership of a guild (itself secured by patrimony, apprenticeship or purchase), and with payment through civic taxation; this citizenship was marked by taking the civic oath. In return, economic privileges and legal rights were granted, especially those to buy and sell property, to trade, and to enjoy the protection of the town's own courts. From 1319, would-be citizens of London had to gain the approval of those already practising their trade, and citizenship was dependent upon support from that trade association. Citizens, moreover, did not have to pay the tolls that were charged on goods brought into the City across London Bridge or tolls anywhere in England, under the charter of Henry I.

Those excluded were called 'foreigners', irrespective of their place of birth, and most were confined to poorly-paid occupations. Furthermore, there was also a tendency to regard marginal groups as a threat to public health, order and morality, and notably so with prostitutes, beggars and vagrants, and those thus defined. The City authorities and those of the particular wards often acted in concert against them. The use of almshouses from the fifteenth century to support only the 'deserving poor' was an aspect of this exclusion.[40] The suburbs, where authority was weakest and lodging cheapest, were a particular resort of marginal groups. In terms of sharing in governmental authority, this (unsurprisingly) excluded most of the population, notably the poor, women and the young.[41]

But in practical terms there could be a degree of agency for members of some of these groups. Not least, they could acquire opportunity in part as an aspect of the social mobility that existed alongside the processes that sought to guide or constrain it. Women, in particular, could acquire wealth through marriage, and the nature of family relations was often more consensual and cooperative than might be suggested by discussion in terms of a patriarchy. Women could further acquire independence by becoming widows.

The governmental system developed apace, the City being divided into 24 wards by 1127, each with its own alderman, the modern complement of 26 wards being reached in 1550 when Bridge Ward Without was added, south of the Thames, in what is now called Borough. The achievement of autonomy by the Londoners under a Mayor elected from among the aldermen, but not always only by them,[42] rested on the strength of the local government offered by the ward system. Although each ward was headed by an alderman, while the Court of Aldermen and the Common Council lent coherence to London's government, each ward also had a wardmote or local forum. Local governmental structures and a political culture which was focused on cohesion helped limit social division within London; but many tensions remained, not least as any tendency towards oligarchy was unpopular among those citizens who were not the oligarchs.

A clear and strong government structure helped in the assertion of what could be presented as rights. In Magna Carta (1215), it was agreed that London was 'to have all its ancient liberties and free customs', and that the granting of aids (a form of taxes) to the Crown from London would take place only under strict conditions. The Mayor was one of the 25 'barons' who were sworn to see Magna Carta was maintained. Without London's support, Magna Carta would never have been granted.

The rise of a national consciousness could lead to hostility towards those judged to be outsiders. Benefiting from royal favour, a Jewish community, possibly starting with immigrants from Rouen, and based on Jews' Street (Old Jewry), was in place in London by 1130. The role of the Jews in usury, nominally forbidden to Christians, and in helping to finance the Crown and other leading figures led, however, to growing criticism. In 1189, this resulted in a violent response, including the burning down of the London Jewry. Anti-Jewish harassment, also seen in other towns, notably Norwich, culminated in Edward I's expulsion of the Jews from England in 1290.[43]

Helped by population and economic growth across England, the twelfth and thirteenth centuries saw significant increases in the foundation of towns, both planned and unplanned. Towns had lords, and landowners were responsible for a number of quasi-new towns, such as Chelmsford and Lichfield, and for towns on new sites, such as Lowestoft.[44] The shape, layout and nature of the resulting towns varied. New Buckenham was founded in the mid twelfth century to support the household of Buckenham Castle. Like New Winchelsea, founded a century later by Edward I, it was laid out on a chequer-board pattern.[45] Landowners (who included clergy) were also responsible for revived towns, such as Wells.[46] In already-existing towns, population growth within the town defences, which meant the walls (whether or not there was also a castle), led to denser occupation, while, from the twelfth century, suburbs developed outside the walls. Suburbs were usually unprotected by walls and also freer and less regulated in their economic activities.

In new and revived towns, it could take a while for self-government to develop even if there was civic consciousness and public buildings. The emphasis on urban privileges, such as market regulations and guilds, lasted for several centuries, angering those such as Daniel Defoe, who, as he made clear in his *Tour*, preferred a free market system:

'The greatest inconveniencies of Britain, are, its situation, and the tenacious folly of its inhabitants; who by the general infatuation, the pretence of freedoms and privileges, that corporation-tyranny, which prevents the flourishing and increase of many a good town in England, continue obstinately to forbid any, who are not subjects of their city sovereignty, (that is to say freemen,) to trade within the chain of their own liberties; were it not for this, the city of Bristol, would before now, have swelled and increased in buildings and inhabitants, perhaps to double the magnitude it was formerly of.'[47]

In fact, by 1722, Bristol probably had doubled its size and population since 1650, but Defoe had last really seen it in 1705.

The physical organisation of towns was classically one of a main street(s), bordered by narrow burgage plots, their narrow frontage backed by a long plot that could include green space. Over time, the plots retained their identity but there could be differing uses for them.[48] This can still be clearly seen in Tewkesbury, where many alleys running back from the main streets between the plots survive, and the routes of many others are known.

Over time, in response to economic and population growth, there was more trade and greater specialisation in occupations, both within and between towns, with particular trades congregating in specific areas in response to the needs of individual trades within towns, or, conversely, being able to disperse across towns.[49] Markets and manufacturing increased. Before 1201, there were only 15 markets recorded in Suffolk, but, over the following century, 47 new markets were found there, while there were 67 grants of market rights between 1200 and 1350. This ensured a denser pattern of commercial opportunities than in the past, for example in Northamptonshire. While weekly markets were the most frequent part of the commercial system, and central both to the role of urban life in wider areas, and of the latter to towns of whatever size, there were also annual fairs, the first at Scarborough being held in 1253. The urban fairs were the longest in duration, Northampton in the fourteenth century having a 28-day fair, while, in the late thirteenth century, Boston fair, which traditionally began on 17 June, St Botolph's Day, sometimes lasted into early September.[50]

While one of the definitions of urban status for small towns is a concentration of trade and service functions, epitomised by a weekly market that supported rural hinterlands, most of the tradespeople were also farmers and graziers. This underlines the extent to which the distinction between urban and rural had to encompass towns with direct rural activities, a theme very much to the fore in suburban areas. Thus, in a legal action of 1275, the burgesses of Appleby complained that Roger Clifford, who held half the barony of Appleby in the right of his wife, had deployed armed men to blockade the town, stopping both their trade and the reaping of their crops.[51]

Yet, both towns and rural areas were directly involved in a growing trade that saw about 30–40 per cent of all grain being marketed by the thirteenth century. Mercantile credit was crucial to trade and the economy more generally. It has been argued that 20 times as much money was in circulation by 1300 as in 1100.

The sophistication of urban credit networks, and the extent to which risk was limited by trust and by the control of disorder and criminality, helped ensure that the transaction costs of credit and debt were contained. This was important to the ability of towns to develop production and trade within hinterlands.[52] An improvement in communications was very much part of the process. Bridges replaced fords as an aspect of an improvement in the road system that contributed to economic activity. Towns operated as crucial centres of the wealth-promoting infrastructures that brought prosperity to the hinterlands, in part by guiding them into more advanced productive practices. In this and other respects, they were hostile to foreign merchants, a hostility that could have a harsh xenophobic character as in the separate strength of anti-Semitism.

The wool trade grew in the thirteenth century, serving Continental cloth manufacturing in the Low Countries and bringing prosperity to towns such as Shrewsbury which, in the early fourteenth century, ranked eighth among English provincial towns in providing tax revenue. The diffusion of wealth was seen in the career of Laurence of Ludlow (*c.*1250–94), a major Shropshire wool trader who also loaned money to Edward I and became involved in deciding government policy where the wool trade was concerned.[53]

Urban growth drew on migration from the countryside, as well as from other towns. Migration was necessary due to high urban mortality. The success of Coventry in the thirteenth century is indicated by the scale and range of migration to the town, with arrivals from as far as Kendal (Westmorland) and Winchelsea (Sussex), and, as with London, with migration not dominated by locals. London drew heavily on East Anglia. At that stage, Coventry had a wideranging occupational structure, which contributed to its economic strength.[54]

In part a recognition of their economic weight and financial importance, towns were given a place in a developing political system. From 1265, selected towns sent representatives to Parliament, their representation in the House of Commons reflecting its tax-raising powers. Yet that was no passive process of automatic approval. In addition, a background to the increased role of towns in Parliament was provided by the political activism over governance that was seen in some towns.[55] This activism contributed to the alignment of municipal with national politics, and also to the political wish to win urban support. This urban support was particularly significant in periods of disorder, such as the 1320s.[56]

The new concept of representation was outlined in the writs to the 1295 Parliament, with an instruction to MPs to appear with authority to give advice on behalf of the communities they represented. This was important to the idea of the group representation of towns, rather than a reliance based solely on links with individual towns. This group representation was highly significant for the nature of English politics, and was a counterpart to that of county communities.[57] The emphasis on Parliament provides a benign account of urban political change, but in practice both could be very difficult. In considering more recent urban hostility to government, notably during the Thatcher ministry of the 1980s, it is as well to remember that this was less disruptive, let alone violent, than many medieval episodes.

As in the 1980s, opposition helped to influence, if not direct, the governmental response, and notably so to London. Its opposition to John and to Henry III underlay much of the attitude of Edward I (r. 1272–1307), who revoked London's liberties and installed a government under his own officers from 1285 to 1299 while earlier, between 1275 and 1285, greatly strengthening the defences of the Tower. From then on, London, or, more particularly, the royal quarter of Westminster, was increasingly the royal capital and not a town following an independent political course. Westminster was the capital, but York was a secondary centre of particular importance when the king was fighting the Scots.[58] The exceptional power and authority of the Crown in England and its strong centralising tendencies were key factors in London's development. Its leading role in the overthrow of Edward II in 1326 and Henry VI in 1461 reflected its continuing capacity for pursuing its own course, but it did so as a central part of the kingdom and not as an autonomous city-state. Indeed, urban support, notably that of London for Edward IV (r. 1461–70, 71–83), was very important to the course of the Wars of the Roses.[59] Monarchs also relied on London for money and loans to carry out wars and military actions, so it was important to keep them 'onside'.

There has long been a wealth of scholarship on medieval towns and across a broad range of topics and approaches.[60] At the same time, an understanding of some points has been affected by the often limited survival of archives, as a result of loss and neglect.[61] Many London archives were destroyed in the Great Fire of 1666. For example, it appears that by the later medieval period, not least as the influence of founding patrons receded, urban politics and governance, in part due to the contentious nature and practice of citizenship and oligarchy, notably as expressed in the freeman's oath, saw a degree of opposition and criticism not so readily present in other branches of governance.[62] Yet such comparative judgments are not easy.

The long-term trend of population and economic growth, with the related social and political consequences, came to an end in the fourteenth century, with profound implications for urban life, although, since all the agencies of government remained in place, without an impact comparable to the end of Roman rule.[63] The population was probably hit very hard by harvest failure, notably the Great Famine of 1315–17, global cooling, and disease, which culminated in the clearly traumatic plague outbreak of the Black Death in 1348–9. The last was the ultimate in an unpredictability that affected so many aspects of urban living, with epidemic, fire and flood to the fore. Thus, York, which had up to about 24,000 people in 1300, had a major flood in 1315. Such floods could be far more deadly and disruptive than those today, as there was no comparable support network.

Alongside rural depopulation as a result of the Black Death, there were serious problems for many towns, problems that provided an important context for the more general variations in developments, including rents, that reflected local circumstances.[64] Trade at most markets and fairs declined, hitting town life. The resulting strains could be seen in the Peasants' Revolt of 1381. Covering much of southern and eastern England, this revolt also affected a good many towns, notably London, Cambridge, Norwich, Bridgwater, Beverley, and Winchester. The effect was a matter both of urban discontent and of the arrival in towns of protesting rural elements, notably, but not only, peasants, as in Maidstone, Rochester, Canterbury, and London. After the crisis, municipal authorities emphasised this latter point, but to do so entailed downplaying an appreciable level of urban activism. The revolt was triggered in part by an attempt to collect the highly unpopular 1377 poll tax in Brentwood, although the key actors there were local villagers. In contrast, rebel townsmen were important in several towns including London and Bury St Edmunds, and in many towns there was no opposition to their seizure, for example in Ipswich and Norwich. In some towns, notably Bury St Edmunds and St Albans, the revolt drew on urban opposition to the power of the abbey, especially restrictions on grinding their own grain and a prohibition on pasturing cattle on abbey lands. At St Albans the abbey records were burnt in the town square, prisoners freed from the abbot's prison, and the abbot was forced to surrender the abbey's rights in a charter. Similar enmity led to a violent attack by townspeople on the privileged University of Cambridge, a revolt backed by the Mayor, again with archives being burned and a new charter issued. In Beverley and Scarborough the poorer townspeople displaced the wealthy élite.[65] These varied factors captured the extent to which town life was fraught with rivalries, and periods of crisis could bring these to a head.

The economic problems of towns continued into the fifteenth century, in turn affecting population numbers by resulting in later marriages and, therefore, a lower birth rate.[66] Warwick was typical of several county towns, an identity that emerged alongside the practice of government, in relying on its role in that governmental position and as a local market, but being unable to grow further because it lacked an industrial base. Yet, there was also a development in the fifteenth century of cloth production centred on towns such as Hadleigh, Lavenham and Long Melford, and ports such as Great Yarmouth and London; although with the particular rhythms of war and peace with France and the Low Countries, and the resulting disruption to trade and export markets, important to the success of trade.[67] Great Yarmouth replaced Boston as the major regional port. So also in the West Country, with Exeter prosperous, although there was a relative decline compared to East Anglia.[68] This was an age that did not have synthetic textiles.

The gradual switch from exports of wool to exports of woollen cloth produced a wealth that encouraged the link between the Crown and mercantile interests, a link that was to be important to the association of government with towns.[69] This linkage took precedence over that between nobility and towns. The freeman's oath included a declaration of loyalty to the monarch, as the freeman was subject as well as citizen.

An assessment of Gloucester based on a 1455 rental suggests that fifteenth-century towns were not necessarily in a grim state – the impression often created of towns other than those in East Anglia. Although there was open ground there, it was mostly in side streets and the suburbs, while the thoroughfares showed competition for housing leading to subdivided tenements, as well as activity by craftsmen and real estate development.[70]

More generally, many townspeople lived in great poverty; but those doing well are revealed by their inventories as living in multi-room environments that offered privacy as well as living in lasting houses in stable property units protected by legal title from seigneurial control. Moreover, urban inventories reveal more goods, such as pottery and stoneware, and furnishings than rural ones.[71]

If there were problems, they were frequently to the benefit of other towns. Thus, York and Beverley were hit by economic problems in the fifteenth century, being passed as commercial centres by a growing Hull.[72] In rare cases, there were also environmental problems. The major instance was that of rivers and harbours silting up in whole or part, for example at Sandwich. More dramatically, the encroachments of the North Sea notably as a result of storms in 1286–7, 1328, 1347 and 1362, had made Dunwich, a once successful Suffolk port, unviable from 1328 not least due to the shifting outlet of the River Dunwich.

The military side of town fortunes and life was shown in Berwick and Southampton, the former as a major position in contention between England and Scotland until finally captured by England in 1482 and the latter as a naval base, one made more significant by the centrality of Normandy to the war effort in France.[73] The ports along the Channel were greatly affected by privateering, raids, and the impressment of ships for royal service.[74] Its population falling from over 2,000 in the late thirteenth century to about 1,500 in 1377, Carlisle was hit by war with the Scots, but was saved by its multiplicity of functions, as military base with a major castle, county town, cathedral city, and a site for markets and fairs. In contrast, Chester was no longer a major military base, as North Wales was finally brought under control with the failure of Owen Glendower's rising in the early fifteenth century. On the other hand, it remained of great significance as a regional centre.[75]

Restructuring, rather than decay, was the prime theme in the fifteenth century, not least due to the growth of service and commercial sectors, and the vitality of the cloth industry; although, as yet, towns were not a prime residence for landowners. They continued to attract migrants, both from within the country and from abroad, most of the latter going to towns, notably to London, where foreign migrants were about 6–10 per cent of the population, but also for example to Bristol, Southampton, and King's Lynn. In Great Yarmouth, there were many foreign brewers. The Low Countries provided the largest groups of immigrants, Flemings being attacked in

1381, particularly in London, where about forty were murdered, in part as a product of the anger of native weavers, although the number killed may have been much higher, one source claiming 400. Others were killed in the same year in Norwich. Hanse merchants from north Germany based in the Steelyard in London were also important[76] but also were met by opposition. Much as today, hostility to newcomers was more pronounced in periods of economic difficulty than in that of urban expansion in the twelfth and thirteenth centuries.

At the level of individual towns, variety extended to civic politics, and notably the degree of oligarchical control as well as resistance to it, as well as alignments with local and national noble factionalism.[77] There was a focus on common profit from and in urban governance, with Christian charity and corporate help regarded as central and as part of a relationship that linked past, present and future, and was eased by gifts and prayers and expressed in them.[78] In practice, political strain, financial pressures and economic pulses all repeatedly complicated the ideal, which helped encourage an emphasis on it. Thus, building on earlier hostility to restrictions on grazing, for example in St Albans, anti-enclosure riots in towns in the late fifteenth and early sixteenth centuries, notably in Colchester, Coventry, Norwich, Nottingham, Southampton, and York, reflected the determination of commoners to be able to continue to graze livestock, and their opposition to enclosures by landowners, which could include town corporations; although the extent of riots in Norwich in 1437 and 1443 has been greatly exaggerated.[79] As on the Continent, there was a widespread attempt by urban élites in the fifteenth century to consolidate control.[80]

Whereas self-governing royal boroughs was effectively independent under the Crown, this was not the case with those owned by landlords, whether clerical or lay. Yet, the latter towns could enjoy considerable autonomy, in part due to the landlords' need for their prosperity and indeed help, both financial and in other respects. This need could extend to leasing out landlord rights, a process that became more common in the fifteenth century.

Communal health, secular and spiritual, were helped by expenditure on sewers and churches, with crises, such as plague and Lollardy (a heretical movement), providing encouragement to action. The most prosperous towns, such as London, Norwich, King's Lynn and Colchester, proved best able to afford action for a cleaner environment. Exeter had a sophisticated public water supply system including a network of underground passages.[81] The management of human and animal waste was a key topic, and there were frequently-repeated steps to improve the running of markets, butchers and tanneries, and for the collection of rubbish, and against urinating in the streets.[82] Poor relief brought together secular and spiritual concerns in action.

Towns were also central to culture, as with the mystery plays staged there as a depiction of good and evil. The Coopers' pageant in York's 1415 Corpus Christi play showed 'Adam and Eve and a tree between them, a serpent deceiving them with apples, God speaking to them and cursing the serpent, and an angel with a sword casting them out of Paradise.' The York mystery plays were written down in the 1460s or 1470s, an aspect of the vitality of a local culture that focused on towns. Parish-supported processions, guild pageants and liturgical celebrations were all associated with the Feast of Corpus Christi in Bristol.[83]

At the same time, towns had a close and symbiotic relationship with their hinterlands, and notably so if they were under the seigneurial control of manorial lords, rather than being boroughs with chartered significance. Those under seigneurial control were generally smaller and primarily local market and trade centres.[84] Coleshill in Warwickshire was under the Clintons, granted powers by Henry II in 1184–5, then, as a result of the marriage of a heiress, the Mountfords, and then, after an execution in 1495 for rebelling, the Digbys.

Patronage by noble landowners was important in helping to create links between urban and rural society. It could also lessen the tensions that could arise from economic links that were, at once, mutually beneficial and yet also subject to a frequent process of negotiation in order to resolve differences.[85] However, as in France, towns tended to look for stable monarchy.[86] They both developed a sense of communal identity and interests,[87] and yet did so within a national and state context that did not require the independence pursued by towns in Germany and Italy. In contrast to Henry VI, Edward IV (r. 1461–70, 1471–83) worked very hard to win the loyalty of London and its leading citizens, on one occasion inviting the Mayor and Aldermen to join him on a hunting party in Waltham Forest. This looked towards the care to woo London shown by the Tudors (r. 1485–1603), bar Mary I

(r. 1553–8): she successfully appealed to London for support against Sir Thomas Wyatt's rebellion in 1554, but became unpopular through her religious policies. Far less support was shown by London under the Stuarts (r. 1603–1714). There was rebellion in London in 1642 and 1688, and serious opposition in 1679–81; but, in contrast, Wyatt and Robert, Earl of Essex, failed to raise support in 1554 and 1601 respectively against Mary I and Elizabeth I.

An absence of urban independence did not mean a lack of identity. Indeed, an aspect of distinctive town identity was provided by urban chronicles and by early town maps.[88] A map of Bristol in about 1480 appeared as part of Robert Ricart's manuscript history of the town, a work produced because the Mayor sought a record of the rights and franchises of the town.[89] Ricart, the Common Clerk of Bristol, brought in the mythical founding of the town and the 1373 charter that gave it county status.[90]

Status was an important aspect of a more general performative culture and society, with the performance linked to institutional politics and corporate profile within towns. Profile was variously secular, religious and, more commonly, both, as with guilds and also care for the poor. Each aspect of profile offered status affirmation and networking.[91] All of these were to be challenged by the Reformation in the 1530s-60s.

At the same time, any emphasis throughout on the change of the Reformation or, indeed, on the arrival of the Tudors in 1485, or any other individual or collective indication of the onset of 'modernity,' seriously risks underplaying the significance of continuity. This was a case of many elements, from the built environment to the socio-economic contexts of life. These showed scant elements of change, although with the important caveat that the Reformation did bring significant elements of change at the level of individual towns, in both economy and society. There were also major elements of continuity in politics and governance.

This then raises the question of why the chapter break is at 1500, as in this book. In part, a break at a century divide is simply a matter of convenience, one in particular that draws on the extent to which the centuries are readily recognised as units. Yet there is also the very point that 1501 was not different to 1499, namely that it is important to understand the role of continuity. This role can be downplayed as books commonly focus on change, and the continuity therefore is implicit rather than explicit. Here, it is brought out as explicit with an understanding that that point should be noted for other chapter divides on century or half-century breaks. The period covered by this chapter, by far the lengthiest in this book, had understandably been one of major change, possibly more so than any century prior to 1850–1950. Yet, the Reformation of the early sixteenth century was to be a fundamental break with the structures and practices of many aspects of urban society and belief.

Chapter 2

Tudor Towns

Written in 1568–88, William Smith's *Particular Description of England with the Portraits of Certain of the Chiefest Cities and Towns* focused on the South, depicting Bath, Bristol, Cambridge, Canterbury, London, Norwich and Rochester.[1] The general interest in towns was reflected in the maps in such works, as also with those of John Speed, with a search for precision rather than iconography, although there were still elements of the latter, or at least of sustaining traditional images.[2]

Distinctions between town and country were less marked than they were to become by the nineteenth century. While towns were centres of manufacturing and trade, both these things were also extensively pursued in the countryside, not least through processes described as protoindustrialization. Similarly, there was much market gardening within town walls. There were also urban orchards and pastures, the latter especially valuable for milk, which could not be refrigerated, treated or preserved, and which therefore went off rapidly. This problem helped encourage the consumption of weak beer. Richard Lyne's Cambridge street map of 1574 shows a pig rooting around in nearby Swinecrofte, as well as fishing. Chickens, ducks and geese were also kept for meat and eggs. John Walker's 1591 map of Chelmsford included not only Bell Meadow but also the 'Backsydes' of the dwellings, which provided them with land for planting and animals. These spaces helped provide family economies with greater resources and resilience, and also ensured work for most of its members. Young children could tend chickens or pick fruit. Economic strain on individuals and families was countered by multiple occupations, as well as by using pawning and theft to raise funds and credit.

Although not built until 1743, the City Mill in Winchester was on the site of earlier corn mills there, on the River Itchen. Watermills were a source of urban power, but not for heating. Indeed, whereas the local environs of Cambridge and other towns provided food, fuel generally came from further afield, due to the exhaustion of local timber and the usual need to move coal from a considerable distance. Thus, Cambridge received wood from nearby Essex and Suffolk, and coal from distant Newcastle,[3] all brought by water which was the only way to handle bulk cargoes.

Urban expansion was a product of general and sustained population growth in the sixteenth century and of the role of towns as centres of manufacturing, trade, government and leisure.[4] Yet, with the exception of London, they were all small: in 1523, Worcester ranked sixteenth among towns by population, but that was only about 4,000; and in 1666 only about 6,000. The next biggest town in Worcestershire, Evesham, had only about 1,400 people in the mid-sixteenth century, the size of a modern village, indeed of a relatively small one.

After London, Bristol, Newcastle, Norwich, York and Exeter grew rapidly,[5] despite the travails of disease, notably plague, which, for example in 1587 killed nearly a third of the population of Norwich, which, with a population of 15,000, had been England's second town in 1550. There was a disproportionately high number of large towns in the southern half of England, particularly so in East Anglia and the South-West. The South-East, in contrast, missed out, in large part due to the inhibiting effect of London on the growth of nearby towns, and because it had less industry than the other two regions, and, in particular, less clothmaking and less fishing. The presence of so many towns in the South impacted not only on the economic, but also the political importance of the area, because it was largely responsible for the high numbers of parliamentary boroughs there. This was also the wealthiest part of the country.

In the sixteenth century, and going forward into the seventeenth, some towns enjoyed rapid growth, although the absence of planned development was a particular characteristic of the generally haphazard and usually rather intermittent urban growth of the sixteenth and seventeenth centuries.[6] This situation brought contingency to the fore, but also reflected and left a poorly-regulated situation from the perspective of the provision of necessary services. More positively, it is unclear that the government was readily capable of providing or supporting planned urban development, of any type, on any scale or continuity. As a consequence, the situation at the time worked possibly as well as could have been anticipated; and as badly.

Economic differentiation was important to success. Thus, Maidstone developed paper-making and brewing for the London market, there was glove-making in Charlbury, Northampton and Yeovil, while Exeter, which had about 8,000 inhabitants, became a major centre for the export of lighter weight 'new draperies' to the Mediterranean. Other towns, such as Coventry and Leicester, were affected by declining industries or largely stagnated. Moreover, some, usually smaller towns, were hit by the market integration that lessened the number and/or significance of smaller markets. Some ports, such as Boston, struggled to compete, as others, such as King's Lynn and Topsham (the outport for Exeter) rose in significance.

London played a key role, not least in entrepreneurial enabling. Thomas Kitson, a London merchant who had a rather equivocal relationship with the town, organised the export of Somerset cloth to the Continent, as well as supplying goods used in its manufacture.[7] The benefit derived by and from London merchants underlines the extent to which the profit from economic activity in a particular town was not only unevenly spread within that town, but also often primarily to the benefit of outsiders. Notably, many traders were transient, investing profit in rural status and activity.[8] This was a sign of symbiosis, but symbiosis on often difficult terms.

Certain towns, notably Hull and Berwick, were well-fortified. The modern new defences of Berwick, constructed between 1558 and 1569, were very different from the castellated medieval ones there and more generally. Most towns, however, had no new defences and thus no response to the challenges potentially posed by cannon and, separately, to the existence of vulnerable suburban areas beyond existing walls. Exposure to cannon had not been a significant issue in the Wars of the Roses in the late fifteenth century, in large part because they were determined by battles, such as Towton in 1461, Barnet and Tewkesbury in 1471, and Bosworth in 1485, and not by sieges, although in 1461 Carlisle was besieged by an alliance of Lancastrians and Scots for several weeks.[9]

In the sixteenth century, the emphasis was on protection from invasion, which encouraged coastal fortifications and that of Berwick. Had the Spanish Armada of 1588 led to the landing of an invading army, then it is not clear that it would have been easy to defend English towns against siege artillery. Yet, there might have been a spectacular siege of London to match the successful Spanish siege of Antwerp in 1585, and sieges could be important in the civil wars of the 1640s, as at Gloucester.

Buildings from the period testify to urban activity and wealth. Thus, the timber-framed Guildhall of Corpus Christi in Lavenham dates from about 1528–9 when the town was at the height of its prosperity and supported numerous clothiers. Paycocke's, a merchant's house in Coggeshall, dating from about 1500, testifies to the wealth of the town's cloth industry. Town buildings from the sixteenth century survive in some quantity, but their numbers were greatly lessened by subsequent rebuilding, especially in the nineteenth century, and by German air raids during World War Two. The latter were particularly devastating to Tudor buildings in Exeter, Plymouth and Southampton, although the timber-framed Elizabethan House on New Street in Plymouth is a fine surviving example. Other good examples are Greyfriars in Worcester, the Elizabethan House Museum in Great Yarmouth, and King John's Hunting Lodge (in fact a merchant's house of about 1500) in Axbridge. In contrast, buildings from the late seventeenth century, a period of major urban building, survive in larger quantities, in part because of the greater use then of incombustible brick. The bombing of Exeter proved particularly destructive to its High Street, as the wooden buildings were highly vulnerable to the incendiary bombs used by the Germans.

The world of 'things' focused on towns. Tudor England was a society that had more possessions than its predecessors, and the results can be seen in the fittings of Tudor houses, both halls and kitchens. The average home had fewer objects than a modern house, in large part because of the combination of low average incomes and an absence of mass production. Yet, more objects survive from the sixteenth century than from the fifteenth, and they do so both in aggregate terms and in per capita counterparts. Moreover, other evidence, such as probate inventories, legal records and literary references, also suggests a marked trend towards possessing more and living an increasingly comfortable life. This was also true of artisans, whose living standard was higher than that of husbandmen.[10]

Increasing material consumption, which focused on towns, invited denunciation by moralists. This consumption was seen as the symptom of an unhealthy craving for luxury and the cause of what was regarded as a major rise in crime, although such a rise has been frequently discerned, and is an instance of the way in which towns focus moral panics, both religious and secular.

The world of things had important cultural consequences, notably due to book ownership and printing, both of which centred in towns. Printing, moreover, became commercially attractive due to the strong demand for books building up in the fifteenth century. Printing helped make urban culture national culture, and made writing more available in a standard form: Londoners and people in Newcastle could read identical copies of the same book, creating a shared and respectable culture that manuscripts with their more limited readership could not generate. Education also centred on towns, and notably so with the rise of grammar schools. Printing was linked to Protestantism, with religion in part a matter of consumerism in that, despite the governmental determination to control developments, there was a degree of choice, sometimes illicit, between beliefs and practices. The intensity of commitment to Protestantism could be linked to book ownership, and to particular books, notably the Bible. Protestantism was a religion of the word.

The Reformation changed the face of cities with the suppression of monastic foundations. Medieval town plans long remained important but with the addition of the new division of former clerical lands. Many religious foundations had occupied much space in towns, whether individually or combined, and helped define their shape. In London, the friaries, notably the Black Friars (the Dominicans), occupied about five per cent of the City's land.[11] Each foundation that was dissolved was an opportunity to rethink, as well as sell, this space and revealed a need to address religious provision and associated social and educational access.

The background was one of energetic lay piety, for example in Norwich, and considerable church building and renovation in the late fifteenth and early sixteenth centuries, for example in Suffolk, Bristol, and the South West, as with the major enlargement of St Michael's, Honiton from 1478, but not only there. Carlisle Cathedral gained splendid choir stalls in the mid-fifteenth century and Rochester Cathedral, another monastic cathedral, was embellished by a Perpendicular-style Lady Chapel in 1490. Within towns, churches served as the centres of identity, linking the generations, as parish churches were the venue for weddings, baptisms, and burials, and their funerary monuments a place of admonition and record as well as memory and loss. The memory represented by a sense of family coherence focused upon churches.

The pre-Reformation Church could also have a continuing major impact on townscapes. Thus, King's College was founded in Cambridge by Henry VI in 1441. To clear space he purchased and levelled houses, shops, lanes, and wharves in the centre of the town, even having a church demolished between the river and the High Street. The purchasing and clearances took three years. The main structures of the mighty chapel itself were not completed until about 1515.

The Reformation transformed the situation, not least by transferring ownership of monasteries, nunneries, and much Church wealth and patronage, and by encouraging the destruction of buildings.[12] Thus, the fifteenth-century tower is all that remains of St Michael's church on Glastonbury Tor, part of Glastonbury Abbey, Somerset, one of the many monasteries ruined at the Dissolution. Other urban monasteries that were turned into ruins included that at Bury St Edmunds. Some of the 12,000 tonnes of stone used by the Cecils to cover the large façade of Burghley House came from monastic buildings in Stamford. Bourne Mill was built by Sir Thomas Lucas as a fishing lodge in 1591 from the ruins of the Abbey of St John in Colchester. The Hospital of St John the Baptist in Warwick, an almshouse, went into the hands of the Stoughton family. Thomas Cromwell gained Lewes Priory.

There was also much change in individual churches. The churchwardens' accounts of Bishops Stortford show that, as required by law and therefore under pressure from the central government, an English-language Bible was purchased in 1541–2, while in 1547–8 a cross, chalices, a pax, censers, an incense boat, and broken altar vessels, were sold by weight, with more following in 1550, while a chantry with its assets went and altars were removed, all causing local anger. In 1554–5, as part of the Marian reaction, a mass-book, pyx, holy-water stoup, altar cloths, a new rood, incense, and an incense boat were among what was bought.[13]

The destruction of the monasteries was a major break with the past, although there could also be a degree of adaptation. The dissolution of the monasteries was accomplished by royal commissioners and contributed to the display of royal power throughout the country. In Carlisle, as far distant from London as any town in England, the Sub-Prior of the Augustinian

Priory, Sir Richard Howthwaite, was executed in 1538 for allegedly spreading rumours of further revolt following the recently suppressed Pilgrimage of Grace, and in 1540 the Royal Commissioners appeared, accompanied by an escort. Lancelot Salkeld, the last Prior, who surrendered the Priory and its possessions that year, became the first Dean of the Cathedral Church of St Mary's, Carlisle, a measure of continuity, but under royal supervision: the Priory was a royal foundation. The Priory possessions in Carlisle reverted to the Dean and Chapter. A similar process was followed at Durham Cathedral Priory.

Church wealth was used for a range of purposes. In the first major redrawing of diocesan boundaries for centuries, six new sees were created, all urban-based: Bristol, Chester, Gloucester, Oxford, Peterborough, and, briefly, Westminster. Moreover, in some cases, monastic churches were purchased by parishes, as in Tewkesbury,[14] and this gave communities an increased ability to control much of their religious life. Rather than for monastic foundations, bequests were now more frequently left for parish churches, educational uses and almshouses. The Wymondham select vestry, founded to manage the property of the dissolved abbey, which had been transferred to the townspeople, took care of maintenance, poor relief, the upkeep of roads and bridges, and other local ends.[15] In Norwich, the 'Great Hospital' was refounded in 1547 under the control of the town, providing care for forty poor inmates, as well as some medical and educational facilities.[16] Indeed, the dissolution of the monasteries helped create opportunities for existing and new corporate bodies. This process underlined the potential of the 'group personhood' that was so important to urban identities. This group identity was a counterpoint to the individualism of townspeople, and this could lead to problems.[17]

Some towns were hard-hit by the loss of wealthy monastic foundations, for example Abingdon, Bruton and Glastonbury, but others with a stronger economy, such as Shaftesbury, managed better. Opposition to religious change led to rebellions from 1536, and these ensured that medieval fortifications not only continued to play a prominent role in the townscape, as in Exeter and Newcastle, but also in conflict. Carlisle was attacked during the Pilgrimage of Grace of 1536 but remained loyal, while York admitted the Pilgrims. The resistance of Exeter to siege in 1549 was important to the failure of the

Prayer Book Rebellion, and of London to that of Wyatt's Rebellion in 1554.[18] King's Lynn and Norwich were both damaged during Kett's Rebellion in 1549, which was still annually commemorated in Norwich a century later.

The Marian persecution of the Protestants also provided an urban landscape of commemoration. Defoe linked 'Hadley', the Suffolk clothmaking town of Hadleigh, to both that persecution and the very recent Jacobite Atterbury Plot of 1721–2, noting:

> 'From Ipswich I took a turn into the country to Hadley, principally to satisfy my curiosity, and see the place where the famous martyr, and pattern of charity and religious zeal in Queen Mary's time, Dr Rowland Taylor, was put to death [1555]; the inhabitants, who have a wonderful veneration for his memory, show the very place where the stake which he was bound to, was set up, and they have put a stone upon it, which nobody will remove; but it is a more lasting monument to him that he lives in the hearts of the people. I say more lasting than a tomb of marble would be, for the memory of that good man will certainly never be out of the poor people's minds, as long as this island shall retain the Protestant religion among them; how long that may be, as things are going, and if the detestable conspiracy of the Papists now on foot should succeed, I will not pretend to say.'

Thanks in large part to its longevity, the reign of Elizabeth I (1558–1603) brought an important degree of stabilisation to a national ecclesiastical settlement. This resulted in a change in urban culture, as Catholic ways of looking at the world faded out or were brought to a close. Earlier in the century, the vitality of mystery plays had been shown, with them being written down in Wakefield in the 1520s, while the Chester and Coventry plays were reworked in the 1530s. Yet, under Elizabeth, the situation changed. The last recorded performances at York, Coventry and Chester were in 1569, 1571 and 1575 respectively, and attempts to revive performances at York in 1579 and Chester in 1591 were abortive. However, as some public rituals were brought to a close, they were replaced by others, such as, after 1558, the Queen's Accession Day anniversary; after 1588, the celebration of the anniversary of the defeat of the Armada; and, after 1605, the celebration of the failure of the Gunpowder Plot. In London, the plays staged in the Inns of Court in part took a role of the earlier town plays, although the context and content were very different.

The Reformation introduced differentiation between towns in the shape of those that became centres of Protestantism and, by contrast, others where Catholicism remained significant. It also led to a measure of standardisation in the shape of the energy devoted to ensuring the new settlement. Regional and local variations in these and other factors were to play a role in the English Civil War of 1642–6. So also with dialect (both oral accent and words printed), which posed a major difference within towns and also between town and country. Born and educated in Stratford-upon-Avon, but living for long in London, William Shakespeare frequently played with dialect as a humorous device, one often linked to travel, distance and the bringing together of strangers, and was able to suggest distance as a result – both physical distance and social distance.

As a reminder of the variety of urban activities and policy, Exeter Council agreed to the construction of 'three commonjakes' or latrines in 1568. More seriously, poor diet encouraged diarrhoea, colon parasitic infection, hepatitis and salmonella, while malnutrition stunted growth, hit energy levels, and reduced resistance to ill-health, especially in the 1590s, a period of poor harvests and bad weather. Crowded housing conditions, the sharing of beds and, also, the effluent from undrained privies running alongside dwellings, helped spread diseases, particularly respiratory infections. The plague remained a serious problem, hitting hard Carlisle and Kendal for example in 1598.

Most dwellings were neither warm nor dry, and it was very difficult to get clothes dry, which discouraged the washing of clothes. Moreover, industrial processes were dangerous to others besides the workers. Dressing and tanning leather polluted water supplies, while urine (usually animal) was widely used for fulling cloth well into the eighteenth century. The kilns of brick and tile works produced smoke and fumes. Fires, more generally, were a major risk to urban life. Among the towns suffering major fires were Nantwich (1583) and Tiverton (1598); although there had been no major fire in London since 1212, at least partly due to effective precautions.[19] The Nantwich fire burned for 20 days, destroyed 150 buildings and made about 900 people, half the population, homeless. Fires challenged town governments and philanthropic practices and resilience.[20] Urban responses to problems drew on medieval precedents, but there were also significant developments. In Norwich, a committee set up in 1552 sought to improve sanitation by identifying problems with the waterways and by paving streets, using powers of taxation and enforcement to that end. Elizabeth I ordered a nationwide collection to rebuild Nantwich, contributing £1,000 and a local group administered the funds and poor relief, and oversaw the purchase of trees for rebuilding the town.[21] In Tiverton, 409 houses were destroyed as the result of a fire caused by the use of straw for cooking rather than more expensive wood.

Whatever the size of towns, they shared the inegalitarian and hierarchical nature of the rest of society.[22] The smallest group were the wealthy and prominent, their power expressed in and deriving from their ability to organise others, legally as Justices of the Peace, generally economically and also often politically. Their strength extended into the rural hinterland, where they would enjoy influence as a result of their power and at least partly because they often chose to go and live there, provide a source of credit, purchase and retain estates, and, if merchants, control rural industry. Within the towns, this group might be employers and/or landowners and generally enjoyed political power as a result of social status and the oligarchical nature of urban government.

The largest urban group were the poor, who tended to lack political weight. Their poverty stemmed from the precarious nature of much employment in even the most prosperous of towns and from the absence of any effective system of social welfare. Most lacked the skills that would command a decent wage and many had only seasonal or episodic employment. Day-labourers, servants and paupers were economically vulnerable and often socially isolated; a large number were immigrants from the countryside. As a result of poverty, the poor were very exposed to changes in the price of food and generally lived in inadequate housing.

In between these two groups, though not separated rigidly from either of them in economic terms, and many of them coming from above or below, was a third one, the 'middling sort', enjoying a more settled income than the poor. Many in this group were artisans, their economic interests and social cohesion frequently expressed through fraternities of workmen. In contemporary discourse, they were the 'people', but part of the poor were 'undeserving',[23] a pejorative description that had scant accurate basis. In *Julius Caesar*, Shakespeare has Casca refer to the crowd as 'the rabblement', 'the common herd', and 'the tag-rag people'.

Alongside relatively static assessments of social structure, as well as the largely fixed spatial distributions of occupations within towns, there were the dynamics, at individual, family and collective levels, of change, in prosperity and independence. So also with the arrival and presence of immigrant groups. Dutch textile merchants in Colchester in the late sixteenth century had their own church and pastor. There were also 'foreign' churches in London. The Reformation led to considerable movement of Continental Protestants into England, while some Catholics left.

The populations of most towns rose during the century but there were considerable problems of dearth (shortages) and poverty in the 1590s, in part due to poor harvests. There were more serious issues in some towns, for example Carlisle, which was affected by famine and plague in 1598. Shakespeare's native Stratford-upon-Avon, a malting town, was hit by shortages of the barley necessary for malting and by high prices for food, as well as by fires in 1594 and 1595.[24]

Tudor London was very much affected not only by immigration but also by the large-scale migration arising from population growth in England. This migration, with its densification of the urban space and demands on jobs, food supplies, and charity placed pressures on the society and governance of London. In part, the pressures led to a hostile response to immigrants, but there was also a more general tension, as in disputes over the delineation of plots of land, an issue still very frequent today. One response was the use of the London Viewers, appointed commissioners who were instructed to resolve boundary disputes.[25] Such problems contributed to the lack of stability, even permanence, in urban living; but the same was true of its rural counterpart.

The unsurprising failure of the Crown to implement an integrated approach to the suburbs ensured that their governance and authority were fragmented, as was that of London as a whole. This situation remained the case until the Greater London Council was established in 1965. Moreover, separately, Westminster remained distinct from London. In Westminster, because of opposition by the Crown and the Dean and Chapter to a borough government, a Court of Burgesses, established in 1585 and nominated by the Dean, had less power than the City Corporation. To contribute to the *mélange* of clashing power there were also in Westminster the Middlesex JPs, a High Steward appointed by the monarch, the vestrymen of the individual parishes, as well as the local gentry who could be reluctant to heed appropriate authority. This interaction both challenged stability and was crucial to it. In Westminster, as elsewhere, it was necessary to mediate the enforcement of regulations through a governance in which competing interests had to be negotiated, not only in relations with social supervisors but also with those of a similar background or more precarious circumstances. Negotiation involved everything from poor relief, its contributions and entitlement, to disputes over enclosures or plague regulations.[26] The same was true of other towns.

The area that was most regulated in London was the City, under the Mayor and Corporation, with its identity celebrated by ritual, including the Lord Mayor's Show. The City was able to call on a network of control in order to enforce regulations, as with the recoinage early in Elizabeth's reign, during which the Mayor instructed the Livery Companies to send representatives into every market in order to ensure that the new coins were accepted, thus showing the City and government cooperating. The Companies served as ways to regulate but also to link, which helped contain differences, the latter role of linkage including between the City and the suburbs. Guild politics, indeed, proved a way to register as well as contain differences, contributing to a metropolitan community, as compromise was a way to deal with the large-scale disruption of economic and religious change. At the same time, concern about the suburbs remained strong, and was part of a wider sense of anxiety about change and uncertainty.

Poor relief reflected and sought to tackle real pressure in towns, not least because poverty was highly visible in small and crowded settlements where much life was on the street. Towns were thronged with migrants from the countryside which shed people as the population doubled from the 1520s to the 1650s. Real wages fell appreciably, further adding pressure on living standards and philanthropy. A series of statutes was aimed at discouraging able-bodied beggars, while providing relief for the 'impotent' poor.[27]

Migrants could find life in the suburbs easier as land and rents were cheaper and regulations less to the fore, although a key aspect was that of the variety of the suburban experience.[28] Much effort and expenditure was required in order to support the social stability and physical fabric of towns, with poverty and vagrancy counterparts in civic attention to the deterioration of the latter.[29] On a longstanding basis, but one accentuated by the tensions arising from religious change and political instability, and then brought to crisis in the 1590s, urban government sought to address these issues and did so in part by increasing its power and lessening any democratic tendencies, or, at least, opposition by those not linked to the governing oligarchy.[30] This rivalry looked toward the political disorder and governmental changes of the following century.

Again, there is the question of continuity. The latter does not imply an absence of change, but rather that change was limited by powerful constraints and/or part of a rhythmic character, rather than one of exponential change. There was a degree to which urban circumstances should be considered in this light, as indeed should those of England as a whole. Thus, arguments about the precursors of the Industrial Revolution include discussion about long-term growth rates that go back to the Tudor period, notably in the steadily rising use of coal. This approach provides a way to look at exponential change and, therefore, to consider the role of towns within it, possibly as enablers of economic change but also as providing services to it. Each can better be understood if it is appreciated that the towns were as much part of the agricultural sector as of the industrial and commercial ones. All three interacted closely.

In demographic terms, the sixteenth century saw significant growth that was to continue into the early seventeenth, but the crises of the 1590s provided multiple warnings of serious weaknesses in economy, society, governance and politics. These affected the experience of urban life for many, although the same was true of its rural counterpart. Indeed, the bleakness of the latter helped explain why there were so many migrants to towns, migrants who remained a key driver of urban society and whose assimilation gave it a character of tension as well as opportunity. If this was true of other periods, then that captures the continuities of urban history.

Chapter 3

Stuart Towns

'Streets of booths were set upon the Thames… all sorts of trades and shops furnished and full of commodities. Coaches plied [on the Thames] full from Westminster to the Temple, and from several other stairs [to the river] to and fro, as in the streets; sledges, sliding with skates, a bull baiting, horse-and-coach races, puppet plays and interludes, cooks, tippling and other lewd places, so that it seemed to be a bacchanalian triumph, or carnival on the water.'

John Evelyn, the famous diarist,
on the Great Frost Fair of 1683–4.

'…the insolence of the common people has risen to a great height about the carrying out of corn especially at Worcester where they not only forced the prisons to let out some of their companions that were committed for these [food] riots but they went in a body where they heard there was a great magazine of corn which they took away and sold it by proclamation for two shillings per bushel.'

James Vernon, the confidential figure in the offices of the
Secretaries of State, at the time of weather-related dearth, 1693.[1]

The most dramatic aspect of the century for towns, as indeed for society as a whole, was that of war, a period of civil warfare of unprecedented scale, though not length. Already, in 1638–40, a breakdown in relations with Scotland had led to increased attention to fortified border towns, justifiably so as the Scots advanced and forced their way across the Tyne in 1640. A plan of Newcastle in 1638 showed the defences of the town including the hills that commanded it as the latter helped establish vulnerability to cannon. The First Civil War, between Charles I and Parliament, followed in 1642–6, the second in 1648, and there was renewed large-scale fighting in England in 1651 when Charles II unsuccessfully invaded, being crushed at Worcester.

In the First Civil War, Parliament found particular backing in London and many of the large towns. There was frequently a divide between towns and hinterlands, one that drew on existing divisions. Thus, prior to the war, Dorchester life reflected the tensions between Puritanism and the Crown.[2] Yet, alongside significant opposition, there were important signs of urban support for Charles I, as when he entered London in November 1641 and Lincoln in July 1642.

Divisions in towns reflected social structures, religious affiliations, political commitments, ideological stances, personalities and contingencies, and could be expressed through performative civic activism, from pageantry to riots.[3] The costs of government demands, notably from the 1620s, as well as the pressures arising from ecclesiastical policies, in the shape especially of the Arminianism of Archbishop William Laud, increased the strains on consensus in the always complex dance of collaboration and contention affecting relations between Crown and towns, as well as within the latter.[4]

At the same time, the causes of disruption did not solely come from the Crown. Thus, in Kidderminster, the Puritans who included the clothiers, were opposed by conservatives who were comprised more of journeymen and were fearful of Puritan moves against their public sociability of drinking and processions. This pre-war tension in Kidderminster became wartime division, and some Puritans, such as the preacher Richard Baxter, left the town, not returning until 1647.[5]

While Kidderminster was Royalist, towns such as Blackburn, Bolton, Exeter, Gloucester, Hull, Leicester, Lyme Regis, Manchester, Plymouth, Reading, and Taunton all backed Parliament, while their hinterlands supported Charles.[6] This situation, at once local and regional, encouraged the Royalists to try to seize these towns as part of their national strategy, but also separate to it. Much of the war indeed was local. Yet, key bridging points made towns major centres for conflict, notably Gloucester, Worcester and Preston, with battles at the last two and a major siege at the first. The same was true for ports, such as Lyme Regis, Plymouth and Hull, all of which were besieged by the Royalists, but which could obtain supplies by sea and were able to hold out.

As in the Wars of the Roses, holding towns could prove fruitless in the event of defeat in the field, as with the Parliamentarian loss of Lichfield after the battle of Hopton Heath in 1643, and the Royalist loss of York after defeat at Marston Moor in 1644. Yet, despite this, many towns had to be stormed, for example Bristol in 1643 and Leicester in 1645, both by the Royalists. It was only necessary to find one weak place to break through. Other towns fell to siege, as Exeter did to the Royalists in 1643, York to the Parliamentarians in 1644, and Hereford to the Parliamentarians in 1646; or they successfully resisted siege, as did Coventry, Gloucester, Hull, Lyme Regis, and Plymouth when besieged by the Royalists.

The war saw much fortification. In Parliamentarian Gloucester and Northampton, and Royalist Worcester, surviving medieval walls were supplemented by new fortifications. The castle in Newcastle was refortified. Other towns saw new works. In particular, London, the key urban support for the Parliamentary cause, not least in taxation, loans and recruits, was protected by major new fortifications built in 1642–3, and far more extensive than the walls. They were a response to the advance of the Royalist army to nearby Turnham Green in 1642.

There was much damage, as with towns that underwent major sieges, such as Royalist Newark. It repelled sieges in 1643 and 1644 but in 1645–6 a six-month siege led to hunger and was accompanied by outbreaks of typhus and the plague that killed about 1,000 people before the town surrendered. A third of Taunton was destroyed in its two sieges. The economic base of towns could also be hit hard, as with Exeter, Gloucester and Reading, the last of which changed hands frequently.[7] Towns that experienced sieges and/or seizures were hit, but so also was the economic base of other towns.

There was also more specific damage. When Chester surrendered in 1646, the victorious Parliamentarians vandalised the Cathedral, breaking the stained glass and damaging the organ and much else. Ely cathedral had been vandalised two years before. A battle at Great Torrington in 1646 led to the destruction of the church and of many buildings. In 1643, Sir John Gell, the Parliamentary Governor of Derby, had paraded the naked corpse of Spencer Compton, 2nd Earl of Northampton, a defeated Royalist, round the town.

There was also organised privation, even destruction, which focused on towns. In 1643, Prince Rupert, a leading Royalist commander, ordered nearby parish constables to provide labour for fortifying Towcester, adding, 'in no ways fail, as you will answer the contrary at your utmost peril; as the total plundering and burning of your houses, with what other mischiefs the hungry soldiers can inflict upon you.' The onerous demands of garrisons such as Hereford and Langport led to the Clubman movement in 1644, as local people in the Welsh Marches and the West Country sought to keep troops out. This may not appear relevant to a history of towns, but that history includes their impact elsewhere and the resulting response to them, a response that included lasting grievances.

There was no comparable damage or loss in English society, urban and rural, until the twentieth century. After the war, as a result of the conflict, there were many who were fatherless, including 56 per cent of the Gloucester apprentices in 1653.[8] The strains of the war had pressed very hard on the population, urban and rural alike, but with townspeople more exposed to conscription, seizures, taxation and billeting, and their churches, clergy and religious observances far more under scrutiny and regulation.[9] Thus, in Parliamentary Norwich, there was iconoclasm, the prohibition of Christmas Day as a festival, and an assault on guild days as festivals. These strains contributed to Royalist rioting there in 1648 as well as helping outline a subsequent topography of political commitment in the city.[10] The prohibition of Christmas celebrations also led to rioting in Canterbury. The same pattern was seen elsewhere.[11]

The disruption of the Civil War greatly complicated, but scarcely ended, civic culture, more particularly the pressing obligations of municipal government, notably poor relief and the maintenance of a basic infrastructure. In many respects, there were major additions to these burdens and tasks due to the extent to which the Civil War hit the Church of England and its provision of services. As a result, there was even greater pressure on town councils, for the secular aspect of municipal governance was now expected to cover more.[12]

The Civil War experience and histories of towns helped affect their later political culture and self-image. Thus, 11 May, the anniversary of the raising of the siege of Parliamentary-held Taunton in 1645, a result which was seen as a great providential salvation against the Royalists, was celebrated with sermons preached into the 1720s and an annual celebration held into the 1770s. Politically, these events were a Nonconformist radical expression of opposition there to the Tory Corporation, for the Nonconformists looked to the Parliamentarians for their history. These local politics relieved, and were enlivened by historical divisions. Taunton's strong Nonconformist commitment led to support in 1679 for the exclusion from the succession of the Catholic, James, Duke of York, the future James II, only, in the early 1680s, for the Tory reaction to see the destruction of Nonconformist meeting houses.[13]

So, conversely, with Worcester, where longstanding Royalist support was in part a response to anger at damage by victorious Cromwellians in 1651 when Charles II was defeated. This anger may have been a factor in 1786 when Thomas Jefferson and John Adams visited Worcester, complaining about a lack of support there for the victorious cause in the Civil War. In contrast, George III received a very good response when he visited. Only in 2018 did Worcester decide to mark the visit of the future presidents with a statue.

The Civil Wars led to a particular reworking of the histories of towns, but this was but part of the process by which history was supplemented and reworked. Thus, Barnstaple had a chronicle, written by the Town Clerk, from 1586 to 1611.[14] This process extended to the visual image of towns, in both maps and illustrations. The two could be combined as many maps included pictogram elements. These related in particular to major buildings, economic activities, such as linen production and fishing nets, and town crests. John Speed's *Theatre of the Empire of Great Britain* (1611–12) contained 73 insert town plans, the majority of them hitherto unmapped.[15] Subsequently, it was necessary to decide whether to show episodes from the Civil War in mapping.

During and after the war, the victorious Parliamentarians 'slighted' or rendered useless Royalist defences, both town walls and, in particular castles, permanently changing town defences and landscape. The castles at Corfe, Kenilworth, Pontefract, Sheffield, Skipton, and Wallingford were among those slighted. On occasion, as in Sheffield, the townspeople were consulted.[16] Among the changes of the Interregnum period (1649–60), there was also the removal of royal iconography and extensive disruption and damage to the Church including the abolition of cathedrals.

In turn, on 29 May 1660, Charles II entered London:

'with a triumph of ... horse and foot, brandishing their swords and shouting with inexpressible joy; the way strewed with flowers, the bells ringing, the streets hung with tapestry, fountains running with wine; the mayor, aldermen and all the companies in their liveries, chains of gold, banners; lords and nobles, everyone clad in cloth of silver, gold and velvet; the windows and balconies all set with ladies, trumpets, music and myriads flocking the streets ... I stood in the Strand and beheld it and blessed God. And all this was done without one drop of blood ... it was the Lord's doing.'

John Evelyn's account of the Stuart Restoration did not, however, capture the serious disruption it brought. This included an attack on many individuals, for example the dismissal of the Postmaster of Sherborne,[17] and towns. The walls and defences of major towns that had backed Parliament, such as Coventry, Gloucester and Northampton, were slighted:

'Upon the 10th day of July 1662 the Lord Lieutenant of the County of Northampton and the Deputy Lieutenant came to this town with some of the trained bands ... pulled down the town walls and gates ... and carried away all the arms and armour that was left in the town.'

This destruction made it harder to police entry and thus control vagrancy.

As part of the reaction against Interregnum changes, Bradford, Leeds and Manchester lost the parliamentary seats they had gained for the 1653 'Barebone's Parliament,' while the poorly-populated 'rotten boroughs' who had lost their seats then, regained them. Defoe, a Nonconformist, commented on the consequences in the *Tour*, as of Castle-Rising, 'an old decayed borough town with perhaps not ten families in it, which yet ... sends two members to the British Parliament, being as many as the city of Norwich itself.' He made similar comments about Queenborough, Winchelsea, Gatton, Bletchingly, Old Sarum, Boroughbridge, Aldborough, and the South West as a whole. Separately, a 1702 pamphlet drew on political arithmetic:

'The Representative of London and Westminster in Parliament, Examined and Considered. Wherein appears the antiquity of most of the boroughs in England, with the proportions, whereby every county is over or under represented according to a scale from the Royal Aid Assessments; by which it appears that Middlesex is found to be represented but one tenth part of its due.'

In another reaction, printing and the supply of paper were strictly limited to the master printers of the Stationers' Company of London and the university printers, while a 1661 Act for the Well Governing and Regulating of Corporations allowed the king to purge boroughs of those regarded as disaffected. Local commissioners were supposed to get borough officials to take the Oaths of Supremacy and Allegiance and to remove the unwilling – or even those who were willing if they saw it as 'expedient for the public safety' to do so. In Gloucester, about three-quarters of the Corporation's members were purged, although most, in practice, had been willing to take the oaths. Thirteen of the 24 burgesses of Tewkesbury were purged in 1662. The imposition of an Anglican order was progressively tightened, with worship not in accordance with Anglican rites forbidden and the Five Mile Act of 1665 prohibiting Dissenting (Nonconformist) ministers from living within five miles of any corporate town or place in which they had served prior to the Act.

In turn, under Charles II (r. 1660–85) and his Catholic brother James II (r. 1685–8), continued political division affected urban politics and governance, and was linked to cultural issues, notably architectural patronage, plans, and projects.[18] Political conflicts, as in Pontefract, were shaped by memories of war and deep-rooted religious differences.[19] In 1586, as a result of a royal charter, the Corporation of Arundel had obtained some independence from its manorial lord. This Corporation was dominated by a Presbyterian group during the Civil War and Interregnum. Removed from power after Charles II's Corporation Act, they returned again after a legal judgment in 1677.[20] More generally, in the early 1680s, in the Tory reaction of the last years of Charles's reign, Charles resorted to encouraging the excommunication of Dissenters to deny them the vote in borough elections.[21] There was also an attack on Whig strongholds in which Corporation charters, such as that of

Norwich in 1682, were remodelled in order to increase Crown influence, while, in 1683, that of London was forfeited because its Council would not accept remodelling. As a result, London's government was brought under direct royal control. Although with significant differences, this was a precursor to the attack on municipal independence in the 1980s.

The remodelling of the London Livery Companies in the 1680s was part of a process of purge and counter-purge that fuelled long-lasting divisions and also helped create an institutional paralysis in the City of London that eased acceptance of the 'Glorious Revolution' of 1688–9; although political variations did not necessarily mean differences or changes in means of addressing urban problems. This point was demonstrated by Winchester where civic cohesion and conservative non-partisan continuity made a success of self-government. The limited ability of central government to create amenable local élites emerged there and elsewhere.[22] In Norwich, on a longstanding pattern, the civic élite sought to limit division by relying on a shared sociability, a moderation in politics, and an emphasis on loyalty to the town and its constitution. Indeed, there and elsewhere, many of those who were most divisive came from outside the élite, offering a different Norwich politics.[23]

Yet changes in personnel could be significant, and these tended to reflect actions by central government. These actions could influence municipal politics. However, once a core group of activists existed in a borough, it generated its own momentum, helping split towns both politically and in religious terms, for example Bedford, but also, if keen on moderation, lessening the impact of royal action.

In 1688, the 'Glorious Revolution' against James II saw not only William of Orange (later William III, r. 1689–1702) and an invading Dutch army overthrow James, but also a Whig seizure of power in many towns. The 'Glorious Revolution' was followed by the 'Revolution Settlement', product, classification and cause of a new political, governmental, religious, financial, economic and cultural settlement. One aspect was a change in regulation that had a major impact on the situation between towns and also within them. London monopolies were felled, for example that of the London Guild of Distillers in 1690. More generally, guilds ceased to be so relevant, and their ordinances and byelaws, which had sought to maintain their power and role, became increasingly redundant. Indeed, by the mid-eighteenth century, most guild regulations were of largely antiquarian interest. The extent to which modern livery companies, such as the Merchant Taylors in London or the Tuckers in Exeter, are charitable clubs, rather than governing bodies for particular trades, reflects the earlier collapse of the guilds as well as more general economic change. Moreover, within towns, the dominant position of the Church of England was weakened, often greatly so, as part of the 'Revolution Settlement'.

After political change imposed from outside, the other major problem for towns was that of fire, most famously in London in 1666, but also elsewhere; Tiverton, Wymondham, Northampton and Warwick being hard-hit in 1612, 1615, 1675 and 1694 respectively. Defoe noted of Alresford, which had a destructive fire in 1689, that:

> 'by a sudden and surprising fire, the whole town, with both the church and the market-house was reduced to a heap of rubbish; and, except a few poor huts at the remotest ends of the town, not a house left standing.'

There was another bad fire there in 1736 which began in a brewery.

Wood and thatch burned readily, while population growth, poorly-regulated building, and the intermixing of manufacturing and commerce with accommodation all provided problems.[24] Moreover, firefighting faced many limitations. Nevertheless, the Rebuilding Acts of Parliament for London acted as the model for large-scale building across the country, notably the stipulations against projecting windows and in favour of brick, as seen for example at Northampton. Parliamentary legislation provided authority for the Warwick Fire Commissioners whose authority lasted until 1704 and who dictated style and encouraged both rebuilding and the widening of streets.[25] This speeded up a more general change in building materials away from timber and towards brick, tile and ashlar. There was a pronounced social dimension to building materials, John Evelyn (a different one to the famous diarist) reporting in 1702 that:

> 'Truro [is] a very pretty neat town built of stone and covered with slate as most of the houses in this county [Cornwall] are, excepting those

which belong to the poor sort which generally consist of mud walls covered with thatch.'[26]

The Great Fire of London also encouraged the taking out of insurance policies, both in London and elsewhere. The resulting creation of fire insurance companies provided new links between London and other towns, as well as records on urban life and values, occupational profiles and building usage that are of considerable value.[27] The *British Mercury* of 4 February 1713 reported that a serious fire in Whitefriars in London was tackled by 25 'fire-men belonging to the Sun-Fire-Office ... and some few of other fire officers.' In Defoe's novel, Moll Flanders finds 'so many engines playing' when there was a fire. At the same time, social access to insurance varied greatly, which was part of the way in which the risk of fire 'structured' and reflected urban societies. Meanwhile, defensive considerations no longer explained the purpose or shape of towns. This was very much seen in the rebuilding of towns damaged by fire.

The emphasis in discussion can be very differently placed. Thirty-eight per cent of the children born in Penrith between 1650 and 1700 died before reaching the age of six.[28] Destroying hopes that bubonic plague was in decline, the brutal and rapidly-spread Great Plague of 1665 had fewer deaths as a percentage of London's population than some earlier plagues, while some other places in 1665 had more than in London, but more people died there than elsewhere, and therefore it was perceived that the plague hit London hardest. The 1636 epidemic had killed over 60,000 people, but 1665 was to see even more slaughtered. As deaths mounted, helped by a long, hot summer, red crosses were painted on the doors of the infected houses in a fruitless attempt at isolation. Beginning in April 1665, the Great Plague did not abate until the November frosts. It saw London's economy ruined. Public places, moreover, were closed, sports banned, a 9pm curfew imposed, and fairs prohibited.

Nevertheless, civil society did not break down during the Great Plague. Indeed, Defoe, a child at the time but whose later account reflected London opinion, praised the ability of the City authorities to provide security and sustenance, and, by comparison, criticised the Crown. Yet, there was an inability to keep records as accurate as is suggested by Defoe's thoughtful use of the Bills of Mortality in order to discuss the course of the epidemic. Although not all deaths would have been from plague, City records indicate that some 68,596 people died during the epidemic, although the actual number of deaths is suspected to have exceeded 100,000 out of a total population estimated at 460,000. This made the Covid epidemic of 2020–22 a mere statistical cough. The authorities could not keep up as deaths mounted in the long, hot summer, while the diarist Samuel Pepys was told by his parish clerk, 'There died nine this week though I have returned but six.' Moreover, the recording did not work well for Quakers or poor transients. Dead paupers were thrown into large burial pits such as one at Tottenham Court.

Many fled London, including the Court, the wealthy, most doctors, and a large number of the parochial clergy. This exodus helped ensure the spread of the plague outside London, both in the South-East and more generally, a process covered by Defoe and which hit hard places linked to London such as Newcastle, the provider of its coal.

The flight of clergy was a serious issue as, in response to the crisis, many of the churches in London were thronged. In a classic instance of his partisanship, Defoe made much of this flight, contrasting it with the determination of Dissenting clergy to stay and continue to minister to all, not only their flock but also the members of the Established Church. After the epidemic, however, there was no let-up in measures against the Dissenters.

This was the last major attack of the plague in England. However, immunity to smallpox, which replaced the plague as the most feared disease, was low, not least because a virulent strain began to have an impact in the second half of the seventeenth century. Towns had quite a number of physicians and, if other medical practitioners were included, there were plenty. However, aside from a lack of appropriate treatments, there were also the issues created by living conditions, not least poor sanitation, crowded residences, and a shortage of sufficient food. Infection was a particular problem in the winter because that was the season of indoor life. In Alcester in 1727–30, a very difficult period health-wise across the country, 21 per cent of the population died.[29]

Living circumstances were grim for most. In towns such as Frome, poor women and children spun wool in their homes. In Defoe's novel *Moll Flanders* (1722), the young Moll is taught to spin worsted, which was the chief industry in Colchester where she grows up. Yet, despite death rates, there was also, as a result of migration, considerable growth in towns, and, as a result of the markets they provided, for producers within their boundaries, in nearby rural areas and in other towns. The demand provided by markets was greatly fostered by urban entrepreneurship and credit which extended the reach of this demand.[30]

Towns in the seventeenth century moved from poverty, conflict and disease to an urban renewal that gathered particular pace from the 1690s but was already in progress before that[31] and of which some aspects can be seen in some towns from the outset.[32] Thus, Norwich recovered from industrial and commercial depression from the 1660s.[33] There were attempts to improve the urban environment: in 1665, it was ordered in Evesham that all householders place lights in front of their dwellings on pain of a fine.[34] In Taunton, the 'East Reach' of the town saw redevelopment on the site of the sieges of the 1640s.

At the same time, governance faced a process of discussion and compromise, or, overlapping but also different, downright opposition and avoidance, that limited both municipal and national initiatives.[35] There were reasons aplenty for division. In the late seventeenth century, there were cross-currents as the result of a reiteration of the oligarchic nature of guilds, one, however, in which traditional regulations were pushed aside by entrepreneurs, leading to journeymen joining together to protect their interests in a context of limited social mobility.[36]

Looking forward to the situation in the next century,[37] but also continuing past practice, the degree of incorporation between municipal governance and urban groups and interests varied greatly. This reflected the composition, conduct, and goals of this governance. The working practices of urban corporations, for example Canterbury and Maidstone, could differ considerably and this affected the extent and nature of organisational cohesion in individual towns.[38]

Until after the Civil Wars, the walls largely delimited towns, as with Newcastle. Nevertheless, there could be significant buildings within towns, as in Newcastle again, where there was the rebuilding of the Guildhall and Exchange (1644–8) and the new Mansion House (1691). Benefiting from plentiful local coal, Newcastle produced about 40 per cent of all the glass made in England in the seventeenth century. The availability of coal was more generally significant. In Defoe's novel *Colonel Jack* (1722), the young boys find warmth in the smouldering ashes resulting from coal-fired glass production in London. The Bear Garden in Southwark was replaced by a glassworks in the 1680s. Edward, Lord Harley's travelling party visited the coal-fired salt pans at South Shields.

Towns provided a setting for industrial development, not least as they offered transport, capital, demand, buildings, labour and norms of economic activity. Their role as service centres sustained these valuable offerings to industry.[39] For example, Nottingham had a major pottery industry, with the production of salt-glaze stoneware starting between 1688 and 1693. Sheffield developed as a major centre of metallurgy.[40]

The successive maps of Bristol produced from 1673 by James Millerd registered the growth of a key port and a major manufacturing centre, including of such products as refined sugar, soap and glass. The castle had been demolished by the Cromwellian government in 1656, which opened the way to new building on the site. This was an equivalent to the dissolution of a major monastic site, although less socially disruptive. Subsequent maps also showed the erection of the Cornmarket (1684) and the changing use of the 'great house'. Used as a term in Bristol and elsewhere to describe the largest mansions of the urban élite, those in Bristol were adapted to act as sugar or soap manufactures in the seventeenth century, and in 1696 one used for the former became the Mint, for the recoinage of 1696, and then, from 1697, the home of Bristol's pioneering Corporation of the Poor: a public workhouse and hospital established as an expression of civic responsibility by the city's wealthy merchants to address public concern about poverty, which were another aspect of the growth that saw Norwich replaced by Bristol in about 1700 as England's second town.

The rebuilding of towns became a more continuous process. Thus, Bristol's Cornmarket was demolished in the 1720s: the world of business digested what had come before. Clarendon House, Piccadilly, a spectacular palace built in 1664–7 for the Lord Chancellor, Edward, 1st Earl of Clarendon, father-in-law to James, Duke of York, was sold after the Earl's death in 1683 to bankers and merchants, who demolished the house and developed the site. More generally for London, Celia Fiennes recorded: 'There was formerly in the city several houses of the noblemen with large gardens and out houses, but of late are pulled down and built into streets and squares and called by the names of the noblemen, and this is the practice by almost all.'

Alongside concern about towns came the longstanding idea that they could be a model of social behaviour, one that looked to religious ideas of the Heavenly City and Classical models based primarily on Athens and Rome. In his *Tour*, Defoe praised the Earl of Pembroke, owner of Wilton House, adding:

> 'The family like a well governed city appears happy, flourishing, and regular groaning under no grievance, pleased with what they enjoy, and enjoying everything which they ought to be pleased with.'

It was not only political issues that help explain differences between towns and their trajectories. The significance of economic fortune remained important and could be seen in trade, external and internal, and industry. There were the classic factors of exhaustion, such as the working out of resources or the silting up of harbours; but also the variations arising from entrepreneurialship and from competition between towns, some of which, such as Lincoln, stagnated.[41] Ports were affected by supply and demand factors for their products, with grain exporters, such as King's Lynn, hit by bad harvests.[42] At a more continual level, the significance of the East Coast trade was very important to the prosperity of a number of ports.[43]

There were also the beginnings of a major enhancement of the transport system within the country. In Yorkshire, the improvement in the Aire and Calder navigation to Leeds and Halifax in 1699–1701 was a major step, as noted by Defoe in the *Tour*:

> 'by which a communication by water was opened from Leeds and Wakefield to Hull, and by which means all the woollen manufactures ... is carried by water to Hull, and there shipped... they can carry coal down from Wakefield (especially) and also from Leeds...'

Under an Act of 1699, the navigation of the Trent to Burton was improved, which enabled it to develop as a major brewing centre.

By 1700, probably about 17 per cent of the population, but possibly more, lived in towns, defined as settlements with more than about 2,000 people. Only six, however, had a population of over 10,000: London, Norwich, Bristol, Newcastle, Exeter and York. Yet, these were the forcing houses of a new society that was increasingly to offer a very different prospect for the future.

Although the extent and nature of the political society created after the 'Glorious Revolution' are matters of academic debate, nevertheless it is clear that this 'public space' focused on towns.[44] At the same time, the process very much varied by town: there was no consistent, let alone united, 'public space'. This was the case with both content and context, not least the degree to which there was religious antipathy and political activism. There was also the local context that was important to the specific character of local culture.[45]

The 'Glorious Revolution' of 1688–9 saw the statues of James II pulled down in Gloucester and Newcastle and the Staff of Authority on his statue in Whitehall broken, as was the sceptre out of the hand of Mary I, another Catholic, in the Royal Exchange in London.[46] Thanks to the subsequent development of an unregulated press, the urban public was able to follow the news with great attention. The *Observator* of 10 June 1702 commented on the public's interest in the War of the Spanish Succession:

> "'Tis an easy matter to pull down pallisades, to attack half-moons, bastions, and counterscarps, in the coffee-houses of London and Westminster, and to bomb citadels and castles with quart bottles of wine in a tavern, where there is seen no smoke but that of tobacco, nor no shot felt but when the reckoning comes to be paid.'

Because it challenged constitutional and social convention, such commentary was politically and socially subversive, or at least potentially so. In the novel *Secret History of Queen Zarah and the Zarazians* (1705) which was probably the work of Joseph Browne:[47]

> 'apprentice boys assume the air of statesmen before they have learned the mystery of trade. Mechanics of the meanest rank plead for a liberty to abuse their betters, and turn out ministers of state with the same

freedom that they smoke tobacco. Carmen and cobblers over coffee draw up articles of peace and war and make partition treaties.'

Indeed, in 1742, Edward Southwell, an MP for Bristol, observed:

'I am sure my station is not to be envied so liable to suspicions and misconstructions and without any compass but my own private judgement to steer by and yet every motion open to the cavils of so divided and populous a city as ours is.'[48]

Criticised for backing the ministry on two measures,[49] Southwell disagreed, adding:

'if I am to suffer or be run down for every single private vote in an affair where none but those who hear the arguments and pleadings can be judges, it is certain that no man can be more a slave than the representative of so populous a city.'[50]

The practice of instructing MPs caused contention, in particular during political crises.[51]

The 'Glorious Revolution' had launched a new period of urban activism, one in which the focus was on a Parliament with annual sessions and regular elections, the latter making it far more dependent on electors. As parliamentary boroughs, rather than the shires, had the majority of the seats in the House of Commons, this was a situation in which towns were over-represented and thus of particular importance. The 203 English boroughs returned 405 MPs, whereas the counties only returned 80. The borough franchise was consciously varied, with different categories of boroughs: householder, freeman, scot and lot, corporation, burgage, and freeholder boroughs. In the twelve householder or 'potwalloper' boroughs, the right of voting was enjoyed by all male inhabitants not receiving poor relief or charity. The qualifications for becoming freemen in the ninety-two freeman boroughs varied greatly, although generally the influence of the Corporation (Council) over the creation of freemen ensured that its views had to be considered. The thirty-seven scot and lot constituencies gave the vote to inhabitant householders, so that occupation of property was crucial. In some of these constituencies, it was necessary also to pay the Poor Rate; in others the franchise was enjoyed by inhabitant householders receiving neither alms nor poor relief. This group included Westminster, the borough constituency with the largest electorate: about 8,000 voters in the first half of the eighteenth century.

In the twenty-seven corporation boroughs, the right of voting was limited to the corporation; in the twenty-nine burgage boroughs to specific pieces of property; and in the six freeholder boroughs to those who owned freeholds. These constituencies had smaller electorates than the householder, freeman, and scot and lot boroughs. Although the boroughs with smaller electorates did not all provide a picture of oligarchic control and corrupt practices, they were generally more stable in their politics and more amenable to outside influence than those with larger electorates.

At the same time, quite populous boroughs could be under the electoral control of particular, often non-resident, families, a control that commonly reflected local property, although it was generally a relationship that had to be managed with care as well as expenditure, as with that of the Dukes of Bedford in Bedford and Tavistock, the Dukes of Bolton and Somerset at Totnes, the Dukes of Bolton and Chandos at Winchester, the Dukes of Grafton and Earls of Bristol at Bury St Edmunds, the Earls Gower at Newcastle under Lyme, and the Robartes of nearby Lanhydrock at Bodmin. The concept of good lordship was crucial to political process and structure. Granting honorary freedoms of the borough to aristocrats, knights, baronets, clergy and gentry compromised the freedom of Ipswich, although, in all these cases, this was more obviously the case in the early eighteenth century.[52]

Merchant representation and mercantile business played a growing role in the Commons, while, after 1690, there was a massive increase in the number of petitions submitted covering overseas trade. Thus, in 1720, James Craggs wrote to his fellow Secretary of State about the need to use diplomatic pressure, observing that:

> 'the principal merchants of [Great] Yarmouth trading in corn to Denmark being apprehensive that a duty will be laid upon their corn, which would amount to a prohibition, I have at their request recommended their

case to Mylord Polwarth [envoy in Copenhagen]. And as that branch of our trade is not a little important to us, I believe your Lordship will judge it proper, as I do, that you should move His Majesty [George I] for directions to Mylord Polwarth to make the necessary instances in that behalf.'[53]

The celebration of the patriot merchant, a theme centring on ports, helped make trade a potent political goal and platform, and this linked to the pursuit of maritime hegemony and imperial advantage, albeit one in which there were significant rivalries between commercial interests.[54] At the same time, most towns were small ones, scarcely imperial ports. Moreover, despite the tendency to focus on major centres, the number and size of small towns remained significant, not least as centres to their localities.[55] Visiting Helston in Cornwall, a small town, on a very busy fair day in 1702, John Evelyn noted: 'Where we dined was the Royal Oak Lottery which one could hardly have expected to have found in a country town so remote from London.' He pressed on to Falmouth where he had 'a small bowl of punch made with Brazil sugar'.[56]

Trading direct with Lisbon gave Falmouth access to Portugal's leading colony, Brazil. Capital energised, and was energised by, an entrepreneurialism, centred on towns, that linked society, economy, and governance. Transport and knowledge focused on urban nodes such as the postal service from Exeter, via Bristol and Worcester, to Chester developed in 1696–1700. Defoe emphasised its value to maintain the correspondence of merchants and 'men of business', and argued the same as that which ran on via Manchester and Leeds to Hull. The image was that of integration: 'The merchants at Hull have immediate advice of their ships which go out of the Channel, and come in… The shopkeepers and manufacturers [of Hull] can correspond with their dealers at Manchester, Liverpool and Bristol.'

Integration was also seen in the handling of immigration, much of which was religious in origin, notably of Huguenots (French Protestants) in the 1680s. This was usually welcomed in dioceses with low Church Bishops, such as Bath and Wells. The immigration built on earlier patterns of Protestant immigration, particularly to London and to East Anglian towns, so that, in the 1630s, they were about 5–10 per cent of the population of Norwich and, by 1690, Huguenots were about 10 per cent of London's population, while by 1709 over 13,000 German Protestants fleeing Catholic persecution, especially in the Palatinate, had reached London, many camping out in the open, for example in Greenwich. Despite short-term tensions, notably over housing and jobs, there was to be a successful integration. Defoe gives Robinson Crusoe an immigrant background:

> 'I was born in the year 1632, in the city of York, of a good family, though not of that country, my father being a foreigner of Bremen [Germany], who settled first at Hull. He got a good estate by merchandise, and leaving off his trade lived afterward at York, from whence he had married my mother, whose relations were named Robinson, a very good family in that country, and from when I was called Robinson Kreutznaer; but by the usual corruption of words in England, we are now called, nay we call ourselves and wrote our name, Crusoe, and so my companions always called me.'

The 'Glorious Revolution' loosened Anglican hegemony, particularly to the benefit of Dissenters: Protestant Nonconformists who believed in the Trinity. Towns became publicly pluralistic. Thus, in Exeter, two Dissenter meeting houses were rapidly opened, while an Independent meeting house was opened in Norwich in about 1693, followed by a Quaker meeting house in about 1699. In Coventry, a large Quaker meeting house was opened in 1698, and a new Presbyterian chapel in 1701.

Flux was to the fore, and this led to opportunity and concern. A sense of uncertainty was captured in June 1693 when James Vernon, a senior official, expressed his concern that Jacobites would exploit the anger of London silk weavers at parliamentary measures to obstruct the import from the Netherlands of raw silk which they could weave.

It was in the towns that authority and power could be most seriously challenged, because, although it was most easy to defy the state, or even rebel, in marginal areas, they were of less immediate consequence. Indeed, towns were in part definable by being different to the alleged barbarity of the countryside. Thus, visiting Brent Tor on Dartmoor, James Yonge claimed in 1674 that the locals were 'rude and brutish'.[57] There was more potential violence outside towns, for example the armed resistance by smugglers seeking to export wool near Hastings in 1697.[58] Yet, towns also posed many issues of control, policing, order and conduct. Within, from and into towns there could, moreover, be a strong sense of the presence in, even threat of outsiders and the rules they could seek to follow and even set.[59]

At the same time, urban life was changing. Wills provide a register of this, those left by inhabitants of Stratford-upon-Avon recording the last bequest of a weapon in 1665, a rise in literacy and the number of books left, and also of wills drawn up by women, from a tenth in the sixteenth century to a quarter in the late seventeenth.[60] Very differently, and as a source of regional and national integration, seasonal migration to London by members of the social élite increased.[61]

As with transport improvement, in the form of river navigation and roads, there was a definite trend after the 'Glorious Revolution' toward the use of Parliament and government, both local and central, to try to create solutions to many problems. In part, this trend drew on voluntary movements, such as the Reformation of Manners campaigns and those for workhouses. These, in turn, looked to collectivist solutions seen from the later Middle Ages and, added to them, the new methods of public politics, including a regular Parliament and newspaper activism.[62]

Continuity and change were linked because change was secured through groups, structures, symbols and practices whose continuity was seen as essential, while these structures, symbols and practices were strengthened by their ability to secure effective change[63] as well as to maintain stability. The affirmation of a corporatist tradition of honest trade, with urban authorities as part of the process regulating markets, including food prices, was an important aspect of urban culture.[64]

That suggests a somewhat benign account of the century, one of problems overcome. Indeed, that is a narrative and approach that is very common in urban history, notably with the disruption, indeed crises, linked to the fall of Rome, Black Death, Reformation, Civil War, and World War Two. As a very slight echo, successive postwar depressions and, indeed, the Covid epidemic of 2020–2 can be seen in the same light. This approach has value but is apt to underplay the degree of continuity in circumstances underlying periods of crisis, stability and growth alike.

The seventeenth century had all three, but also this continuity, whether of the facts of life and death, social structures, gender values, lifestyles, methods of work, and practices of religious observance, economic control, and political governance. All were constitutive of urban life, but so also were the consequences of the circumstances of individual towns. The latter were not to have the same ability to surmount without major problems the mass urbanisation and economic transformations of the nineteenth century, both of which greatly altered urban topography, literally bursting its bounds. Prior to then, in contrast, there was considerably more continuity, and it is that theme that should be to the fore.

Chapter 4

1700–1750

If we generally remember the eighteenth century through its stately homes or rather palaces, we also think of the townscapes of the period, especially the squares of the West End of London and the crescents of Bath. Many other towns also have or had important, eighteenth-century areas, including Liverpool and St Ann's Square, Manchester, which was largely built in the 1710s. A major expansion of urban life lay behind these Georgian buildings, brick-built, often constructed in a new, regular, classical style, not least in terraces that lined new boulevards, crescents, squares and circles.

This expansion, however, was scarcely trouble-free. Disease became less abrupt, with no repetition of the plague of 1665, but fire remained a problem, as did politics. In 1745, a Jacobite army, largely of Scots, overran towns from Carlisle to Derby, while in 1756 an express arrived in Dorchester to announce that French troops had landed near Bridport and were marching inland. In fact, a French privateer had driven a coaster ashore and sent some of its hands to pillage the ship.[1] Yet, what was captured was the anxiety that could be present behind the attractive facades.

Urban life became more important as the percentage of the population living in towns (settlements with more than about 2,000 people) rose from about 17 in 1700 to about 27.5 in 1800, a major increase, especially as it occurred when the population was rising, and, in the second half of the century, rising fast. Much of this percentage was due to London, which, in 1700, had more than half a million people, nearly 10 per cent of the population and more than all the other towns together; and only five of the latter had more than 10,000 people: Norwich, Bristol, Newcastle, Exeter and York.

At the other end of the size spectrum, the situation was more complex, because contemporary ideas of a town cannot be readily summarised in terms of a settlement with more than 2,000 people. Indeed, many settlements that were recognised as a market town, or were incorporated or parliamentary boroughs, or were regularly referred to as towns, had smaller populations. The size criteria is also problematic, because population figures prior to the 1801 census are approximate, and are complicated by the lack of a clear equivalence of town and parish: many towns were either part of a parish or part of several.

At the lower level, many towns grew considerably, but others were stagnant and some declined. As with the population as a whole, growth was most pronounced after 1750. The town prospects made between 1728 and 1753 by the Buck brothers show how towns then looked very little changed from after the Reformation in the sixteenth century,[2] but, by 1800, many were very different.

By 1800, London's population had doubled to make it the most populous town in Europe, or the Americas. It was over ten times larger than the second town, although London's share of the national population did not rise in the eighteenth century. This should be seen not as a sign of failure, for London continued to expand and to attract many migrants, but rather of its already large size, and of the growth of manufacturing and commercial centres that were central to industrialising regions and to the Atlantic economy, Liverpool being the prime example of such a commercial centre.

Despite the growth of the Atlantic economy, the reiterated stress on the commercial importance of London ensured that its trade was generally seen as synonymous with that of the country. In the third edition of his influential *Universal Dictionary of Trade and Commerce* (1766), a work that first appeared in 1751, Malachy Postlethwayt, an active writer on economic issues, added a dedication to George Nelson, Lord Mayor of London, and to its aldermen and councillors, that included the passage:

> 'London tradesmen appear to constitute the very active soul of the commerce of the whole British state; and they are an essential medium between the merchant, the country shop-keeper, and the consumers ... Of such high concernment are the London tradesmen to the whole traffic of the nation, that all our native commodities and manufactures almost of every sort, more or less, centre at first in London, and amongst the London tradesmen, brought to them from all the inland manufacturing and trading towns; and cities throughout the kingdom,

where those commodities and manufactures are not made or produced. The countrymen shear their sheep, sell their wool, and carry it from place to place; the manufacturer sets it to work, to combing, spinning, winding, twisting, dyeing, weaving, fulling, dressing, and thus they furnish their numberless manufactures in the whole woollen branch. But what must they do with them, if London did not take them first off their hands, and the London tradesmen, warehousemen, factors, and wholesale dealers, did not vend and circulate them amongst the London merchants, as well as to all the remote parts of the nation? London is the grand central mart to which the gross body of all our native commodities are first brought, and from whence they are again sold ... this is the case be it Manchester for cotton wares; Yorkshire for coarse cloth, kersies etc. ...'[3]

This was an exaggeration of London's economic centrality, but, nevertheless, the market and finance of London was central to English economic activity. Earlier, in his *Tour Thro' the Whole Island of Great Britain* (1724–6), Daniel Defoe provided an account of Ipswich:

'swallowed up by the immense indraft of trade to the city of London ... if it be otherwise at this town, with some other towns, which are lately increased in trade and navigation, wealth, and, people, while their neighbours decay, it is because they have some particular trade or accident to trade, which is a kind of nostrum to them, inseparable to the place, and which fixes there by the nature of the thing; as the herring-fishery to Yarmouth; the coal trade to Newcastle; the Leeds clothing-trade; the export of butter and lard, and the great corn trade for Holland, is to Hull; the Virginia and West India trade at Liverpool, the Irish trade to Bristol, and the like.'

London was significant in influencing notions of urban life, although there was also much provincial autonomy. London's squares were imitated in towns such as Bristol. As an aspect both of these notions and of an underlying reality, London posed the greatest problems of law and order and social conditions. London's dominant position owed something to the enormous growth of its trade, but also reflected its role as the centre of government, the law and consumption, and its dominance of the world of print, which became even more important as a shaper of news, opinion and fashion. Political programmes were conceived and debated in London, the seat of the Court, legislature, executive and judiciary. Nevertheless, there were frequent opposition claims, especially under Sir Robert Walpole, the leading minister from 1721 to 1742, that the government neglected London and was unpopular there.

London newspapers circulated throughout the country and were also crucial sources for the provincial press. The turnpike and postal systems also centred on London. This dominance of communications reflected and sustained London's economic importance. Thus, London-based insurance companies, such as the Sun Fire Office, and banks were able to organise insurance and banking elsewhere by delegating the work to agents in other towns with whom regular contact could be maintained. Profits from trade and government helped bridge the gap between London as a centre of production and as a centre of consumption.

London grew significantly physically, especially at the beginning of the century, when the West End estates of landlords such as Sir Richard Grosvenor and Lord Burlington were developed as prime residential property. Mayfair and St. James's became the select side of town and the streets there still bear the names of the politicians of the period, for example Harley Street and Oxford Street, both named after Robert Harley, 1st Earl of Oxford. Building and gentrification helped make the area safer. Leading aristocrats built or re-built grand London houses, such as Burlington, Carlton, Chandos, Chesterfield, Derby, Devonshire and Spencer Houses. Buckingham House was bought by George III.

Other areas further east, such as Clerkenwell and Hackney, became less fashionable, a process paralleled in Paris. Westminster Bridge provided a new route across the Thames and helped development on the south bank. It was followed by Blackfriars Bridge, opened in 1769 after nine years' construction. The ½d toll demanded from those who crossed led to a riot.

This is a very secular account, for the most impressive building was the triumph of architectural accomplishment for the glory of God that was Christopher Wren's St Paul's Cathedral, begun in 1675, consecrated in 1697 and declared officially complete in 1711. Far from looking to rebuild the old Gothic cathedral, this borrowed the style of church architecture seen in Baroque Rome, but did so for the Church of England. James Paterson's *Pietas Londinenses* (1714) captured the huge diversity of religious services on offer in London – it was a parish by parish guide to services, lectures and prayers in the city. Built in 1711–24, Thomas Archer's St Philip's in Birmingham was another major Baroque work.

The different worlds of London co-existed on uneasy terms, as was noted by commentators. In his novel *Moll Flanders* (1722), Defoe presented its social world as very bleak for women:

> 'that marriages were here the consequences of politic schemes for forming interests and carrying on business ... as the market ran very unhappily on the men's side ... women had lost the privilege of saying No.'

The novelist Henry Fielding focused on London presented, not as a predatory bourgeois environment, but as a world threatened by Westminster: he atomised London in terms of the corrupt Court and aristocracy of its West End, with their commerce in vice, and the more acceptable commercial metropolis.[4]

Civic splendour was celebrated in the Mansion House, built in 1739–53, but stability and growth were not problem-free, being affected by periodic crises. In the aftermath of the bursting of the South Sea Bubble, a pamphleteer wrote of London's freemen in 1722, 'as South Sea has stripped them of their superfluous riches, long wars, continued taxes, and high duties, impaired their stock, and shaked their credit.'[5]

In addition, the independence, divisions and vitality of urban politics were particularly true of some of the larger towns, notably London.[6] These led to the City Elections Act of 1725 which defined the freeman franchise of London as narrowly as possible and imposed an aldermanic veto on the actions of the more popular and Tory-inclined Common Council in order to limit the volatility and independence of popular London politics. More generally, the role of freemen in politics was such that the choice of them was a significant matter and therefore a cause of dispute; as is not the case today.

Alongside the dramatic change of the Great Fire of 1666 and the major transformation of the West End, the creation of London in many respects was an evolutionary, not a revolutionary, process, with development out of existing housing types and traditional layouts. The ability to change and upgrade the structure of new houses, plus the high level of maintenance they required, particularly in the painting of woodwork, made them perfectly suited to a consumer society geared towards the continued renewal and replacement of products. The designs of London's new houses were given wider impact through Richard Neve's *The City and Country Purchaser and Builder's Dictionary*, which first appeared in 1703, with a second edition in 1726.

Consumerism and class also interacted in open spaces, notably with squares tending to be public, rather than private, arenas until the 1720s, when London began to be shaped as a series of bounded spaces, both physically and socially, where enclosure ensured exclusion and exclusion provided exclusivity.[7] Meanwhile, the extent to which London was changing, while yet retaining traditional features, was captured in Marco Ricci's painting *A View of the Mall from St James's Park* of about 1710. The Mall was a walk where fashionable society went to see and be seen, to intrigue, to flirt and to proposition. The park contained three avenues for pedestrians and, in the 1700s, Queen Anne's gardener, Henry Wise, planted 350 limes to provide shade. In his painting, Ricci has Wren's St Paul's in the distance and shows London society on display, but this is also a world with cattle grazing in order to provide the city with milk. Elizabeth Cromwell, wife to Oliver, had kept cattle there. The large number of women depicted in Ricci's painting reflected the extent to which many public places were not segregated. An additional take on the scene may be provided by Bird Cage Walk in the park being a major centre for homosexual sex, and by Roxana's nearby role in decadent parties in Defoe's 1724 novel of that name.

There was a series of settings for cultural activity that were intended as accessible, the most significant remaining churches. Thus, in his *An Essay on Criticism* (1711), Alexander Pope noted:

> As some to church repair,
> Not for the doctrine, but the music there.

Henry Purcell, organist of Westminster Abbey in 1680–95, and the composer of a large number of anthems and hymns, had a considerable influence on the next generation of English musicians, although it was superseded in terms of style by that of Handel. John Weldon (1676–1736), another successful composer of much both sacred and secular music, was organist of New College, Oxford and later in the Chapel Royal, St Bride's Fleet Street, and St Martin's-in-the-Fields. Maurice Greene (c. 1696–1755), the son of a London vicar, who was educated by Richard Brind, the organist of St Paul's Cathedral, succeeded the latter after being organist of two other London churches, before becoming organist and composer to the Chapel Royal in 1727 and Master of the King's Band of Music eight years later. Noted as an organist, his works included numerous anthems.

London developed further as a centre of consumption and leisure. The amount of fixed specialised investment in the latter rose greatly with theatres, including the Theatre Royal, the King's Theatre and the Pantheon (a grand assembly room in Oxford Street completed in 1772), pleasure gardens, picture galleries and other facilities, ranging from gambling houses to coffee houses, auction houses to brothels. Although some facilities were, or sought to be, socially exclusive, most, as elsewhere, were readily accessible to anyone with money to spend. Separately, London, though large, was compact: it was still immune from the congestion and sprawl of the following century, and the proximity of the countryside lessened the demand for private gardens. There were suburban settlements, such as Islington, but they were close in to London by later standards, and the same was true for other towns.

The social basis of London's development was not only that the rural élite increasingly came to spend part of the year there, but also that the 'middling sort' expanded considerably.[8] This, moreover, was true of regional capitals, such as Norwich and Nottingham; county centres, such as Warwick; and developing entertainment centres, particularly spa towns, such as Tunbridge Wells, Scarborough, Bristol Hot Wells, and Bath. Thirty-four new spas were founded between 1700 and 1750, and even more in the second half of the century. For all these types of town, there was an increased social and cultural infrastructure. In *Moll Flanders*, there is mention of the 'little country opera-house' at Bury St Edmunds, where Moll is able to pickpocket a gold watch, although she prefers the opportunities of London.

There was, however, criticism of some of the forums of urban sociability. Thus, Defoe's praise, in his *Tour*, of society in Maidstone became a way to challenge the fashion for assemblies:

> 'This neighbourhood of persons of figure and quality, makes Maidstone a very agreeable place to live in, and where a man of letters, and of manners, will always find suitable society, both to divert and improve himself; so that here is, what is not often found, namely, a town of very great business and trade, and yet full of gentry, of mirth, and of good company. It is to be recorded here for the honour of the gentry in this part of England; that though they are as sociable and entertaining as any people are, or can be desired to be, and as much famed for good manners, and good humour; yet the new mode of forming assemblies so much, and so fatally now in vogue, in other parts of England, could never prevail here; and that though there was an attempt made by some loose persons, and the gentlemen, and ladies, did for a little while appear there; yet they generally disliked the practice, soon declined to give their company, as to a thing scandalous, and so it dropped of course.'

Writing of York in the *Tour*, Defoe observed:

> 'the keeping up assemblies among the younger gentry was first set up here, a thing other writers recommend mightily as the character of a good country, and of a pleasant place; but which I look upon with a different view, and esteem it as a plan laid for the ruin of the nation's morals, and which, in time, threatens us with too much success that way.'[9]

The 'middling sort' were largely professionals and gentlemen merchants. Doctors, bankers, lawyers, clergymen, and Customs and Excise men, could all be found in major towns, and their numbers increased. They were largely responsible for new building and rebuilding, the replacement of timber-frame by brick in houses for the well to do, for example in Norwich from the late-seventeenth century and in Lancaster. Queen's Square, begun in 1699, set the fashion for brick-built houses in Bristol, and was responsible for the growth of brickworks there.

Alongside light, roomy and attractive private houses for the affluent, numerous public and philanthropic buildings were built. Theatres, assembly rooms, subscription libraries and other leisure facilities were opened in many towns, alongside public outdoor space: parks, walks and racecourses. The social world that fostered the demand for new buildings and spaces, was matched by entrepreneurial activity, artistic skill, and the wealth of a rapidly-growing economy.

New buildings often marked a major change in local consciousness, not least as a replacement for past settings of authority, as with the new Guildhall in Worcester designed by Thomas White and constructed between 1721 and 1727. In mid-century, Nottingham replaced its medieval timber-framed Guildhall by a brick one with a colonnaded front. It would be easy to leave that remark as an instance of general improvement, but, instead, there was, as so often, a response to specific circumstances, Defoe noting:

> 'There was once a handsome town-house here for the sessions or assizes, and other public business; but ... being over-crowded upon occasion of the assizes last year, it cracked ... it must be said (I think) that Providence had more care of the judges, and their needful attendants, than the townsmen had.'

More generally, the image of towns altered. Timber and thatch were seen as dated, unattractive, non-utilitarian and, increasingly, non-urban; as were long-established street patterns. Furthermore, although some churches were rebuilt, new stone and brick buildings increasingly offered new definitions of town function, with an emphasis in particular on leisure and retail, and, more generally, on private space open to those who could pay (shops/subscription rooms), rather than spaces open to all (market places, churches).

New forums for sociability were created. The influential Assembly Rooms at York were largely built in 1731–2. Assemblies were first held in Newcastle in 1716 and new assembly rooms opened there in 1736 and 1776, while Norwich gained assembly rooms in 1754. The townscape literally became brighter as street lighting was introduced, on the main streets of Lancaster from 1738. Human noise was also focused on towns, as remains the case today. In his play *The Relapse* (1696), John Vanbrugh referred to London as 'that uneasy theatre of noise'.

Service activities, rather than industrial expansion, were the basis of growth in many towns. The economic basis of the shift was growing prosperity, especially in commerce, and this interacted with increased and differentiated consumption. Most of the non-food goods bought by affluent households were made in towns, and, even more, sold there or through them. The Coalbrookdale ironworks sold its pots, kettles, and firebacks through fairs in market towns such as Bishop's Castle, Congleton, Oswestry, and Wrexham, as well as to shops including, in 1718, in Birmingham, Bromsgrove, Evesham, Gainsborough, Ludlow, Macclesfield, Manchester and Shrewsbury.[10] Facilities for, and patterns of, service activity responded to the example of London. The capital was presented as the benchmark for conditions elsewhere, although it would be mistaken to ignore the provincial capacity to preserve local practices and to take initiatives, and, in part, London's impact was itself a product of its openness to influences from outside. This element of its history tends to be downplayed, but it was significant to the inter-urban history of England, an element of its urban history that should not be neglected.

Towns also benefited from the strength of the rural economy, providing not only a commercial but also a social focus. A degree of urban-rural rapprochement and cohesion at élite level was an important factor encouraging stability, and possibly contributed to a degree of cultural merging. Joseph Pickford (1734–82), the London-born architect who designed the Derby Assembly Rooms, also designed the Riding School at Calke Abbey, a stately home, as well as Josiah Wedgwood's house and factories at Etruria.[11] It is important not to exaggerate: differences remained between urban and rural values, not least in politics and religion, and the landed magnates visited towns on their own terms. Yet there was a degree of interchange based on shared values that was arguably greater than that of the two previous centuries.

The co-existence of a growing urban sector with landed society helped to ensure a two-way flow in social and cultural attitudes. Urban development altered the institutional and cultural landscape of well-populated regions. In his *Tour*, Defoe praised the wealth of Londoners displayed in the Home Counties. This included new stately homes, such as Wanstead House, the palatial seat of the Child family, bankers who had only reached the peerage in 1718, and the 'fine houses of the citizens of London' near Carshalton, 'some of which are built with such a profusion of expense, that they look rather like seats of the nobility, than the country houses of citizens and merchants.' The positive interaction of town and country was crucial to a growing national self-image as an improving society.

As a related, overlapping but also distinct process, rather than sharing a coherent standpoint, the urban population participated in the spectrum of existing opinion. It was divided by confessional, economic and political views, with the extent of division also varying greatly by individual. This very lack of urban homogeneity aided integration with the views of the rest of society, and also helped ensure that urban interests could be wooed by élite politicians.

The urban dimension of politics was important, especially thanks to the location of so many parliamentary seats in towns, albeit, often, small places, and also due to the very specific and important economic interests of towns, interests which could be furthered by political means. Purges of corporate government undertaken after the restoration of Charles II in 1660, and again in the 1680s, had helped accentuate the politicisation of many towns, undermining attempts to present town life as harmonious and unified. This fed through into the so-called 'rage of party' of the reigns of William III (1689–1702) and Anne (1702–14), when party groups sought to use the tactic of removing their opponents from town councils in order to ensure unity. The important political role of town Corporations, not least in the creation of freemen, cut across their function as institutions of local government. However, the co-existence of the two elements helped provide much of the character of urban politics, and, indeed, government,[12] which extended to religious issues. In King's Lynn, the significance of religion was shown in the Corporation spending much money on clerical stipends and church building and repair, as well as its time on appointments and on stipulating details of worship. More generally, and lessening division, the Whig position did not mean hostility to the Church of England, despite many Whigs being Dissenters. The last was subject to variations by town, Defoe noting that in Northallerton many Whigs were not Dissenters, although he also commented that this was unusual.

At another level of politics, a town's use of its MPs to advance or defend its local interests with government or in Parliament, particularly in relation to the passage of Acts of Parliament, provided the basis for a strong relationship, one that required both parties to give and take. At that level, politics was reactive and consensual, with the search for compromise part of a dynamic relationship in which local issues were crucial. A Chester item in the *Birmingham Journal* of 21 May 1733 reported:

'Saturday's Post brought us the agreeable news that the petition against our Navigation Bill was defeated, and that the Bill had passed through the House of Commons; this occasioned an universal joy in this city, which was expressed by bonfires, illuminations, etc. Two large bonfires were lighted, and still continue burning, viz. one at the White Talbot, the other at Gloverstone, and will be kept in night and day till it pass the House of Lords, when they will be greatly augmented.'

The (London) *Daily Courant* of 18 May 1734 reported of the election of Edward Thompson as MP for York:

'The company of substantial and loyal citizens that went with Mr Thompson wore orange-coloured cockades, and carried a flag with the motto Navigation, in memory of his great service in obtaining a bill for the improvement of their river, hallowed Thompson, Liberty and Navigation.'

This relationship between MPs and towns, and the recognition on both sides that it had to be constantly nurtured, was a long-term structural feature of politics that added stability to the system.

There were, however, particular problems in managing large urban constituencies. Popular opposition politics, indeed radicalism as generally understood in this period, was particularly associated with large towns, especially London, where disturbances were linked to parliamentary opposition in 1733, and again during the Wilkesite troubles in the 1760s. Such radicalism could also be significant in other towns, for example Bristol. There was intimidation, if not violence, at elections, a theme that can be underplayed by a scholarly focus on provincial culture. In 1727, 'the mob at Peterborough elections' gave a lady a fright resulting in a miscarriage. In 1730, a ministerial newspaper reported of an election in Winchester:

> 'The populace rode in multitudes against many gentlemen who were voters, several of which had dirt thrown in their faces, other coaches were overturned, whilst numbers who were guarded by constables and other officers, met with the greatest disrespect.'

Four years later, Sir Robert Walpole wrote from Norwich on the day of the poll: '…great expenses made, great threats ushered in the day, but a due provision to repel force by force made it a quiet election.'[13] The flavour of public politics was glimpsed at in a letter published in the *Public Advertiser*, a London paper, on 12 January 1757:

> 'I am the Chairman of a club of reputable persons, consisting of some gentlemen of fortune, and some not inconsiderable tradesmen, who talk freely enough, at times, of the public affairs; but always under a restriction that I am afraid is seldom observed elsewhere; namely, to propose remedies rather than inflame complaints; and even this, with all the diffidence becoming public individuals'.

Aside from the centres of county government and/or provincial culture, there were also important industrial towns, although their growth, as with Birmingham, owed something also to their role as centres of trade and distribution: on a longstanding pattern these were closely linked to industry. The trading role was particularly important for ports. In the South West, the ports became relatively more important: Plymouth replaced Exeter as the region's largest town in the second half of the eighteenth century, while Falmouth, a small settlement in the mid-seventeenth century, was Cornwall's largest town a century later. Whereas the inland regional centre and manufacturing centre of Norwich was the second most populous town in England in 1700, Liverpool, an Atlantic port that was not a county capital, was in 1800. The county capital of Lancashire was Lancaster, although, since its foundation in 1889, the County Council has been based in Preston. Defoe was particularly impressed by Liverpool, praising it in his *Tour*. Under the Liverpool Improvement Act of 1748, a town commission was established and the new Exchange (1749–54) confirmed the town's commitment to commerce. A charitable infirmary opened in 1749 on Shaw's Brow was testament to the civic benefits of trade. Other Atlantic ports had less spectacular or sustained growth, but, nevertheless, still saw a major rise in population. Whitehaven's population rose to 16,000 in about 1785.

Both Liverpool and Whitehaven were slaving ports. There was a major expansion in the slave trade, and between 1691 and 1779, British ships transported over two million slaves from African ports. The regulatory framework that had maintained London's control was dismantled in 1698, when the African trade was freed from the control of the Royal African Company, legalising the position of private traders and making shifts in the relative position of ports far easier. In the 1710s, the merchants of Bristol, who had long criticised the monopolistic role of London trading companies, replaced London in the leading position in the trade. Bristol, which was where slaves from Ireland were landed in the Anglo-Saxon period, had ships carrying about 17,000 slaves in 1725. In turn, with Bristol hit hard by wartime disruption due to privateering in 1739–48, Liverpool, which was less exposed to French and Spanish privateers, took the leading role from the 1740s.

Many smaller ports were also involved, including Barnstaple, Bideford, Dartmouth, Exeter, Lancaster, Plymouth, Poole, Portsmouth, Topsham, and Whitehaven, the last of which sent about 69 slaving voyages to Africa between 1710 and 1769 when the trade was abandoned as unprofitable.[14] The country's largest industry, woollen textiles, benefited greatly from the opportunities provided by exporting cloth to West Africa and also to the slave colonies.[15] This sits uneasily with the sense of Enlightenment confidence.

It was not only Atlantic ports that saw major rises in population. On the east coast, Sunderland, North and South Shields, and Tynemouth all benefited greatly from the export of coal, principally to London, and from coal-based industries, such as glass-making. Hull and Newcastle, both more established urban centres, also saw major population growth.[16]

Coal-based industrialisation was significant in some towns, as in Birmingham, where the first rolling mill was opened in 1740. At the same time, water power not only remained important but also increased, as when a large water-driven factory was opened at Derby on the River Derwent in 1721 by Thomas Lombe for his Italian silk-throwing machinery. More generally, the stocking industry moved from London to the Midlands, especially Nottingham, and, in 1750, there were said to be 1,200 frames in the town.

Some towns, such as Oxford, Hereford, and Warwick, were fairly static communities, while growth rates were relatively low in some formerly important centres, such as Worcester. Other towns were affected by adverse economic circumstances. Gloucester's trade, sugar refining and glass manufacturing could not compete with that of Bristol, and its cloth industry also declined. The net effect of such shifts was to accentuate the long-established changing character of the urban network.

The fate of individual towns was a matter of multiple factors. For example, York was hit by the growth of Leeds, but it was able to benefit as a major centre for the local gentry, and, again unlike Leeds, to profit from developments in the trade in food. York became in mid-century the largest national collecting point of wholesale butter and the provincial source of London's butter. This reflected the agricultural character of the lush grasslands of the Vale of York.

Towns, particularly the major ones, constituted the living space of the most articulate and informed members of society, and tended to have their associated paraphernalia, such as printing presses. The press indeed is one index of urban success. Excluding London, the number of newspapers rose from about 24 in 1723, to 32 in 1753, 35 in 1760, and 50 in 1782. The presence of newspapers was important to political consciousness in towns. The provincial expansion was due both to the increase in the number of towns with papers and to more towns having more than one paper: this was particularly true of Bristol, Exeter, Newcastle, Norwich and York.

Yet there were also failures. After the *Union Journal: or, Halifax Advertiser* (1759–*c*.1763) ceased publication, Halifax had no paper until the early-nineteenth century. After the failure of the *Darlington Pamphlet* (1772–3), the needs of Teesside continued to be met by the Leeds, Newcastle and York press, and no other paper was launched at Darlington until the *Darlington and Stockton Times* appeared in 1847. The *Hereford Journal* (1739) was also short-lived, but the *British Chronicle, or Pugh's Hereford Journal* launched in

1770, lasted into the twentieth century. In Cumbria, the *Kendal Courant* (1731–6), *Kendal Weekly Mercury* (1735–47) and *Whitehaven Weekly Courant* (1736–43) all failed, but the *Cumberland Pacquet or Ware's Whitehaven Advertiser*, launched in 1774, was successful.

Other towns only acquired their first papers later: Carlisle in 1798, Falmouth – the first in Cornwall – in 1801, and Barnstaple – the first in north Devon – in 1824. After two or possibly three failures in the eighteenth century, the continuous publication of papers in Plymouth began in 1808. This is a reminder that the character and fortune of towns varied.

As the foundation of newspapers showed, it was not only the large towns that expanded, while many towns saw graceful as well as profitable urban expansion. Lieutenant Richard Browne wrote from the Isle of Wight in 1757, 'Newport is a very clean pretty town, regular and well built, the Bath players are in it and we have plays every night.'[17] Overall, the growth in the numbers of schools, hospitals, dispensaries, infirmaries, theatres, reading rooms etc. may not have been massive, but it was significant and changed the institutional and cultural landscape not only of the towns but also of most of the well-populated regions in the country. This was important to the period's self-image as an improving society. Such self-understanding should neither be taken at face value, nor regarded as descriptively or analytically sufficient, but it did reflect something of the realities of eighteenth-century life.

In some respects, urban life offered freedom. If towns obviously did not provide equality of opportunity, they did, in a Dick Whittington fashion, have the lure of opportunity, and the sustained migration to them was a testimony to this. Each migrant, and Whittington, a younger son, was born in Gloucestershire in 1354, becoming an apprentice in London, represented an individual decision that life might be better in a town. For many, this proved illusory: rural penury translated into urban poverty. Towns contained impoverished, squalid and dangerous areas. Indeed, urban degradation was more pernicious, because of the absence of the social and community support that was more prevalent in rural parishes, although not without its own harshness and exclusions. Indeed, alongside consumerism and the middling orders, it is necessary to remember the important role of manufacturing in towns, and the extent to which economic shifts and problems, which were many and varied, could push artisans into what would today be called the 'underclass'.[18]

However, the social system was more fluid in towns: mobility was greater, traditional hierarchies weaker, and control laxer. Urban populations were not on the whole radical in their politics or beliefs, but town life did provide the context for most new ideas, both élite and popular, and offered new experiences. It was also easier to bridge the divide between élite and non-élite in towns, whether in the dissemination of fashions, such as tea drinking and the wearing of imported cloth, or of new political views. The concentration of people in towns, their higher rates of literacy, and more marked traditions of political autonomy and independence of attitude, helped to foster, at least in part, a consumer society, the consumerism of which went beyond goods and services to include attitudes and beliefs. In the last, the eighteenth-century town prefigured the situation today.

Towns were also the forcing houses of the commercial economy and culture of print through which the country became not only a world power but also a political society that saw domination as its national destiny. The relationship between town development and urban politics has been presented very differently. It is possible to emphasise the way in which urban renaissance aided élite integration and thus growing stability.[19] Yet, it is also reasonable to stress the resilience, and indeed vitality, of differences and divisions within the urban community, including within the élite.

As elsewhere in the book, the argument here is that both approaches are correct, and that it is unhelpful to isolate either stability or strife, continuity or change, and, also, to treat them as in some way incompatible. Instead, as was only to be expected, in a complex society with a high degree of political awareness and participation, there was both change and continuity, division and unity, and their dynamic interaction provided much of the flavour of urban consciousness and politics. The rhetoric and politics of division did not pre-empt the practice of co-operation.

The most prominent model of urban life was London, but other major towns also developed, in part through institutions and building, Norwich gaining a lunatic asylum in 1714, a new shire hall in 1749, assembly rooms in 1754, a theatre in 1756, a hospital in 1771–2, a public subscription library in 1784, and a new county jail in 1792–3. Smaller towns also expanded. Stockton, an important port for North Sea trade, acquired a new parish church in 1712, a customs house in 1730, a town hall in 1735, a theatre in 1766, and a grammar school in 1786. Norwich was a long-established town, but there was also the rapid growth of newer centres, notably Liverpool and Birmingham. Local circumstances – the money and energy of individuals and of the community – were crucial, as not all towns moved at the same pace towards what has been seen as an urban renaissance. In Taunton, there was hardly any new building of importance until the market house was constructed in 1771.

Urban economies were helped by the growing commercialisation of life. The infrastructure of, and for, money transformed the nature of the domestic market and of townscapes. New covered markets and shops were opened, as were banks and insurance offices. Advertising grew and trade directories were produced. In a world of 'things', where increasing numbers could afford to purchase objects to bring them pleasure, rising prosperity helped towns grow. Much of this prosperity reflected their role as social centres and providers of service activities, as much as commercial and industrial functions. Published in Bury St Edmunds, the *Suffolk Mercury or Bury Post* noted in 1733 that it was:

'Printed by T. Baily in the Butter-Market; where may be had bibles and common prayerbooks of all sizes; all sorts of school books, books of devotion, history, law, physick etc. Shopbooks, pocket-books, paper, pens, ink, sealing-wax and all sorts of maps and fine prints for parlours, staircases, chimney-pieces; and all sorts of printed blanks. Where may be had also the London and Gentleman's Magazines.'

Thomas Ashburner's 1749 poster advertising a weekly Kendal magazine, *The Agreeable Miscellany*, promised to:

'contain essays etc on various subjects, Divine, Moral, Historical, Political etc., Geography, Voyages, Mathematics, Husbandry, Gardening, Mechanics, Trade, Poetry, Criticism, Transactions, Wit and Humour.'[20]

Yet, as always, circumstances varied, in both content and context, and with both intrinsic and extrinsic factors playing a part. These ranged greatly, from fire in the case of the first, to communications in the latter. Fire remained a major issue, as at Blandford Forum in 1731, after which the town was rebuilt, with the help of a donation by George II and an Act of Parliament, producing a brick-and-tile town centre including a larger market place that has lasted to the present. In Devon alone, Tiverton was hit hard in 1726, 1730 and, especially, 1731, the last leading to an Act of Parliament that all roofs thereafter should be of lead, slate or tile; while Crediton lost 460 houses to a savage fire in 1743, and much of Honiton was rebuilt after fires in 1747 and 1765.

Communications were a dynamic context. Thus, the comparatively slow growth of many Cheshire towns was due, to a degree, to their relatively poor links with the more dynamic centres in Lancashire.[21] Communications and the related attitudes were important, not least in facilitating the reciprocal economic relationships through which dynamic towns created and sustained a regional network.[22]

Enlightenment confidence can be qualified, in general, in terms of a more complex urban reality, not least as captured in the genre of 'strange newes'. On 30 May 1723, the *Weekly Courant* of Nottingham carried a London report of five days earlier:

> 'For several nights last week, a bird was heard to sing in the Dissenters' Burying Ground in Burnhill Fields; it began at 11, and continued its song for most of the night. This drew a great concourse of people that way; and some of the old women would needs have it the spirit of a female child that was found there a few days before, supposed to have been murdered. On Thursday, it ceased its note, and the old women in the neighbourhood being assembled, according to custom, were puzzled to assign a cause for the loss of their feathered songster, one of more age and gravity than the rest, declared she thought he had absented on account of Mr Layer being to be hanged next day.'

Christopher Layer was a Jacobite.

Disease remained a serious issue, the year divided by the prevalence of particular illnesses. The limited nature of the housing stock led to a sharing of beds that encouraged a high incidence of respiratory infections and explained wealth-related epidemiological variations within towns.

Meanwhile, the 'Revolution Settlement' that followed the 'Glorious Revolution' of 1688–9 made a Parliament with regular elections a permanent feature of the political system, and that greatly enhanced the political influence of towns. It was seen, for example, in 1704 when Robert Harley, a Tory Secretary of State, wrote to George Stepney, the envoy in Vienna, concerning a petition from Exeter and several other West Country parliamentary constituencies complaining about Austrian tariffs on British woollen cloth:

> 'There is the greater reason to consider the petitions, and endeavour to obtain redress herein, because, besides the general interest of the nation, the members from the West have a great influence in the resolutions of the House of Commons, and especially in the granting of money.'[23]

Yet Parliament also provided a setting for rivalry between towns. Thus, legislation of 1721, introduced by Waller Bacon, MP for Norwich, after petitions from woollen manufacturers, prohibited the import of plain white calico by the East India Company, and thereby hit the domestic calico printers who competed with these manufacturers.

The understanding of towns in part is a matter of debate over the nature of society, whether it was a commercial society dominated by a 'middling order,' or whether the emphasis should be on élite influence.[24] Towns were certainly important in the definition of political attitudes.[25] However, the extent of their influence over rural areas is difficult to evaluate; especially as most of the sources are of urban origin, as with the *Craftsman* of 7 October 1727 when it declared of London that 'the eyes of the whole nation are constantly fixed on the conduct and proceedings of this city, as the *Primum Mobile* of Great Britain.' Towns were a social focus for the surrounding countryside, as with the assizes and race meetings. Yet it is too easy to focus on urban perspectives and norms as well as the interests of 'Trade', as opposed to the 'Landed Interest' which bore a relatively heavy tax burden.

A clash of interests and cultures was presented by Tobias Smollett, in his novel *Launcelot Greaves* (1760–1), which looked back to the last general election, that of 1754. The Tories arrive first in the market town, which is unnamed and therefore everywhere, with their emphasis on the 'Landed Interest' met by a hostile 'multitude' who throw stones, dirt and dead cats, while the Whig candidate, backed by the town authorities, and emphasising the Williamite-Hanoverian tradition, is a Jewish stock jobber. Anti-Catholicism is shown as vying with anti-Semitism, which indeed were themes in the highly contentious 1754 Oxfordshire election.[26]

Moreover, the *Salisbury Journal* of 7 January 1754 recorded the celebrations in nearby Devizes following the swift repeal the previous year of the Jewish Naturalisation Act of 1753:

'Last Friday the gentlemen and principal tradesmen of this borough, met at the Black Bear Inn to rejoice on account of the repeal of the Jew Bill; and though numbers of different persuasions were assembled on this occasion, yet party and prejudice were entirely laid aside, and all were unanimous in expressing their joy and highest approbation. The effigy of a Jew was carried through every street in town, attended with all sorts of rough music; several men had torches that the inhabitants might see the effigy, and read the paper that was stuck on his breast, containing these words

NO JEWS!
Reformations to the B--ps [Bishops];
Christianity for ever.

They made a halt two or three times in every street, drank and repeated the above, amidst the acclamations of a great number of people: a large fire was made, and they burnt the body of the Jew, and set his head on the top of the pillory; the bells rang, and beer was given to the populace; several loyal healths were drank by the gentlemen, etc. and likewise variety of toasts, applicable to the occasion. The Thursday following (being Market Day) the head was again put on top of the pillory, which gave great delight to the farmers and other country people.'

In addition, William Lorimer commented on the failure of Sir William Calvert, a former Lord Mayor, prominent brewer, and government supporter, to win re-election as an MP for London: 'Calvert came pretty near, and it is certain he had the majority of merchants and substantial people, but the mob could not forgive his joining in the Jewish Bill.'[27]

These elements were part of a more general tension over religion within towns. Alongside the more striking elements, anti-Catholicism and anti-Semitism, there were also important rivalries within Protestantism, particularly between supporters of the Church of England and Dissenters. Thus, Edmund Harrold, a Manchester wigmaker, was unsure whether he should marry a Dissenter.[28] Dissenters tended to congregate in towns.

A sense of place was certainly seen in electioneering, as in 1767 when Viscount Hampden noted grumbles in Lewes that a candidate came 'as far from home as Hertfordshire'.[29] The following year, in a bitterly contested election in Preston, local links were an issue, a flysheet in favour of the Corporation candidate opposing 'an Alien', as well as this borough ever being 'annexed to any family', which was a reference to the influence of the Earl of Derby.[30] There were also (unsuccessful) attempts in 1766–77 to end the dominance over Morpeth of the Earl of Carlisle.[31]

Smollett was also spot-on with reference to his presentation of electoral corruption, a theme also seen with Fielding. Thus, the electors of the constituency of Weymouth and Melcombe Regis, about 300 freeholders, despite an agreement of 1744 among the different electoral interests ensuring uncontested elections for over half a century, still expected the customary election-time treats. In the 1761 election, £295 12 shilling had to be spent on ten public house bills, an unopposed re-election of one of the candidates the following year costing £201 19 shillings and 6 pence.[32]

The blunt side of electioneering was shown in the Yorkshire election of 1742, William Buck reporting:

'One Flint a famous York Bully had during the Poll been committed for assaulting Mr William Turner… Bailed … When Mr Turner was chaired, this rascal appeared at the head of the mob and attempted to assault Mr Turner; but Tom Pulleyn … a Man of Weight knocked him down twice.'[33]

William Turner was the successful Whig candidate. Discussion of urban politics frequently related to the social background of opponents. Much of the criticism was directed against the opposition to the Walpole ministry. The pro-government *Daily Courant* was particularly critical in 1734, referring, on 30 April, to 'mechanical statesmen ... all undone by following politics, instead of the trade they were bred to', and, on 19 October, adding:

> 'Wonderful indeed is the power of Patriotism [a reference to the opposition use of patriotic ideas]. It opens and enlarges all the faculties of the mind... Inspired by this illustrious passion, the attorney's clerk will talk like an oracle on the nature and origin of government, on the power of kings, and the liberties of the people, and fancy himself capable of holding the Great Seal [being Lord Chancellor], before he knows how to fill up a bond.'

Repeated attempts to prevent the sale of unstamped newspapers,[34] which were significant in London, served as a way to restrict the circulation of the news.

However, ministerial commentators also defended their supporters, notably in response to opposition criticism of the City Address to the new king in 1727.[35] The *Flying Post*, in its issue of 13 July 1727, reported:

> 'Though many false and malicious, as well as foolish insinuations, have been made, in order to bring into contempt the late method, for joining in an Address to his Majesty, by the Citizens of London, as if the Address had been chiefly signed by porters, cartmen and illiterate people; we are well assured that the whole is so much forgery.'

Two days later, the *London Journal* provided a detailed account of how the Address was drawn up, making it clear that Gibraltar and the national debt had both been hotly contested, and that a dispute over the rights of aldermen had played a part. Key themes in foreign policy were also at dispute.

That was not the only tempo in the published debate about urban identity and consciousness. The publication of urban history was a new version of the long-established pride of place also reflected in ritual, sociability, institutions, and politics, including feasts and feast sermons.[36] Bristol had its first complete history, *The History and Antiquities of the City of Bristol*, by the antiquarian and surgeon William Barrett, published there in 1789, a work that included the hoaxes perpetrated by Thomas Chatterton. In contrast, Andrew Hooke, a pro-government Whig newspaper owner, who had started to publish a history in 1748, could not make it pay. Both writers praised the role of trade and argued that it was a moral as well as practical good, one reflecting virtue and industry. It was in accordance with the conventions of urban history that Barrett argued that trade and navigation caused towns to prosper. He also claimed that urban history was more valuable than its county counterparts, as it demonstrated the value of economic activity. Hooke advanced similar themes. Depth was provided by the reiteration of the longstanding tradition that Bristol had an ancient origin, an approach that challenged that of William Camden. Very differently, Chatterton provided a past for Bristol by his forgeries of purportedly medieval works. Hooke, in contrast, argued from the absence of evidence, suggesting that early chronicles were only concerned by the doings of the Church and had therefore ignored trade.[37]

Town charters and histories very much linked the past to present legal rights.[38] Thus, John Whitaker received the thanks of Manchester in 1793 for his *The Charter of Manchester translated, with Explanations and Remarks* (1787), a work produced in vindication of the rights of the town against the lord of the manor. This was a traditional cause for historical work, but one now pursued in print as part of the process of justification and lobbying. Civic portraiture and the foundation of newspapers were other aspects of urban identity.[39]

The emphasis on distinctive urban identity was in interplay with the degree to which national links were strengthening, notably through improved communications which became particularly apparent from mid-century as more turnpike roads were established. To a degree, the local was giving way, not to the regional, but to the national.

There was also a process of political and religious easing, one facilitated by the weakness in much of England of Jacobitism, the peaceful accession of George II in 1727, the linkage of Tories and opposition Whigs, the peaceful replacement of Walpole in 1742, the defeat of the '45, and an easing of religious tensions from the early 1720s following the failure of Whig attempts in the late 1710s to limit the Church of England. In towns such as Great Yarmouth, a workable accommodation with Dissenters was gradually teased out.[40] By the 1720s, there was scant interest in any enforced uniformity. There was also a degree of compromise in the treatment of Catholics, although, in the 1740s, the Whig Archdeacon of Cleveland broke up a Catholic convent in York. Defoe noted that Durham was:

> 'full of Roman Catholics, who live peaceably and disturb nobody, and nobody them; for we being there on a holiday, saw them going as publicly to mass as the Dissenters did on other days to their meeting-house.'

This image of religious calm is a very satisfying one, which, however, described more a tolerance at a given social level than the frequently more difficult relations within towns as well as societies, notably in periods of crisis. Sir Dudley Ryder, the Attorney General, recorded in his diary of 3 December 1745, the day before the Jacobites reached Derby: 'people in great pain for the City [of London].... Papists suspected of an intended rising as soon as the rebels are near London.'[41]

This point serves as a reminder that the circumstances of the present can readily be found in the past. Just as today, there can be good relations between different groups, whether religious, ethnic, social or political, as well as poor relations, so the same was true for the past.

Partly as a result, there are difficulties with the evidence. This is particularly so in the vexed case of perception, a category at once important and difficult to assess. And particularly so when much of the population had only limited, or no literacy, or, if literate, left no sources. The eighteenth century, as a result, is misleading, for the 'culture of print' did not encompass all. Even for those involved, there were conventions that can be misleading, as well as the weight of the London example. What is instructive is a cult of the town linked to an ideal of politeness as lifestyle and morality. The last was more aspiration than an accurate description, but, nevertheless, was an important model.

Chapter 5

1750–1800

'Before I could determine to embrace the condition of a prostitute, I was one day accosted in the park by an elderly gentleman who sat down by me upon a bench, and, taking notice of the despondence which was evident in my countenance... he, in return for my confidence, saved me from the most horrible part of my prospect, by taking me into his protection, and reserving me for his own appetite.' Parks and Polite Society: Tobias Smollett novel, *The Adventures of Ferdinand, Count Ferdinand* (1753).

'The riots so usual at contested elections have been uncommonly violent in many of the country boroughs, but none perhaps have been so dangerous as those at Leicester and Nottingham.

The four candidates at the former town ... entered into a coalition to return one member for each party. This junction was no sooner made public than it became the signal for one of the most mischievous riots we ever heard of. The mob were so exasperated at being bilked of further extortion on the several candidates, that they broke open the town-hall and completely gutted it. They made a bonfire of the Quarter Sessions Books, and the Records of the Town, burnt the public library, and would have murdered the Coalitionists, could they have got at them. Several persons have been most severely wounded, and one man is killed. It was not till after the military were called in, and the Riot Act read, that the mob was dispersed.' *Jackson's Oxford Journal*, 3 July 1790. Each seat returned two MPs.

By 1800, about 27.5 per cent of the English population lived in towns, defined as settlements with more than about 2,000 people. By 1800, there were also many more towns with over 10,000 inhabitants, including important industrial and commercial centres in the North, such as Manchester, Leeds, Sheffield, Sunderland and Bolton, and in the Midlands, notably Birmingham, Stoke and Wolverhampton.

Urban England meanwhile changed. Travellers earlier in the century had focused on London and, more particularly, on its mercantile sites, especially new ones such as the Bank of England. The Midlands and the North were largely unknown. When industrial information was sought, as with shipbuilding by Peter the Great, the focus of attention was the London area, in his case Deptford in 1698.

A century later, the situation was very different. Touring in 1784–5, the brothers François and Alexandre de La Rochefoucauld saw John Wilkinson's mill at Birmingham, describing it in detail and discussing it with his agent, recording also that the majority of workers in the city's nail manufacture were women and that they generally turned out 2,000 daily, earning a shilling. The brothers also described Coventry ribbon manufacture, Liverpool slavers, and the Sheffield metal industry. In 1815–16, Archduke John of Austria visited Birmingham, Liverpool and Manchester, including James Watt's works.[1] Shipbuilding became very important in Sunderland and on the Tyne.

Manufacturing impressed travellers recording dynamism, as with Thomas Pennant writing of Macclesfield and Chesterfield in 1769:

'That town [Macclesfield] is in a very flourishing state; is possessed of a great manufacture of mohair and twist buttons; has between twenty and thirty silk mills, and a very considerable copper smelting house, and brass works.... Chesterfield; an ugly town. In this place is a great manufacture of worsted stockings, and another of a brown earthenware.'[2]

There was also industrial growth in the South, including of textile production in expanding towns such as Devizes.[3]

In general, however, there was a divide over industrialisation, which became more significant for towns in the Midlands and the North, while they and the districts centred on them became more important to industry. Towns including Derby, Newcastle, Nottingham and Stockport became more major centres of activity. In Stockport, the population rose from 3,144 in 1754 to 14,830 in 1801, and in Liverpool to 83,250 in 1801. Ten years earlier, William, Marquess of Lansdowne urged a traveller to 'see Liverpool. It is an amazing phenomenon.'[4]

Yet, part of this activity derived from slavery. By 1752, Liverpool had 88 slave ships, with a combined capacity of over 25,000 slaves, and in 1750–79 there were about 1,909 slave trade sailings from there, compared to 869 and 624 from London and Bristol respectively. The last declined in relation to Liverpool and its better port facilities, including the Old Salthouse, St George's and Duke's Docks. Moreover, inland towns could benefit from slavery, with cloth, manufactured in Kendal from local wool, exported for the use of slaves in British colonies.

Liverpool was a key port in North American and Caribbean trade as a whole, as well as that of the Irish Sea. Thus, much Lancastrian coal was exported through Liverpool to Dublin. In place of the earlier emphasis on rural manufacturing districts that lessened the urban-rural divide,[5] the relationship between urbanisation and industrialisation now became closer, with the growing major towns closely associated with manufacturing or with related commerce and services, although small towns remained important, not least in the goods and services they could provide.[6]

Liverpool was the port for Manchester, in part thanks to a new canal link. Manchester became a major industrial centre, with an older core that lacked the rectilinear street plan and the regular layout planned and provided for more recent developments. The latter reflected plot size, landowner convenience and initiatives, and the largely flat topography. Agricultural land was turned into the high income (rental) and capital (sales) of urban property.

Yet, some towns did badly, especially, on a longstanding pattern, if they suffered from poor communications, such as Hereford, or were affected by competition, as Gloucester was from Bristol. Improved communications exposed towns, such as Gloucester, to London's competition, both commercial and industrial. In turn, London benefited from political connections and plentiful credit.

There was also more local competition. Yarm declined once the bridge over the Tees at Stockton opened in 1769 and created a lower crossing point.

Some towns appeared dated. In his novel *The Expedition of Humphry Clinker* (1771), Smollett wrote:

> 'The city of Durham appears like a confused heap of stones and brick, accumulated so as to cover a mountain, round which a river winds its brawling course. The streets are generally narrow, dark, and unpleasant, and many of them almost impassable in consequence of their declivity.'

Moreover, even expanding towns could face crises in particular sectors, in part due to developments elsewhere. Thus, Charles Roe acquired a colliery at Wrexham from where coal was taken to a copper smelter he built at Liverpool in 1767. However, the company moved its operations to South Wales in the 1780s, benefiting from less expensive coal and labour, and in 1793 the company's Liverpool works were closed. In contrast, Liverpool had successfully challenged Bristol for dominance of trans-Atlantic trade, but Bristol still saw important industrial growth, with sugar refining, a tobacco industry, including milling and snuff making, chocolate and cocoa production, cotton mills, soap making and salt refining, as well as metallurgy. However, Liverpool was better placed, both as a port and through the developing economic geography and transport system of England. By 1772, Liverpool had a greater trading tonnage than Bristol, and, by 1791, it was three times as great.

Coal was the major fuel in many industries including sugar refining, glass-making, brewing, salt-boiling, brickmaking and chemicals. Yet, far more was required, not least entrepreneurial ability and transport, both of which were significant for example to the development of the Staffordshire pottery industry from a craft into an industrial process.

Alongside general growth, there were important differences between towns. Thus, the major increase in textile production in Lancashire and Yorkshire was in part achieved at the expense of traditional centres of production such as Colchester, Exeter and Worcester. The peak year for the export of serge, a type of durable cloth, from Exeter was 1777.[7]

Coal power and water power were not the sole factors in favour of Lancashire and Yorkshire, and handlooms continued to be important, not least due to the costs and problems involved in early power looms. Instead, labour was cheaper in Lancashire and Yorkshire and, linked to that, the textile industry less restricted by corporatist traditions than in long-established centres, such as Norwich. There, the manufacture of worsted stuffs continued to be important and its output rose until the 1780s, but the industry remained essentially domestic and quasi-domestic, no factories of any size were built, and competition from the West Riding of Yorkshire had passed it by the mid-century. Partly as a consequence, population growth in Norwich was limited: the number of inhabitants rose from nearly 30,000 in 1752 to 41,000 in 1786, before falling to 37,000 in 1801, which affected local demand and capital availability. Due to competition with the uniform quality and lower prices of machine-spun yarns from the West Riding, the Suffolk yarn industry, although still active in the 1780s had collapsed by 1800.[8] At the same time, as was/is frequently the case with industrial expansion, there was significant competition within the West Riding of Yorkshire, leading to the building by subscription of six large halls in different towns for the more convenient marketing of cloth.

In contrast to an annual average population increase for England and Wales in 1750–70 of 0.75 per cent, that for the West Riding was 1.7 per cent. By the 1790s, industrial change had a clear regional pattern that was reflected in indicators such as expenditure on poor relief per head of population. In 1801, the average figure for England and Wales was 9 shillings 1 penny (45 pence) but in the industrial counties it was far lower: 6s 7d in the West Riding and 4s 4d in Lancashire. In contrast, counties with hardly any industry, such as Sussex and Kent, where the Wealden iron industry had declined greatly, or with declining industries, such as Essex, Norfolk and Suffolk, had to pay far more than the average. A visitor from Derbyshire in 1750 reported, 'what a great deal of good the cotton spinning does at their town and Youlgreave. He says it would be very hard to maintain the poor about them if it was not for that business.'[9]

Economic growth had major consequences for population structure, not least migration from other parts of the country, and was linked to a fall in the age at first marriage and to rising birth rates. Economic growth was also linked to lower mortality rates in the first months of life, as the better nutrition both of mother and child was a consequence of growth. The parish registers of the Yorkshire shipping centre of Selby indicate this benign relationship,[10] although, at the individual level, the benign was often absent.[11]

At the same time, towns were centres of discontent with new developments. There were many industrial disputes, usually defensive actions against unwelcome changes. In 1758, there was a major strike by check weavers in and near Manchester, seeking a return to the prices of the 1730s and recognition of the Manchester Smallware Weavers' Society; but their strike was defeated after a prosecution for illegal combination (proto-trade unions of skilled operatives who wanted to protect their status over the unskilled), a method also used to stop a worsted weavers' combination in Manchester in 1760. Mechanisation brought investment but also hostile responses by some workers. James Hargreaves's spinning jennies were destroyed by rioters in Blackburn in 1768–9. In Leicester, there were riots in 1773 and 1787 against improved stocking frames, and in Shepton Mallet spinning jennies were smashed. In 1791, in Bradford-on-Avon, a carding machine was 'tried' and ceremoniously burnt. There were also protests in the region at Chippenham, Frome and Trowbridge, delaying the adoption of new cloth-making machines, which contributed to a slower growth rate than in Yorkshire. Such a potential for social tension ensured that the management of urban unrest was of great significance and played a role in accounting for differences between towns, as well as helping reflect and explain their character as communities. Politics, religion, philanthropy, social structure, demographics, and coercion, whether by rioters or respondents, could all play a role.[12] So, for example, with differences in the administration of the Poor Law and in other aspects of relief. The poor could be able to ease their situation by negotiating the terms of relief with those who were locally prominent,[13] but this varied by town.

Meanwhile, towns were not only places of manufacture, but also served as display cases as well as consumer centres, including for the rural élite who spent much on living in towns, notably the West End of London,[14] and who came 'into town', treating them as social centres. Edward Phelps of Montacute wrote of Taunton in 1775:

'Our Sessions [meeting of the Quarter Sessions which heard most crimes that could not be tried summarily] was more brilliant than any

I have ever heard of – The Natives as they were emphatically styled pouring in on us from every side. Baronets as plenty as hops, but of worse growth and no flavour.'[15]

Provincial architects, such as Joseph Pickford in Derby, and Richard Gillow and Thomas Harrison in Lancaster, were responsible for fine buildings in a large number of centres.[16] Thus, the social world that fostered the demand for buildings, such as theatres and assembly rooms, was matched by entrepreneurial activity, artistic skill and the wealth of a growing economy. Houses were decorated according to a whole new range of styles and fitted with new products. Wallpaper became fashionable, carpets more common, and furniture more plentiful. Alongside light, roomy and attractive private houses for the middling orders – such as Fenton House in Hampstead, Maister House in Hull, Lawrence House in Launceston, and Wordsworth House in Cockermouth, and the Georgian terraces of Bath, the Clifton section of Bristol and other cities – numerous public buildings were constructed; although it is too easy to forget that, among other accidents, bricklayers broke their necks as a result,[17] because safety at work was limited.

While old gates and walls were demolished, theatres,[18] assembly rooms and subscription libraries were opened, as were parks and walks. In Newcastle, a fortress against Jacobitism in 1715 and 1745, most of the gates and walls were demolished between 1763 and 1812. In their place, major public buildings were constructed, including the Assembly Rooms in 1776 and the Theatre Royal in 1788. Stamford received a smart new Palladian assembly room just as the medieval gates obstructing traffic on the Great North Road were taken down. Norwich city gates were taken down between 1791 and 1801.

Like Tunbridge Wells, Bath was a prime instance of display, cultural consumerism and the impact of change on old towns. Dating back to pre-Roman days, it was new as an eighteenth-century experience, both as a place of leisure, indeed *the* place of leisure, and as a new townscape, one made dramatic by its rise up an impressive hill. By 1800, Bath had a population of about 33,000 and was about the tenth largest town; although the numbers there fluctuated by visitors, and therefore the season, the opposite of the situation in manufacturing towns. Popularised by the visits of the poorly Queen Anne in 1702–3, Bath became a city where it was fashionable to be seen. The social élite went, but so also did many in the middling orders. Although it was already successful, the development of Bath as a city of orderly leisure, and therefore a respectable and safe place to visit, owed much to Richard 'Beau' Nash who, in 1705, had succeeded Captain Webster as Bath's second Master of Ceremonies. Nash's 'Rules' for the behaviour of visitors were first published in 1707, part of the process by which the codification of social propriety was expressed and debated, explicitly or implicitly, and centred in towns; although in Smollett's novel *The Adventures of Roderick Random* (1748), Nash and Bath both appear as odious. In Defoe's novel *Moll Flanders* (1722), Bath is 'a place of gallantry … where men find a mistress sometimes, but very rarely look for a wife.'

Health might be the basis of the resort, but Bath was often a destination for those seeking marriage, and this goal attracted men and women of all ages, as well as the parents acting as chaperones for the young women. The first Pump Room at Bath was built in 1706, followed in 1708 by Harrison's Assembly Rooms, and in 1730 by additional rooms in the Palladian style by John Wood the Elder. Both sets of rooms ran in parallel until the later eighteenth century.

The suburbs laid out to the north of the old core of Bath were to be influential for the establishment of urban forms. Circles, even if not the invention of Wood, were first used on any scale by him in Bath. Wood began the King's Circus in 1754, the design and decoration reflecting his masonic and druidical beliefs. His son began the Royal Crescent in 1767. Palladianism greatly influenced the extension of Bath. This was famously so with the Circus (1754–64) and the Royal Crescent (1767–74), and also with Wood the Elder's Queen Square[19] (1728–34) and Assembly Rooms (1730), his son's Assembly Rooms (1769–71), and the Palladian Bridge created in the nearby gardens of Prior Park. Other buildings included new churches, notably St Michael's (1734–42) and St James's (1768–9), as well as Robert Adam's Pulteney Bridge. 'The white glare of Bath' was a product of its being built largely of light yellow oolitic limestone, albeit in a process in which competing individuals and interests created multiple problems, aside from those of financial availability, notably linked to the collapse of the Bath Bank in 1793, technical issues and the particular problems of individual sites.

By mid-century, a series of walks and gardens were major social attractions there: the Gravel Walks and the Grove, Harrison's walks and gardens, the Terrace Walk, the Parades, and the Spring Gardens. The public spaces were lined by luxury shops, assembly rooms and socially-acceptable accommodation.[20] Alongside its development as a fashionable resort, Bath became, after London, the town that attracted most discussion, the effects of construction and activity helped make an attractive topic and space for the descriptive poetry, prose and painting of the period. Like the West End of London, Bath became normative as a setting for the urban play of the social élite through their repetition in novels, plays and paintings.[21]

Yet, Bath, like the West End, also focused not only frenetic gossip,[22] but also moral panic, as so much else of the different aspects and sites of urban life did in this far-from-secure age, and across history. The town attracted concerns about conduct and misrepresentation, both of which centred on the marriage market, and thus sex. Countering concerns, however, about its setting as a place for vice, notably gambling and sex, and the depiction of the worrying problems of luxury, the life of Bath was based on the fusion of gentility and equality. The assurance of the former made it possible in theory for the company to set aside status and act as equals, sidelining or, rather, marginalising, the concerns about social fluidity that played such a corrosive role for critics. Social mixing, in practice, had its limits there and elsewhere.

Town life in general saw attempts to organise space. Built in 1713, the Priory Estate, that of the onetime Priory of St Thomas of Canterbury, dissolved in 1536, centred on Old Square, played a major role in the gentrification of Birmingham. Occupants were not allowed to keep pigs, dump sewage, or open butcher's or blacksmith's shops. Another area of select housing in Birmingham developed around the new St Philip's Church, built in 1711–15. Indeed, the organisation of space, both within towns and in individual sites such as buildings, excluded the bulk of the population in the cause of what in effect was an uneasy mix of hierarchy, status and profit. So also did the norms of behaviour that were encouraged.

Court and other institutional patronage had long been centred in London, but the new Theatre Royal in Newcastle, opened in 1788, was indicative of the major expansion of provincial culture, which was focused on the middling orders,[23] a section of society that both grew and acquired more disposable wealth. This in part reflected the development of professionalism in a range of activities including the law and medicine. Many towns benefited from renewed cultural energy. In Hertford, there were subscription concerts in a specially built concert-room from 1753 to 1767 and in the 1770s concerts took place in the new Shire Hall, completed in 1771, which had assembly rooms established for such functions. Built in 1766 with a capacity of about 1,600 people, the Theatre Royal in Bristol was modelled on the leading London theatre at Drury Lane.

When, in 1786, the major theatrical company in East Anglia, the Norwich Comedians or the Duke of Grafton's Servants ceased to tour smaller towns, it was still able to concentrate its attentions on Norwich, King's Lynn, Yarmouth, Barnwell (Cambridge), Colchester, Ipswich and Bury St Edmunds, for the last of which, a theatre built in 1819, survives as the Theatre Royal. James Boswell's visit to Falmouth in 1792 provided a vivid account of a theatrical performance.[24]

A greater number of provincial towns also could now boast professional painters, patronised by the local gentry, as well as townspeople. This was not only true of major centres such as Bath and Norwich. Mathias Read (1669–1749), a Londoner settled in Whitehaven in 1690, was patronised by the Lowthers and painted scenes in the Lake District. Hamlet Winstanley (1694–1756) died at Wigan possessed of 'a competent fortune.' In Hampshire, artists were established in Southampton, Winchester and Portsmouth.[25]

Service activities were fostered by the improvement of communications in the surrounding countryside and could become more significant than a town's manufacturing role. In the case of Exeter, both were important. Alongside its continued role in textile manufacture, it became a centre for the 'middling' sort, largely professionals and gentlemen merchants. The growth in urban functions ranged widely. The Royal Hampshire County Hospital was established in Winchester in 1736. The Devon and Exeter Hospital opened in 1743, the first banks in the city opened, Exeter Bank in 1769 and the Devonshire Bank in 1770, and the Law Courts were built in 1773–5. The changing urban fabric in Exeter included the removal of the four city gates from 1769 to 1819, the construction of Bedford Circus from 1773, and the building of brick crescents – Barnfield in 1792 and Colleton from 1802. In Plymouth, Durnford Street and Empire Place were laid out in

1773 as a fashionable residential area. The development in service functions was also seen with the growth of resorts along the South Coast, for example Sidmouth where Fortfield Terrace was begun in 1792. There were also attempts to provide genteel housing in Exmouth and Torbay in the 1790s.

Paving was extended to existing thoroughfares in Tiverton under an Act of 1794. Legislation was important as part of the process of urban improvement. Thus, in Southampton, the development of a spa triggered a demand for tighter control and improvement, and this was seen to require the creation of new machinery. Following the earlier example of Portsmouth, the Common Council of Southampton approved the establishment of commissioners in 1769 and an Act of Parliament was obtained the following year, despite concern that the Commission might lead to an encroachment on the Corporation as well as higher taxation. The Commission was empowered to deal with the paving, repairing, widening and cleansing of the streets, and with the policing and lighting of the town. Overall, the result in Southampton was a marked improvement in the efficiency of street sweeping and a renewed vigour in the prevention of the dumping of rubbish. The line of building was gradually controlled.[26] Paving and lighting improvements were usually a matter of local initiatives, as with the Cambridge Paving and Lighting Act of 1788.

The growth of circulation, proprietary and subscription libraries, built outside the tradition of parish libraries, very much focused on towns. The first of the many proprietary libraries, whose members owned shares, was the Liverpool Library, formed in 1758: membership was over 400 by 1799, and, between 1758 and 1800, the library acquired an average of almost 200 books annually. Proprietary libraries followed in other towns, including Warrington (1760), Manchester (1765), Leeds (1768), Sheffield (1771), Hull (1775), and Birmingham (1779). Towns, moreover, offered their potential readers choices. In Kendal, where a book club was formed in 1761, a newsroom followed in 1779, a subscription library in 1794, and an 'Economical Library' for the less affluent in 1797;[27] although with at least some rural subscribers.

With their race courses, assembly rooms and other facilities, towns were also centres of a regionalism different from the traditional shires, one underlined by the circulation zones of provincial newspapers. Geography as advertisement, booster and boast was very much seen with newspapers as they sought to establish that their circulation areas were extensive and growing. Thus, the Hereford-based *British Chronicle* of 28 January 1779 named agents, by whom advertisements were taken in and the newspaper distributed, in 31 places. Their distribution, across Wales and the Welsh Marches, demonstrated the extent to which some provincial newspapers had a regional span. So also with the circulation of newspapers such as the *Sherborne Mercury* and the *Cumberland Pacquet*. The former circulated across the South West,[28] and in a fashion greater than the Exeter papers which focused more on their urban market. The list of places with agents offers a basis for a presentation of local and regional geography in terms of economic opportunity, at least in terms of advertising and the spread of news, and provides a way to delimit the areas of influence of the towns of the period. For example, the *Bristol Chronicle, Or, Universal Mercantile Register*, a Bristol weekly launched on 5 January 1760, added a list of named agents at Bridgewater, Taunton and Wells in the issue of 3 May 1760. At the beginning of 1773, *Drewry's Derby Mercury* named agents in Ashbourne, Ashby-de-la-Zouch, Bakewell, Burton-upon-Trent, Chesterfield, London, Loughborough, Rotherham, Uttoxeter, Winster and Wirksworth, and announced that it was: 'dispersed by Joseph Housely, through the towns of Alfreton, Higham, Chesterfield, Dronfield, Sheffield and numerous intermediate villages.' This was a more constricted circulation zone than those of the Hereford, Bristol, Gloucester and Sherborne newspapers. In contrast, on 16 January 1773, the *Newcastle Journal* claimed: 'The circle of this Journal's distribution is near 600 miles, within which circumference are upwards of 250 towns.' There were no effective and lasting rivals to the Newcastle press closer than newspapers published in Edinburgh, Glasgow, York, Leeds and Manchester.

That summer, the *Cambridge Chronicle and Journal* named agents in Bedford, Boston, Bungay, Bury St Edmunds, Caistor, Downham, Ely, Gainsborough, Grantham, Huntingdon, King's Lynn, Leicester, Lincoln, London, Louth, Newark, Newmarket, Norwich, Peterborough, Retford, St Ives, St Neots, Spalding, Stamford, and Wisbech, a very extensive area, and, in effect, a greater East Anglia. The newspaper also offered an account of its distribution network, an account that threw light on the variety of means involved:

'This paper is distributed northwards every Friday night, by the Caxton post, as far as York, Newcastle, and Carlisle; through the counties of Cambridge, Huntingdon, Bedford, Buckingham, Rutland, Leicester, Nottingham, Lincoln, Northampton, Norfolk, Hertford, Essex, and the Isle of Ely, by the newsmen; to London the next morning, by the coach and fly; and to several parts of Suffolk etc by other conveyances – persons living at a distance from such places as the newsmen go through, may have the paper left where they shall choose to appoint.'[29]

By January 1777, the *Bristol Journal* was listing named agents in Abergavenny, Bath, Brecon, Bridgwater, Carmarthen, Chippenham, Exeter, Gloucester, Haverfordwest, Liverpool, London, Marlborough, Sherborne, Taunton and Wells,[30] again a very extensive area. Like other newspapers, the *Salisbury Journal* had a complex administrative network that radiated from the hub of the newspaper printing office. Underlying this was an associated system of smaller news-agency centres.[31] Diaries and accounts shed further light. In 1791, Thomas Fenwick of Burrow Hall, Lancashire was reading the Leeds newspaper.[32]

Such papers, all town-based, can be termed provincial if that is taken to mean regional rather than local.[33] The provincial, rather than local, nature of newspapers is in part explained by the extent to which the news published was national or international, rather than local, however defined. Newspapers were read in order to discover news of the outside world, and this world was one that was essentially defined by the metropolis and foreign countries, rather than by other parts of provincial England, near or far. Nevertheless, alongside the under-reporting of parts of the country,[34] it was certainly the case that the space devoted, both to local news and to news from other provincial parts of England, increased greatly toward the close of the century; with the news from other parts derived in part from other provincial papers. Already, between May 4 and September 14, 1749, the *Worcester Journal* carried news about Shrewsbury, Birmingham, Stratford-upon-Avon, Cheltenham, Benson, Bredon, Stow on the Wold, Droitwich, Cardiganshire, Gloucester, Hereford, Warwick, Pershore, Lichfield, Horton and Marlborough. Booksellers at a number of towns, including Bridgnorth, Shrewsbury, Warwick, Stourbridge, Stafford and Evesham, took in advertisements or sold this newspaper.

Much local news was of economic value. The *Portsmouth and Gosport Gazette and Salisbury Journal* in 1752 reported the price of wheat at Devizes (24 February) and ship news at Poole (May 25), and also pressed policies, for example the enforcement of the law against the buyers and hawkers of smuggled goods, a practice that hit fair traders (18 September). The *Leeds Mercury* of August 18, 1775 included, in its local news, items from Newcastle, Selby, Thirsk and Wooler, which provided considerable coverage.

Publications regularly underlined the idea that social cohesion was linked to prosperity and to politics, as in a pamphlet of February 1757 that printed 'The St Giles's Address to Andrew Stone', a Lord of Trade. This depicted despair among the London poor as their livelihood was threatened, and showed how the war, in the shape of the loss of the British base in Minorca to French attack in 1756, had wide-ranging consequences:

'We the lamp lighters, link-boys, dustmen, chimneysweepers, cinder-sifters, carmen, porters, shoe-cleaners, hackney-coachmen, and (late) bruisers of ... St Giles's ... By means of this capture to the enemy, many Turkey merchants, who had used to have twenty fires blazing at once, and of course, so many chimnies to sweep, now are forced to do their business at coffee-houses, for want of money to buy coals at home. Their wives call aloud for no coaches, though their own are laid down, their maid servants, which they never did before, sift their own cinders. Their very apprentices, when they cross the way, never pay the link-boy, but cry, like courtiers, another time. And, their porters carry the letters and messages, who used to stay in the warehouse; and, to our utter ruin, pocket the money themselves.'[35]

Higher levels of information availability and flow became more common. For example, the *Dorchester and Sherborne Journal* of 27 November 1801 noted:

'In compliance with the request of many of our readers, and it being our wish to render our journal as extensively useful as possible, we have inserted the current prices of all the leading articles of merchandise, which we mean to continue weekly; and as the greatest care will be taken as to accuracy, we have no doubt it will prove highly interesting to merchants and traders to every description.'

As an example of the resulting regional net, *Drewry's Derby Mercury* of October 8, 1773 carried details of the price of cheese at nearby Nottingham fair, and of the willingness of the principal inhabitants of the nearby industrial town of Wolverhampton to take Portuguese coins; while *Woolmer's Exeter and Plymouth Gazette* of 30 November 1809 provided not only London grain, meat and butter prices, but also Salisbury, Basingstoke, Devizes, Newbury, Andover and Warminster grain prices. Both economy and society benefited from newspaper advertisements about crime, for example horse-stealing and fraud.[36]

Although reaching across a considerable rural hinterland, newspapers were more available in towns, which was where they were published. Literacy rates were higher there, while newspapers were less expensive as it was not necessary to pay for delivery by newsmen. Regional and local reporting focused on the towns. This emphasis was taken further in newspaper titles, as with the *Kentish Post* which was subtitled the 'Canterbury Newsletter'.

Moreover, the towns were the source of news. Thus, in 1791, responding clearly to interest after the Priestley riots, the *London Chronicle* of 23 July printed an account of Birmingham:

'Birmingham being unhappily at present a general topic of conversation, we are favoured with the following short account of it from a correspondent who has long resided there.

Birmingham is a large town in Warwickshire, and the most flourishing of any in England for all sorts of iron-work and curious manufactures. It has no corporation, being only governed by two constables and two bailiffs, and therefore free for any person to settle there, which has contributed greatly to the increase of its trade and inhabitants.

The town stands on the side of a hill forming nearly a half-moon. The lower part is filled with the workshops and warehouses of the manufacturers, and consists chiefly of old buildings. The upper part of the town contains a number of new and regular streets, with a handsome square, elegantly built.

It has two churches, one in the lower part of the town, which is an ancient building with a very tall spire; the other is a very grand modern structure, with a stone tower, cupola, a set of bells and musical chimes, which play seven different tunes, being one for each day in the week. It has many meeting-houses for every denomination of dissenters, who are very numerous there.

The houses in this town are supposed to have increased within these 20 years above 10,000; so that admitting the inhabitants then were 80,000, at the rate of five to a house, they must now be increased to 130,000. It is 109 miles north-west from London.'

In fact the 1801 census revealed a population of 73,670. Birmingham also had an active urban culture that included artisans and traders, upwardly mobile working men, often self-educated Dissenters, such as the bookseller William Hutton who also wrote the first history of the town and whose home and shop were looted in the riots, in part due to the opposition to Dissent but also because he had called for a cut in the Poor Rates and been an official in the debtors' court.[37] The hostility to Dissent underlined the extent to which religion was not necessarily a social cement. Denominational differences remained important.

Aside from economic and press links from town into the countryside, there were many others, including the placing of very young children with rural wet-nurses, as by London in Berkshire from 1744 to 1768.[38] Wet-nursing was an instance of the social issues of the period. Alongside development, towns also faced and posed serious problems of regulation and control. Poverty and crime were concentrated there, as were problems of sanitation and health. Remedies were generally from within the community. The *Salisbury and Winchester Journal* of 20 December 1790 reported:

'A correspondent of Frome informs us, that in consequence of several persons of that town having lately been bitten by a mad dog, the parishioners, at a vestry, entered into a resolution of relieving no pauper who should keep a dog. A laudable example for other parishes to follow!'

Rabies more generally was an issue. On 17 February 1792, the *Chelmsford Chronicle* offered its readers a cure for rabies 'handed to us by a neighbour'.

Meanwhile, as part of a more general transformation, philanthropic foundations were responsible for new hospitals and schools. The former attracted the attention of foreign visitors, such as the French surgeon Jacques Tenon who, in 1787, travelled as far west as Plymouth and as far north as Birmingham and Worcester.[39] With the exception of Birmingham, this matched the travels of George III over a wider period, reflecting the dominance of the South in the collective imagination.

Many townspeople lived in precarious circumstances, often in disrupted family situations and outside established patterns of hierarchy. Urban crowds could prove volatile and pose serious challenges to control, ones that led to the deployment of troops. At the time of the disturbances linked to John Wilkes, Elizabeth Montagu complained from London in 1762 about a classic feature of town life:

> 'all mankind are philosophers and pride themselves in having a contempt for rank and order... Alexander the Great was treated with contempt by a certain philosopher [Diogenes of Sinope] in a tub, but in this enlightened age, the man who made the tub would use him with the same scorn.'[40]

She was depressed by a similar situation in Newcastle.[41] Fire and firefighting were so prevalent that they could readily be used as an image for politics, such as by George Lyttelton writing from Worcester to Elizabeth Montagu in 1763. She was then in London, and he was clearly referring to newspapers:

> 'I find your chief entertainment has been houses and ladies burnt to ashes, and incendiaries endeavouring to set the nation on fire. What engine can be found to quench that fire, if it spreads much further, the watchmen of the state will do well to consider.'[42]

Towns, with their voluntary associations, notably Dissenting chapels that undermined the cohesive role of parishes (Marlborough had its parish church at one end of the Square and Dissenting chapel at the other), and also the politicisation centred on clubs and newspapers, were centres for reforming pressure of a more radical direction.[43] At the very least, towns were affected by the national dimension of politics.[44] Yet, pressure for reform could lead to curtailing the activities of others. Newspapers such as the *Leeds Intelligencer*,

Leeds Mercury and *Sheffield Advertiser* criticised such popular pastimes as cock-fighting, drunkenness and profanity, continuing a more general tendency of admonishing and controlling the poor.[45] The *Cambridge Intelligencer* in 1798 published a call for action:

'A correspondent at Banbury in Oxfordshire, has sent us a most shocking account of a *Bull-baiting*, which we find annually takes place there at Michaelmas. After the poor animal has been baited for several hours, it was dragged round the town with ropes, amidst the shouts of a barbarous (barbarous in every sense) multitude... What are the magistrates and what are the clergy about on such occasions? If the latter would but use their influence to humanise the lower classes it would do more good than all the Philippics against French Atheism etc.'

Yet, alongside the standard emphasis on urban Enlightenment, it is important to note the strength of a faith in which evil had a real presence. Newspapers published articles on the need, in light of thunder and lightning, to contemplate the Day of Judgement and the Torments of Hell.[46] The development of Methodism showed a concern for religion among artisans in particular, with John Wesley especially active in London, Bristol and Newcastle. In Nottingham, the Methodists focused much attention on those working in the important stocking industry. Their first chapel in the town, the Octagon, was founded in 1764; it was replaced by a larger chapel in 1784, and again in 1798. There could also be a violent response to Methodist meetings, as in Sheffield in 1744, Exeter and Leeds in 1745, York in 1747, Norwich in 1751–2 and Birmingham in 1764. Meanwhile the Church of England remained active, with most churches kept in good repair, and many were rebuilt, for example five in Worcester in 1730–72[47] and St Nicholas, Bristol in the 1760s.

At the same time, there was considerable precariousness for both individuals and communities. In July 1785, a hot, dry month, fire broke out in a tallow chandlery in King's Sutton and then destroyed most of the town, spreading quickly in part because the town was overcrowded. 150 houses were wrecked. Churches were crucial centres, especially for devotion but also for philanthropy, sociability and culture, the *Leeds Intelligencer* reporting on 17 October 1769:

'On Thursday and Friday last, the Oratorios of Judas Maccabeus and the Messiah were performed in Trinity Church for the benefit of the Infirmary in this town, with the most exact regularity and to the satisfaction of very polite and crowded audiences.'

Somewhat different priorities were also to the fore for Sir Roger Newdigate of Arbury in Warwickshire who, in the early 1750s, attended the races at Warwick, Lichfield, Rugby and Nuneaton, went bowling and patronised a book club at Atherstone, attended a Birmingham club and the annual Feast of the Drapers' Company of Coventry of which he was a member.[48]

Towns also continued their longstanding position as centres of investment, but, as with so much else in this period, institutionalisation played a big role, in this case the development of banking and establishment of banks, the first of which were opened in Norwich in 1756, Exeter in 1769, Chichester in 1779 and Richmond, Yorkshire in 1792. Furthermore, there were no local credit monopolies: individual banks were rapidly followed by others, the Exeter Bank (1769) by the Devonshire Bank (1770), City Bank (1786), General Bank (1792) and Western Bank (1793). By the end of the century, there were several hundred provincial banks in England, helping to keep the money supply buoyant and circulating, and to spread credit.

In turn, and underlining the symbiotic relationship between London and other towns, an inter-regional credit structure based on London developed, ensuring that local economies were very much linked to national financial developments, and also thereby to each other at the national level. The establishment of a bank clearing house in Lombard Street in London in 1775 led to a great improvement; banks were allowed to balance credits and withdrawals by a ticket system.

The politics of towns in the last decades of the century had very different aspects. Urban interests were able to press for governmental support. Thus, in 1784, Francis, Marquess of Carmarthen, the Foreign Secretary, complained about an Austrian regulation against the import of manufactured goods, writing that 'the towns of Manchester and Sheffield have taken the alarm and have applied to government on the subject.' The envoy in Vienna was instructed to threaten reprisals. In 1785, Joseph II of Austria was 'very freely attacked by the Birmingham manufacturers on account of his late prohibitory edict'.[49] In 1786, William Eden made efforts on behalf of the Nottingham stocking industry in the governmental trade negotiations he was conducting with France,[50] while in 1788, when Eden was envoy in Spain, he was sent representations from committees of the Chambers of Commerce at Leeds and Exeter, and in 1789 Sir George Yonge, the Secretary at War and MP for Honiton, also registered pressure from nearby Exeter.[51]

Yet, the period ended with the divisions and drama of responses to the French Revolution, a crisis that stirred up anxieties and led to paranoia about opposition. In some towns, there was government action against opposition newspapers. In many towns, elections became more contentious, as in Northampton where, in 1796, the Whigs were in part dependent on cobbler support in order to win the election, a recourse that captured the social dimension of politics. In Warwick, the Earl, who lived in a large castle there, sought to maintain a traditional family patronage, but his leadership was challenged by urban interests no longer willing to follow this lead, although other voters were prepared to maintain the established pattern.[52] This tension was a more widespread one, and had political, generational and ideological dimensions, and features at once local and national. Alongside a rise of partisan politics from the 1790s, there was the same within parishes, as a separatist Methodism and a distinctive evangelical tendency both weakened cohesion.

Differences and rivalries within individual towns were drawn into broader currents by the politicisation of these years, although the extent of both politicisation and alignment varied. This ensured that there were many contrasts between the politics of individual towns, a situation that has continued to the present including for towns with similar social structures. Thus, whereas in some towns urbanisation increased social tension, in others the spatial pattern of urbanisation led to an increased separation that could lessen tension.

The politics, including religious politics, culture and society of individual towns, provided local forcing-houses for a variegated urban middle-class culture, one that extended to the purposes, character and achievements of philanthropy and institutionalisation.[53] The same was to be true of later developments; but local factors were to be squeezed hard, particularly in the twentieth century, by a combination of national regulation, oversight and financial provision, as well as by the disruption at the local level produced by the amalgamation of authorities to produce what was very much a new local.

Looking at the period in terms of what came earlier and later is valuable, but also incomplete because it can lead to a failure to understand these years on their own merit. All too often there is a tendency to think in terms of a failure yet to achieve developments that were to follow, notably industrial change, indeed revolution, and political radicalism. Such an approach tells us little about attitudes at the time. Judging by the press and by public petitioning, there was an engagement with national politics, but that, of course, was the nature of those particular sources, a point that remains relevant today.

The press also revealed a very different set of concerns in terms of local advertisements, including for the sale of animals, land and other rural criteria. This underlines the degree to which many of the towns of the eighteenth century saw continuity with earlier periods in being centrally concerned with their rural hinterlands, although London's concern was far less. This situation was to change in the nineteenth century, and notably so from the 1870s when rural England had the stuffing knocked out of it by the Great Agricultural Depression. Until then, there was a fundamental relationship in which much of urban life was linked to rural hinterlands, each affecting the other.

Yet towns were also in inter-urban networks (there was never only one network), and these provided a way for the definition, pursuit and defence of particular interests, issues and identities. Moreover, individual towns sought to define their regions and, in that context, to influence and delimit hinterlands. This was a peaceful pursuit, but that did not make it any less urgent or important.

Chapter 6

1800–1850

'Nothing can be conceived more grand or more terrific than the yellow waves of fire that incessantly issue from the top of these furnaces … it is impossible to behold it without being convinced that … other nations … will never equal England with regard to things made of iron and steel. They call it black Sheffield, and black enough it is; but from this one town and its environs go nine-tenths of the knives that are used in the whole world.'

William Cobbett, Sheffield, January 1830.

'Railways are shifting all Towns of Britain into new places: no Town will stand where it did, and nobody can tell for a long while yet where it will stand… Railways have set all the Towns of Britain a-dancing. Reading is coming up to London, Basingstoke is going down to Gosport or Southampton … while at Crewe, and other points, I see new ganglions of human population establishing themselves, and the prophecy of metallurgic cities which were not heard of before … the unfortunate Towns subscribed money to get railways; and their business has gone elsewither… Towns thus silently bleeding to death.'

Thomas Carlyle, *'Hudson's Statue'* (1850), in Carlyle, *Latter Day Pamphlets* (London, 1850), p. 226.

Towns increasingly throbbed to the beat of machines. By 1821, Manchester had over 5,000 power looms, each an investment in change. In Bradford, which became the global centre of worsted wool production and exchange, a reference to the wealth of which was to be made in T.S. Eliot's poem *The Waste Land* (1922) with 'a silk hat on a Bradford millionaire', factory horsepower rose 718 per cent in 1810–30. Its population climbed from 16,012 in 1810 to 103,778 in 1850, by when there were 17,642 automatic looms there, mass-producing women's dress fabrics, the mechanisation of yarn spinning there followed in 1826 by that of worsted weaving. In Charles Dickens' novel *Hard Times* (1854), the new form of utilitarianism is vividly described: 'so many hundred hands in the Mill; so many hundred horse Steam Power. It is known, to the force of a single pound weight, what the engine will do.'

Jane Austen had been less engaged with urban industrialisation. In *Pride and Prejudice*, finally published in 1813, although written earlier, Elizabeth Bennet visits Birmingham. So, in reality, had William Gilpin, Thomas Jefferson, and the La Rochefoucaulds. The factory of Matthew Boulton and James Boulton at Soho in Birmingham was a major and much-visited site that was described in print.[1] Austen does not comment on what Elizabeth saw, but Birmingham comes up in *Emma* (1815), when the ridiculous Mrs Elton complains about social upstarts:

'People of the name of Tupman, very lately settled there, and encumbered with many low connections, but giving themselves immense airs, and expecting to be on a footing with the old established families ... how they got their fortune nobody knows. They came from Birmingham, which is not a place to promise much.... One has not great hopes from Birmingham.'[2]

Ironically, Mrs Elton's brother-in-law, Suckling, who was very annoyed, is described as having made his fortune from trade.

It is the images left by Dickens that prevail. His powerful novel of industrial strife, *Hard Times* (1854), was based on the Preston textile weavers' strike of 1853–4, an attempt to reverse recent wage cuts.[3] Dickens presented an insistent pollution of life:

'It was a town of red brick, or of brick that would have been red if the smoke and ashes had allowed it; but as matters stood it was a town unnatural red and black like the painted face of a savage. It was a town of machinery and tall chimneys, out of which interminable serpents of smoke trailed themselves for ever and ever, and never got uncoiled. It had a black canal in it, and a river that ran purple with ill-smelling dye, and vast piles of buildings full of windows where there was a rattling and trembling all day long, and where the piston of the steam-engine worked monotonously up and down, like the head of an elephant in a state of melancholy madness. It contained several large streets still more like one another, inhabited by people equally like one another, who all went in and out at the same hours, with the same sound upon the pavements, to do the same work, and to whom every day was the same as yesterday and tomorrow, and every year the counterpart of the last and the next.'

So also with his *The Old Curiosity Shop* (1840–1), which was based in part on his visit to Wolverhampton and Birmingham. Dickens described the arrival of Little Nell in Birmingham by canal, and the disorientation caused by the town:

'The water had become thicker and dirtier ... the paths of coal-ash and huts of staring brick marked the vicinity of some great manufacturing town.... Now the clustered roofs, and piles of buildings trembling with the working of engines, and dimly resounding with their shrieks and throbbings; the tall chimneys vomiting forth a black vapour, which hung in a dense ill-flavoured cloud above the housetops and filled the air with gloom; the clank of hammers beating upon iron, the roar of busy streets and noisy crowds, gradually augmenting until all the various sounds blended into one and none was distinguishable for itself, announced the termination of their journey... The child and her grandfather ... stood amid its din and tumult, and in the pouring rain, as strange, bewildered, and confused, as if they had lived a thousand years before, and were raised from the dead and placed there by a miracle.'

More briefly, Robert Shackleton, a visiting American, in his book *Touring Great Britain* (1914), observed of Manchester: 'Manufacturing has done this thing ... Great, black, sooty place ... What an astonishing congestedness of population,' a congestedness in part owing to migration into Manchester (and other towns) from smaller settlements and rural areas.[4]

Dickens provides an account not only of polluted towns but also of the hard labour of urban workers. Referring in *Nicholas Nickleby* (1838–9) to Kate Nickleby, he wrote of:

'… many sickly girls, whose business, like that of the poor worm, is to produce with patient toil, the finery that bedecks the thoughtless and luxurious, traverse our streets, making towards the scene of their daily labour, and catching, as if by stealth, in their hurried walk, the only gasp of wholesome air and glimpse of sunlight which cheers their monotonous existence during the long train of hours that makes a working day … their unhealthy looks and feeble gait.'

At the same time, in his short story 'Dullborough Town' (1860), Dickens provided variety: 'Most of us come from Dullborough who come from a country town,' although even there change was to the fore: 'the station has swallowed up the playing field.'

The variety of town life in this period is sometimes presented in terms of the industrial North and the agrarian and/or residential South. This is inaccurate, other than in the most general terms, much depending for example on the definition of 'the North'. In Devon, there were towns that conformed to the idea of an agrarian South, but Plymouth, the largest town in the county, was different. Its naval functions led to the town becoming distinctly urban working class in character. Plymouth spread considerably but, in part because of the physical constraints of site and the space demands of dockyards, not sufficiently to keep pace with the growth in population. As a consequence, as with other large urban areas, there was a decline in quality of life, in particular as a result of overcrowding. Multiple-occupancy was combined with indifferently built houses, and the net result was insanitary housing conditions. Cholera hit Plymouth hard in 1832. At the same time, its growth provided employment for those seeking work across Devon, while also serving to draw in labour from further afield. Thus, some skilled Welsh migrants moved to the city.

The importance of new technology and entrepreneurial energy was demonstrated at Tiverton where John Heathcoat founded a machine-made net and lace factory. The threat to jobs posed by his patented bobbinnet machines had led to the destruction of his Loughborough factory by rioters in 1816, and Heathcoat moved his machines to a disused Tiverton cotton mill. Production from this factory hit lace-making in East Devon and showed what could be achieved in the absence of coal. John Boden, a former partner of Heathcoat, opened the Derby Lace Works near Barnstaple in 1825 and by 1830 he was employing 1,000 people. Largely as a result, the population of the town rose from 5,079 in 1821 to 7,902 in 1841. More dramatically, by mid-century Sheffield produced half of Europe's steel and by 1900 its population was 400,000.[5] The growing population of towns made food prices very sensitive, although that was scarcely a new issue.

Indeed, in general, there was a new divide over manufacturing, with access to coal a key issue, notably for London, but not the only one. Bruton, in Somerset, had been a major centre of silk production, with the largest manufacturer employing 700 to 900 hands (workers) on about 15,700 spindles in 1823. However, due to foreign competition, it was soon down to 230 hands, 7,000 spindles and a four-day week.

The lifestyle and densely inhabited working-class neighbourhood that developed in Tiverton was different from the gentility, politeness and refinement conspicuously displayed in South Devon resort towns, with their approximations to Bath society. Assembly rooms opened in Exmouth in 1801 and Dawlish in 1811, and circulating libraries at Sidmouth, Dawlish, Exmouth and Teignmouth by 1815, while Den Crescent in Teignmouth was built in 1826. This coast became a fashionable place to live and retire, and this helped lead to a distinctive social and demographic structure. In contrast, the North Devon coast was less fashionable, although it attracted trippers from South Wales.

At the same time, growth was scarcely easy. Competition between towns continued to be incessant, and government agencies could intervene. Thus, in 1839, the installation of a customs officer at Hartlepool made that port independent of Stockton. The routing of railways and location of junctions were to be other major causes and forms of acute competition.

Meanwhile, like changes to communications, industrialisation involved much disruption and hardship, often with scant improvement in real wages or labour security.[6] There were widespread disturbances and a degree of radical violence. In Carlisle, the handloom weavers rioted in 1819, there were abortive radical conspiracies in London and Huddersfield in 1820, and the invention of friction matches in 1826 by the Stockton chemist John Walker and their subsequent manufacture as 'strike anywhere lucifers', made arson easier. Henry Addington, the Home Secretary, had warned in 1820:

'The accounts from Manchester, Leeds, Glasgow etc are unsatisfactory. A simultaneous explosion appears to be meditated.'[7]

In political, economic, social, and cultural terms, the role of towns in part remained that of linking London to the rest of the country, and that was emphasised in provincial towns. Thus, the *Devonshire Chronicle and Exeter News*, which appeared every Saturday evening, carried, at the start of its issues in 1831 and 1832: 'This is the only newspaper in the West of England in which the London Gazette, Price of Stocks, and Markets of Friday etc are printed and published on the following day.'

Separately, and linking towns across the country, continued tension over the role of London took many forms. Under the heading 'London Advertising Money-Lenders', the *Taunton Courier* of 2 March 1831 reported:

'One of those blood-suckers has sent us an advertisement which he requests may be inserted for a series of weeks. We have uniformly resisted the invitation of these fellows to allow our columns to become the vehicles of their depredatory practices.'

Due first to canals and then to rail, there was a new geography as landlocked industrial towns, such as Stoke and Wolverhampton, found their relative position transformed. *Smart's Trade Directory* for 1827 noted that goods could be sent from Pickfords' canal wharf in Wolverhampton, a leading centre for the manufacture of iron products, direct to 73 towns, including Bristol, Liverpool, London and Manchester. The opening of a canal to Northampton in 1815, linking it to the Warwickshire coalfields and to London, was important to the development of Northampton's footwear industry. Thanks to the convergence represented by better and more rapid communication, the prices in the Michaelmas cheese fair at Derby in the nineteenth century were very similar to those of national indices, although local conditions, notably drought and poor production methods, could encourage disparities, and this encouraged the introduction in the 1850s of new methods for cheese-making. The population of Carlisle, a centre of cotton manufacture, rose from near 10,000 in 1801 to over 35,000 by 1841, while Jonathan Dodgson Carr, adapting a printing machine to cut biscuits, replaced cutting them by hand. Helped by Carlisle's position as a major rail junction, he sold his product throughout the country, transporting it by rail. Another biscuit-maker in another key rail station was Huntley and Palmer, supplier of sponge fingers to the nation, based in Reading.

The formidable effort represented by the new rail system was captured in 1837 when the *Gentleman's Magazine* declared of the London and Greenwich Railway: 'no less than 60,000,000 bricks have been laid by human hands.' Companies and towns that wished to stay at the leading edge of economic development had to become and remain transport hubs. The ability to obtain large supplies of coal was fundamental. Thus, mills located earlier to benefit from fast-flowing streams in upland areas, faded because they lacked the access enjoyed by large-scale steam-driven urban mills.

Ports were particularly important as they joined domestic transport systems to international markets. Those reached via the Atlantic were of especial significance. Liverpool, the third most populous English town in 1801, after London and Manchester, continued to expand rapidly. Built in 1709–15, the Old Dock was filled in during the 1820s as the city's docks expanded ninefold from 1756 to 1836 to cope with a 30-fold rise in tonnage. Rural areas in John Eyres's 1765 map, including around Shaw's Brow and Toxteth Park, became densely populated.

Crowded towns, however, posed particular issues for health. Population growth was met by increased population density. In Lancaster, back gardens were turned into houses, with access through doors and arches on main roads, but lacking water supplies, sewerage or lighting. Similarly, the rapid growth in Nottingham's population was met by back-to-back housing in courts with access to streets via narrow tunnels through the houses on the street frontages. In Austen's novel *Mansfield Park* (1814), the Price household in Portsmouth has small rooms and a narrow passage and staircase.[8] More seriously, the Bradford Sanitary Committee visited over 300 houses in 1845 and found an average of three people sleeping per bed. Due in part to infections, mortality under five was about 50 per cent in Manchester from 1789 to 1869. In a development that is relevant for today, population density rose as the urban population grew. Thus while the population of Sunderland nearly trebled between 1825 and 1865, the built-up area did not keep pace and the overcrowded east end was the centre of the 1831 cholera epidemic in the town. The crowded, insanitary part of Carlisle was badly hit by cholera:

the city had an unsatisfactory water supply. An orphanage was founded in Wolverhampton after the 1849 epidemic in order to provide for cholera orphans. There was a similar need elsewhere.

Southampton, like many towns, had an area known as the 'rookeries' from the networks of courts, alleys and paths inhabited by the poor. In 1843, Pipewellgate in Gateshead had 2,040 people crammed into a street 300 yards long and mostly only eight feet in breadth; there were only three privies in the street. That year, fewer than 10 per cent of the homes in Newcastle had water directly supplied, and a reliance on Tyne water was linked to major cholera outbreaks in 1832, 1850 and 1853. Robert Baker's 1842 'Sanitary Map of the Town of Leeds' was reproduced by Edwin Chadwick in his *Report on the Sanitary Conditions of the Labouring Population of Great Britain*. Baker plotted clusters of cholera outbreaks and contagious diseases and argued for sanitation. Commissioned in 1839 by the government to investigate the lives of the poor, Chadwick found that individual immorality or idleness was less to blame than modern urban life, a revelation that prompted programmes of public health reform and schemes for urban improvement. Changing definitions of epidemic disease played a role in pressure for local and national public health measures.[9]

Nearby towns shared in the concerns about public health, but their contexts varied greatly. Thus, Huddersfield, a West Riding industrial centre that did well, was very different to nearby Wakefield, a market centre that did not grow comparably, although both had to respond to the major social changes of the period.[10]

George Thomas Clark, the General Board of Health's Superintending Inspector, who produced an enquiry into Durham's sanitation in 1849, bleakly concluded:

'This city is associated in men's minds only with architectural splendour and ecclesiastical dignity; and few persons beyond the bounds of the county are aware of the contrast between that Durham which strangers visit to admire, and that Durham in which 10,000 human beings pass an existence demonstrably shortened by one-seventh part.'[11]

Moreover, there were serious health issues in the smaller towns, for example Battle in Sussex, of which a 1850 report noted:

> 'There is no provision for the removal of any offensive or noxious refuse from the houses and gardens of the poorer classes; all the decomposing and putrescent animal and vegetable matter which is brought out of the house is thrown into a pool, around which is engendered an atmosphere favourable to the production of febrile epidemics.'

There were also problems with the care of the poor under the 1834 Poor Law Amendment Act, with many workhouses harsh as well as bleak. In Wimborne, workhouse beds had to be shared, meat was only provided once a week, there were no vegetables other than potatoes until 1849, men and women were segregated, and unmarried mothers had to wear distinctive clothes. The Andover workhouse scandal of 1845 revealed an abusive and corrupt master of the workhouse, and totally inadequate rations. In Stroud workhouse in 1849, cruelty encompassed a scalding to death.

Urban responses, indeed renewal, were political, not least because of the cost entailed and the patronage involved. Thus, in Nottingham, there was delay in building a large modern workhouse as stipulated by the Poor Law of 1834 because Tories preferred the previous system of outdoor relief. The new workhouse was not completed until 1843.[12]

Towns more directly engaged political concern due to their being centres of political stress. As the sources of press criticism, the towns led the opposition to the Tory establishment in the early nineteenth century. Town politics included the voting of official thanks, as in 1809 when Salisbury Corporation voted thanks to the (opposition) parliamentary denouncers of the sale of army commissions by the mistress of Frederick, Duke of York, son of George III and head of the army. In the provinces, the demand for peace with Napoleon, another opposition cause, was led by the *Leeds Mercury* under its editor-proprietor Edward Baines. Most of the eleven individuals who funded his acquisition of the paper in 1801 were Dissenters. Newspapers which supported the call included the *Nottingham Review*, founded in 1808 by a Methodist printer, Charles Sutton, and the *West Briton*, launched in

1810. Other papers critical of the wartime government included the *Leicester Chronicle*, *Liverpool Mercury* and *Manchester Evening Herald*.

Rates of reading and writing and thus ready access to the press, were higher in town than countryside due to the differences in schooling. Thus, by 1811, Warwick had a grammar school, a borough school, free schools, a 'School of Industry' (effectively a poor law school for pauper children and orphans), and denominational Sunday schools.[13]

The end of the Napoleonic war in 1815 saw a continuance of opposition press activism, including in the newly-launched *Sheffield Independent* (1819) and *Manchester Guardian* (1821). In this and other respects, moral improvement gained a pointedly political content and energy, and at both local and national levels.[14] There was also an important economic dimension with worker opposition to new technology. In 1812, the Luddite riots saw extensive attacks on factory equipment in the North and Midlands. At a general meeting on 27 February in Huddersfield, a major centre of the woollen industry, a subscription association hostile to the Luddites was established to obtain information about the riots. The resolutions accepted an account that was scarcely one of calm:

'It appears to this meeting, that a violent and determined spirit of insubordination has gained much ground amongst the workmen employed in various trades and manufactures, and particularly amongst the shearmen and that the same is organised and supported in a matter, not only alarming to trade in general, but to the peaceable inhabitants of this town and neighbourhood in particular.

That we cannot sufficiently deprecate all attempts to limit the ingenuity of our artificers, the employment of our capital, and to prescribe the mode to which the different operations of our trade shall be conducted, and particularly those now making in this neighbourhood, for the destruction of the machinery used in the finishing of woollen cloth.'

Nottingham, a centre of Luddism, saw a more general radicalism including opposition to the Corn Law and, in 1815, to war with France.[15] Subsequently, urban tension and reform demands led to the brutal government response that caused the Peterloo Massacre of 1819 in Manchester, while in London the very differently radical Cato Street Conspiracy was suppressed the following year.[16] There was to be fresh violence in the early 1830s, with major riots in Bristol, Derby and Nottingham in 1831 as part of the pressure for a reformed electoral system. Henry, 4th Duke of Newcastle, a politically-active ultra-Tory, very much sought to direct constituencies in which he had an influence, evicting tenants for openly supporting an opposition candidate at the Newark by-election of 1829, stating he should be able 'to do what I will with my own'. The following year, Newcastle noted during the 1830 General Election that he would 'place in the House of Commons 5 of its cleverest members'.[17] In contrast, in Newcastle-under-Lyme, the interests of the nearby Leveson Gowers, as well as of the self-elected corporation, were challenged and weakened by social change and voter politicisation. More generally, broadsides and other propaganda emphasised the role of ordinary citizens. Printing was far less expensive than treating the electors.[18]

In the event, the Reform Act of 1832 saw growing towns, such as Birmingham, Blackburn, Bolton, Bradford, Leeds, Manchester, Oldham, Sheffield, South Shields, and Sunderland that had not, hitherto, had their own MPs gain separate representation from the county seats. 22 large towns gained two MPs and 19 English towns gained one. In contrast, many 'rotten boroughs', seats with small populations, such as Minehead, a seat under the control of the Luttrells of Dunster Castle, and Old Sarum, lost separate representation. That led to the loss of many separate seats in the South, notably in Cornwall where localism had been particularly evident in small boroughs and, helped by the major advantage for local candidates, political practices and alignments were of considerable durability.[19] 56 boroughs lost their seats, and 30 lost one of their two MPs. Political favouritism played a role in the 1832 legislation, as with Stockton, where the Tory Marquess of Londonderry was influential, remaining without its own MPs, whereas Whig strongholds in County Durham gained seats.

The Municipal Corporations Act of 1835, again passed by the Whig government, standardised the situation, replacing self-selecting oligarchic Corporations, mostly run by Tories, in the 178 towns where such Corporations had been dominant, by elected borough councils – based on a franchise of rated occupiers. These had control over the local police, markets and street lighting. The creation of police forces, in London in 1829 and in provincial towns in the 1830s-40s, reflected anxiety about urban crime, a sense that something had to be done, and could be achieved, as well as towns copying each other and competing with each other.

The Municipal Corporations Act was to be the basis of an upsurge in urban politics and a wave of urban reformism that drew on a continuity of commitment on the part of many, for example the self-made Mancunian (Manchester inhabitant) Absalom Watkin (1787–1861), a critic of Peterloo, supporter of the Reform Act and the Anti-Corn Law League, and proponent of undenominational state education.[20] The political content of local government was transformed, as the vote became a way to ensure participation. This helped align local with national politics, with the latter, and the resulting alignments, coming to dominate the former in most towns, for example Shaftesbury. A sense of public accountability was captured in the *Sherborne Mercury* of 6 February 1837 under the heading 'Reform Meeting at Lyme Regis':

'A public meeting was held … in the Guildhall, the Mayor in the chair, for the purpose of enabling their respected representative, William Pinney Esq., to state his opinions upon the leading political questions of the day, and to take the sense of his constituents on his parliamentary conduct during the past session.'

The article continued by providing details of the meeting. Elected MP in 1832 as a Whig, Pinney was unseated in 1842 for bribery.

Aside from the specifics of political pressure, the press was more generally a support for 'improvement'; 'improvement' as understood by those who wanted reform and stability, reform more particularly as perceived by those with wealth and property. Thus, the *Birmingham Commercial Herald* of 16 January 1804 supported the local plan for an association 'to protect the property of the honest and industrious' laid out in an advertisement for a 'society for preventing, detecting and punishing fraudulent bankrupts, swindlers etc'. Yet, 'improvement' also involved criticism, notably of vested interests, as in the *Birmingham Chronicle* of 11 March 1824, which, under the headline 'The Free Grammar School of Birmingham', declared:

'A considerable interest having been excited in the town relative to an intended application to Parliament for enlarging the objects and appropriating the funds of this noble and invaluable institution, and several correspondents having addressed letters to our journal on the supposed intentions and object of the governors, we have been at some pains and expense to procure correct and entire copies of the charters and documents of its original foundation and present government. We now place them collectively before our readers, certain that publicity is the best guarantee of integrity in public trusts and that the executive management of the school can have no objection to a free statement of their powers and the objects of the trust... Some deference is due to public opinion.'

On 13 May, the paper called for an annual statement of receipts and expenditure from the school. Similarly, John Edward Taylor, the founder of the *Manchester Guardian*, was subsequently Deputy Chairman of the Improvement Committee of the Manchester Commissioners of Police. His colleague Jeremiah Garnett was one of the Commissioners. In Preston, gas-lighting, based on Wigan coal and supported by the *Preston Chronicle* and local capital, was introduced early, and also helped the cotton manufacturers by lighting their mills in the winter.[21]

Social pressure arising from economic change became more acute in the 1840s, focused on the Chartist movement. However, it did not lead to a political crisis.[22] Moreover, the élite's engagement with new developments was seen with the visit of Prince Albert, reforming husband of Queen Victoria, to Birmingham in 1843, in an affirmation of a link between monarchy, industry and modernity. Due to radical agitation, Albert had been advised not to visit Birmingham, but he did so, touring five major factories, and being favourably received.

'Improvement' became a national policy. In 1848, the Public Health Act created a structure, including local boards of health, to improve sanitation, and they took action. Thus, the Board of Health established in Leicester in 1849 was instrumental in the creation of a sewerage system and in tackling slaughterhouses and smoke pollution. A critical report on Derby by Edward Cresy, a Superintending Inspector under the General Board of Health, led the Council to embark on a programme of works, including public baths and washhouses.

Contemporaries were also concerned about the religious situation. The expansion of towns stretched existing church provision, while the mission of the churches did not necessarily elicit a response. The Religious Census of 1851 revealed that in the growing Suffolk towns of Ipswich and Mildenhall there was only sufficient space in Anglican churches for a minority of parishioners, a widespread problem. Larger parishes were those where Anglican devotion was less apparent in Suffolk, where the sole non-Christian worship was a synagogue in Ipswich.[23] Personal circumstances were important: John Davis, the Anglican Rector of St Clement's Worcester, reported that his working-class parishioners: 'seldom ever attend Sunday Morning service. The Saturday Market and the late payment of wages on the evening of that day contribute probably in no small degree to produce this.' In short, drink kept devotion at bay, which contributed to the temperance movement that became stronger in the second half of the century. Urbanisation, moreover, could stimulate anticlericalism as well as declining church attendances.

Towns also saw tension between churches to the fore, not least due to the re-establishment of the Catholic hierarchy in 1850 and anxiety about massive Irish immigration as a result of the Great Irish Famine of 1845–51. Despite efforts by Poor Law authorities to return Irish migrants,[24] there was a substantial change to many towns, as well as to the image of urban life. Hostility to Catholics was seen at the level of particular towns, for example the Murphy Riots of 1867 in Birmingham, but also seen more generally. To many, this was an important element in urban 'culture.' Indeed, this hostility was one of the factors that helped define urban politics, and in a way that looked forward into the twentieth century. Urban Conservatism was in part a matter of anti-Catholicism, as well as being opposed to Dissenters and their commitment to temperance.

Such a definition fails to capture variations between and within particular towns, the within attracting far less attention than the between. Yet, at the same time, there was a degree of nationalisation of politics linked to national political parties and movements, such as the Primrose League of the Conservatives. This nationalisation was criticised as sapping urban identities and replacing cohesion by partisanship, but that was a longstanding argument, rather than one simply of this period. Indeed, the difference was not so much a degree of division but rather the extent to which national labels were willingly embraced by those who were thus divided.

This also meant a potential degree of subordination on the part of specific urban identities. On the one hand, there was a longstanding ability to deploy and retain multiple identities, both involving urban life and encompassing other concerns. Yet, such an ability did not mean that these identities were of unchanging relative weight. Here, indeed, there appears to have been significant change in the late nineteenth century, one that was in part linked to specific administrative changes related to the establishment of county councils. This scarcely exhausted disruptive developments. The provision of education changed at a greater rate than since the Reformation. Railways created some new alignments, while some existing ones disappeared with the wagons and stagecoaches, and lost significance as a result.

Again, change was in part a matter of the churn of the generations, because individuals maintained experiences, values and hopes in part grounded in their life-cycle. As a result, there was an accumulative character to 'modernity' (an idea itself that was contested), and many of the changes of the late nineteenth century were fully felt only in the twentieth. This lapsed character to the urban experience is less than obvious in the sources, and is regarded as less prominent than the rural counterpart. Yet, it is a character that is worth considering. So also with both townscape and housing stock. There were massive changes in both, and these obviously attract attention, notably when space is limited, but also much that was at least a survival and often a continuation based on considerable support. And that is one aspect of urban life for many.

Chapter 7

1850–1900

'Great improvements have been made within the last 30 years; narrow lanes have been pulled down to make way for broad avenues; noble public buildings, which would be ornamental to any capital in the world.'

Manchester, described in 1859 by John McCulloch, was followed by *In the Nineteenth Century the Northumbrians Show the World what Can Be Done with Iron and Coal* (1861), a painting by William Bell Scott, set in Newcastle, that sought to capture, as Scott stated, 'everything of the common labour, life and applied science of the day.' It depicted as purposed, indeed heroic, workers at Robert Stephenson's engineering factory, one of the largest manufacturers of railway engines in the world, an Armstrong gun, also produced in Newcastle, the steam of modern communications, the High Level Bridge, and telegraph wires.

Another, somewhat different view of the role of urban institutions was presented by the Reverend H. Harris at the annual meeting of the Darlington Horticultural Society: 'this society ... was calculated to improve and elevate the taste of all classes, especially the poorer classes, by withdrawing them in their leisure hours from grosser indulgences to a pleasurable and improving pursuit.' At the same time, and less positively, 'Condition of England' issues were very much presented in an urban context, and another cleric, the Rector of Bethnal Green in London, was less optimistic in 1895:

'a vast majority of the men in your district will have spent their Sundays for the last twenty-five years and their fathers before them, in the following way: they will have lain in bed till about eleven or twelve, having been up early all week; they will then go round when the public houses open, which they do at one; they will have what they call a "wet" till three ... they will then have dinner, the great dinner of the week, which the missus has been preparing all morning. Then comes a lie down on the bed in shirt sleeves until five, with a pot of beer and *Lloyd's Weekly*; then follows tea, and after tea a bit of a walk round to see a friend or a relation; then fairly early to bed to make up for a very late Saturday night.'

Urban differentiation became more pronounced in the nineteenth century with the expansion of large towns particularly important within a context of general growth to a total of nearly 80 per cent of the population in towns with over 2,500 people by 1901. As a result, in the modern period, it becomes more difficult to distinguish the urban experience from national history as a whole. Yet, once England was an overwhelmingly urban nation, then the urban environment, its changing character, including transport, housing and planning, and the fortunes of different types of town, were of even greater consequence.

Alongside the continued development of the leading town, London, there was the continuing spectacular rise of other major towns such as Manchester, Liverpool and Birmingham.[1] This was a rise that was of global significance, not least as British shipping dominated oceanic trade. Liverpool and London were ports of world importance, while Sunderland was by 1850 the greatest shipbuilding town in the world, with high wages and a high rate of owner-occupation of housing.

The economic health of towns owed much to communications, which increasingly meant rail rather than canal. For example, with railways creating ready access to nearby iron ore mines and to coke supplies from Durham, four major iron and steel works were established at Workington in 1862–74, and the population there rose from 6,467 in 1860 to 23,749 in 1891. Opened in 1861, the line from Durham to Barrow-in-Furness also took Furness iron east.

Ports tried to develop rail links in order to enhance their significance. Thus, Hull sought links with the industrial zones of Yorkshire. Under legislation in 1836, the town gained a rail link in 1840, the Hull and Selby Railway, which linked with the Leeds and Selby Railway that had opened in 1834. The Hull terminus was adjacent to the Humber Dock, the Victoria Dock Branch Line opening in 1853. The York and North Midland Railway expanded to reach Hull by leasing the Hull and Selby Railway from 1845, a lease acquired by the North Eastern Railway in 1852. As a major game-changer, the very large Alexandra Dock in Hull, which, excavated by steam-powered excavating machines, opened in 1885 and was backed by Hull Corporation, served the new Hull, Barnsley and West Riding Junction Railway and Dock Company (later Hull and Barnsley Railway), which was formed in defiance of the North Eastern Railway's attempt to control the local rail system. The new company focused on coal exports.

There was also specialisation at other levels, as in leisure, more particularly, seaside resorts, for example Newquay, Ramsgate, Bournemouth, Hove, Eastbourne, Margate, Southend, Yarmouth, Skegness, Cleethorpes, Bridlington, Scarborough, Whitley Bay, Morecambe and Blackpool. In contrast, spas were of declining importance.

Nevertheless, much of the population still lived and worked in small towns, and large numbers in areas that suffered deindustrialisation, such as East Anglia, were quiet market towns. Many, such as Diss and Swaffham, had little growth and, indeed, were not to change greatly until they expanded again from the 1960s. The sustained Great Agricultural Depression that began in the 1870s hit such towns hard, as did an integration of the country through the intensification of the rail network, which meant that functions hitherto supplied very locally could be better obtained from a distance. Thus, in Berkshire, branch lines were built to Faringdon (1864), Abingdon (1873), Wantage (1875), Wallingford (1886) and Lambourn (1898).

Yet, at the same time, many towns that are not now seen as manufacturing centres were important then for industry. Thus, there was the mechanised manufacturing of stockings at Messrs. Owen and Uglow's factory at Tewkesbury. Owen invented and patented the reinforcing of the underfoot and heels of stockings, and his factory employed 600 workmen and 150 women. Tewkesbury was served by river and, from 1840, rail. Industrial centres tended to be less conservative in political and religious terms. Luton, which specialised in the making of straw hats, had a strong Nonconformist element and was also a centre of Liberalism.[2]

At a different scale, *Newcastle upon Tyne from Windmill Hill, Gateshead*, a painting of about 1871 by the North Shields-born Myles Birket Foster, who generally focused on sentimental rural scenes, showed formerly prominent buildings – the castle keep and cathedral, now joined by factory chimneys and the railway bridge. As yet, there were not the prospects that were to be obtained from skyscrapers. Its population rose from 28,294 in 1801 to 215,328 in 1901, and such an increase was only achieved by large-scale migration, much of it of people with scant experience of towns. So also elsewhere. Of the 225 iron workers at the Britannia Foundry in Derby in 1871, over half were born outside the town, although most came from the county, and this pattern of migration from nearby was more generally the case.

Yet, there was also migration from a greater distance, although far from on the scale of the situation today. The 1851 census revealed that 18.9 per cent of Liverpool's population was Irish-born, largely a response to the recent potato blight and resulting famine in Ireland. Other port cities, such as Portsmouth and Plymouth, also had many migrants. Overwhelmingly poor, and attractive as labour precisely because they were paid badly, the Irish migrants lived in the areas of cheapest rent, which were invariably the most crowded and least sanitary. In Newcastle, where the percentage of Irish-born migrants rose to 8 in 1851, the majority of them were housed in poor living conditions in areas such as Sandgate. The men were generally employed as labourers or in other casual work, the women as washerwomen, flower sellers or other poorly-paid jobs. The migrants focused and exacerbated anti-Catholic feeling to which Irish violence contributed, not least in Liverpool, Middlesbrough and Wolverhampton.[3] However, as a reminder of the perennial variety, many Irish immigrants did not live in ghettos but were dispersed across working-class areas, and a certain number 'married out'. Others emerged into the middle class.

Population density continued to grow in many cities, ensuring serious overcrowding. Sombre statistics hinted at the human suffering that accompanied in Liverpool the massive growth in trade. In 1846, Liverpool contained 538 brothels, and in 1857 there were at least 200 regular prostitutes under the age of 12. The wealth of Liverpool resulted in new residential park suburbs, such as Princes Park (1842), and many fine public buildings. This was in particular prior to the major expansion of rail-linked suburbs, an expansion that required available finance and land. Squalor also led to Liverpool becoming one of the first places anywhere to embark on a programme of municipal house building. Agricultural depression in 1873–96 was to facilitate the availability of land, the purchase of which was an aspect of the close relationship between landed interests and towns, one indeed that helped compensate the former for the problems created by this depression. This depression also encouraged rural depopulation. There was also a development within towns themselves by aristocratic landowners, such as the Earl of Darlington on the Bathwick estate in Bath, Lord Calthorpe at Edgbaston in Birmingham, and the Dukes of Devonshire at Eastbourne.[4] The Calthorpes had been wool merchants in the seventeenth century. A critical stance was adopted by George Bernard Shaw in his play *Widowers' Houses* (1892) with the aristocratic Henry Trench appalled that Blanche Sartorius' father is wealthy through slum landlordism, only for Sartorius to point out that Trench's money has come from similar sources.

The extent to which many towns could spread in most directions was important to their geographical growth and therefore density. This was true of London, Birmingham and Manchester, but conspicuously not of Liverpool, due to it being built by the sea and not, as with London and Newcastle, near to it.

Rail also brought change to town centres as lines were driven to them and stations and associated yards built. Thus, St. Pancras station and its hitherto unprecedented single-span overall roof was opened in London in 1868 on the site of Agar Town, a slum, but also home to many. Indicators such as height and physical well-being revealed to contemporaries the punishing experience of urban life for many. This was an instance of how concern, indeed disgust, about urban life, for example the 'Great Stink' of the Thames in London in 1858,[5] vied with confidence in the potential of towns and the ability to handle urban problems.

About 7,840 out of the 20,000 families in Newcastle in 1854 lived in only one room. In 1852, 8,032 of the 9,453 houses in Newcastle lacked toilets. In 1866, 43 per cent of the city's population was still living in dwellings of only one or two rooms, and in 1885 30.6 per cent. Newcastle's mortality rates fell from 30.1 to 19.1 per thousand between 1872 and 1901, but mortality contrasts between registration districts there were from 17.1 to 41.5 per thousand in 1881. Urban poverty was described by novelists including George Gissing in *Workers in the Dawn* (1880) and Andrew Mearns in *The Bitter Cry of Outcast London* (1883).

Mortality rates varied between town and country,[6] by town and within them, which opened up discussion of causes; discussion that could reflect managerial issues and public policy, but also social stigmatism at the expense of the poor.[7] Gastrointestinal disorders linked to inadequate water and sewerage systems were responsible for Bradford's very high infant mortality rate. The burial records of the Bonner Hill cemetery in Kingston indicate that from 1855 to 1911 one-third of all burials were of children aged four or under. For August and September 1899 when 44 infants under one died of diarrhoea in Kingston, the Medical Officer of Health reported:

> '…only one infant was brought up entirely at the breast, and six partly at the breast and partly by artificial feeding. In only eight houses was there a decent larder where milk could be stored, and this is a defect found in houses of even a high rental, where the larder is often placed so as to be practically useless. It may be placed so as to be exposed to the hot sun for the greatest possible number of hours, or it may be just over the sink waste, or in close communication with a w.c. or where ventilation is only obtained with the accompaniment of dust.'[8]

Across the country, diphtheria and measles were particularly serious, and exacerbated by damp houses. Reports on Bruton in the 1870s and 1880s graphically described insufficient and defective toilet arrangements, inadequate sewerage disposal and a lack of clean water. A reluctance to spend money ensured that plans to improve the situation were delayed, and, though the sewerage system was finally improved, Bruton did not construct a water supply system in the Victorian period. Similarly, for financial reasons, there was opposition in Ealing to the improvement of sanitation and water supplies.[9] More generally, urban living as well as urban growth posed major problems,[10] and their scale was unprecedented.

The rapidly-growing populations of the industrial cities had to be housed, and one of the ways in which the changing country of the late nineteenth and early twentieth century is still with us, is that much of the housing stock today derives from that period; whereas a relatively small percentage of the current stock survives from earlier periods, and notably so in urban areas. By the 1860s, the terraced streets we know today were being built and, by the 1870s, a standard version of working-class housing was the 'two-up-two-down' 'through terrace' – with its access at both front and rear, and of solid construction and adequately ventilated, sometimes with small gardens or back yard. Increasingly, this was becoming the standard dwelling. I lived in such a house in Durham in 1981–3. It had a ground-floor bathroom as a later addition, with water-pressure issues affecting the location of the bath.

The traditional terraced house reflected the rise in average real wages in the 1850s-1860s as the economic boom of industrialisation brought prosperity. These houses were a great improvement on the back-to-backs, the lodging-house, and the damp cellar, in which all too many had lived. In part, this was because terrace houses were built at a time of prosperity and rising construction standards in new residences included covered sewerage systems and adequately piped clean water. Indeed, from 1875, under the Public Health Act, which also restricted 'cellar dwellings', it was mandatory to provide not only damp proof courses in new houses but also lavatories on the same plot as a new house. This often meant outside lavatories, and many houses were not converted to have inside ones until the late twentieth century. These houses, with their separate rooms, enabled greater definition of the spheres of domestic activity, from chatting or reading to eating or sleeping, all of which had major implications for family behaviour and gender roles, as well as for a sense of privacy.

This pattern replaced an earlier style of layout frequently described in terms of a warren, a style that had been difficult to keep clean or to light because it contained so many self-enclosed alleyways, closes or courts. In contrast, the straight streets of terraced houses, equally apportioned and relatively spaciously laid out, were easier to light and to provide with supplies of gas, water and drainage, a situation that was true not only of areas as a whole, but also of individual properties. Legislation was important with the removal of the Brick Tax in 1850, encouraging the large-scale utilisation of bricks in construction, and their use helping to keep damp at bay, while the end of the Wallpaper Tax in 1861 affected the interior of houses. Technology also played a role, as in the provision of inexpensive linoleum from the mid-1870s as an effective floor-covering.

Terraced houses were usually built in straight streets. The move towards straighter streets owed much to the growing volume of horse-drawn and wheeled traffic, which benefited from such streets, as changing direction was not easy for this traffic, which was also helped by better road surfacing, although increasing the speed of traffic entailed banishing pedestrians from the street to an often non-existent pavement. Indeed, there was the development of a segregation that is even more apparent today given the lethality of cars.

Rather than seeing the working class as beneficiaries of municipal government or the entrepreneurialism of developers, it is necessary to note the degree to which they had 'agency'. They could take the initiative in order to improve their living arrangements,[11] and also adapt their social structure to the possibilities of the housing stock.[12]

Nevertheless, many of the urban poor and casually employed still lived in one-roomed dwellings, tenements, back-to-backs, rookeries and courts, and would continue to do so until World War Two (1939–45). Their walls frequently ran with damp, sanitation was often primitive, lighting was limited, and poorly-swept chimneys contributed to the fug in many homes, with health greatly affected as a consequence. In 1920, a Ministry of Health report on pollution from domestic coal fires, which was serious, recommended that housebuilding schemes not be permitted unless they provided for smokeless methods of heating. Moreover, a large part of the urban working-class population, notably casual labourers, whose job security was lowest, occupied the same housing for only a few months.

In response to difficult circumstances, there was much religious activism, with committed clerics and laity seeking to make Christian teaching more accessible. This reflected the degree to which towns were seen as the centre for competition with irreligion and also between faiths. It was necessary to think of confronting the varied nature of ecclesiastical provision. Leeds was such a large parish by the 1840s that it had 12 chapelries and curates, and the vicar of Leeds was in effect close to being a bishop. The 1851 Religious Census was followed by increased Church activism, but success was mixed.[13] Provision was most pronounced in the towns and not only for Protestantism. Thus, Brighton, the sole major town in Sussex, was revealed by the 1851 Religious Census, to have the only synagogue and Catholic Apostolic church in Sussex, one of the two Mormon congregations, and two of the five Unitarian chapels.[14]

Anglican and Catholic 'slum priests' took the Church's message to the urban poor, and bishops insisted on clergy working through cholera outbreaks. Anglican Church interiors were rebuilt in order to replace box pews, which belonged to families, with rows of identical, open pews, most of which were rent-free and open to all. Careful appointments were intended to improve the Church, and it definitely improved on the situation in the early nineteenth century, not least in having less non-residence, but divisions within the religious world as well as the inherent difficulty of the task continued to create problems. St Peter's Northampton kept up with urban growth there by introducing a chaplaincy for shoemakers and a railway chaplain.[15] Missions, notably to the East End of London, such as Oxford House, sought to reach out to those who did not go to Church, lecturing for example on Sunday afternoons in Victoria Park, Bethnal Green. Working-class areas, such as the Rope Walk district of Ipswich, had Nonconformist chapels, in its case a Congregationalist one.[16] However attempts to proselytise in working-class areas were of often limited success.[17]

Concern about atheism and irreligion focused on towns, particularly London, and was an aspect of a wider sense of urban malaise. Drink maps were used to fight the cause for temperance in a number of towns, including Leicester, Liverpool, London, Manchester, Norwich, Oxford and Sheffield. They sought to shock by demonstrating the widespread availability of alcohol and suggesting that tackling this would help tackle crime, poverty and poor-health.[18]

There were also moral panics about political radicalism, sexual behaviour, moral depravity and much else. Despite the failure of Chartism in 1848, London, in particular, continued to be a centre of radical thought, not least republicanism.[19] Yet, in practice the scale of disaffection was modest, certainly prior to the 1880s. At the same time, it was an element in urban life and in the reaction to it. Furthermore, the idea that a 'criminal class' was a product of moral degeneracy was linked to the reading of a particular environment, namely the townscape of the unrespectable working-class.[20]

In response to health issues, and based on town councils and existing local boards of health, the 1872 Public Health Act sought to tackle sanitation. In particular, there was an emphasis on clean water. In part, this was an engineering and organisational triumph, but there was also the process by which the countryside was increasingly subordinated to the towns. Many towns looked far afield, Manchester to the distant Lake District to supplement water supplies from the nearby Pennines: the Corporation purchased the Wythburn estate, stopped the local lead industry in order to prevent water pollution, and, despite overwhelming local opposition, gained parliamentary approval in 1877 for the drowning of the Thirlmere valley. Meanwhile, Brighton obtained adequate water in the 1860s and an intercepting sewer in 1874.

More generally, there was legislative pressure for improvement to the housing stock, notably with the provision of toilets or, for example under the 1894 London Building Act, of window area. The Public Health Act of 1875 took forward into general legislation many of the provisions of the Town Improvement Clauses Act of 1847 including those relating to the layout and naming of new streets and the effect on utilities. The Adulteration Act of 1878 stipulated the appointment of local analysts. A Royal Commission on the Housing of the Working Class was held in 1884–5 and led to the Housing of the Working Classes Act of 1890 which enabled the President of the Local Government Board to authorise local authority housing schemes.

There was also a strong attempt to address the problems of urban life, although not those that might have been posed by a need for defence. General Sir John Burgoyne, the Inspector General of Fortifications, pointed out in 1856 that the navy and fortifications were necessary for defence as hostility to conscription made it impossible to match Continental armies.[21] In 1860, he proposed a defensive ring around London of twenty-eight forts and batteries, mounting 1,050 guns, a formidable number, and to be manned by a permanent garrison of 17,000 troops. Colonel Sir Shafto Adair followed in 1862 with a more extensive proposal for 71 guns and batteries, 2,192 guns and 25,600 troops;[22] but neither proposal was implemented, and there was reliance instead on the navy with the major defensive focus for the army on the protection of the major naval dockyards of Plymouth and Portsmouth, with Dover also seen as an exposed position and plentiful troops in the London area. Within towns, the focus was on the police, and crime fell appreciably in the later decades of the century.

Although there were tactical and other differences, Liberal and Conservative governments both supported reform which focused on towns due to the size of their population and what were seen as their particular problems. The Recreation Grounds Act of 1859 and the Public Health Act of 1875 encouraged the laying out of public parks but the key elements were local. The first Manchester park opened in 1846, while Moor Park in Preston was established as a park in 1867.[23] Halifax opened the People's Park, paid for by Sir Francis Crossley, the MP and owner of the local carpet mills. Liverpool Corporation purchased farmland from the Earl of Sefton and in 1872 the 265-acre Sefton Park was opened, typically by a member of the royal family, the Duke of Connaught. Wolverhampton gained parks in 1881 and 1895. Municipal parks and buildings testified to the strength of local identity and to the desire and ability to improve the local environment.

So also with clubs and activities. In Street in Somerset, the Brass Band was formed by 1870. There was also an entrepreneurial response with music halls and football clubs founded in large numbers to address the opportunities offered by urban working-class leisure within the context of new mass, commercialised interests. Cinema was to join the music hall.

There was a boom in sport. In 1901, 111,000 spectators stood on the banks of Crystal Palace – the football stadium that hosted the Cup Finals from 1895 until 1914 – to watch Tottenham beat Sheffield United in the final. So also for middle-class sports. Northumberland Cricket Club had a ground in Newcastle by the 1850s, while Newcastle Golf Club expanded its activities in the 1890s.

Moreover, food outlets multiplied, the first permanent Lyons teashop being founded in 1894. As the largest city in the world up till then, London had the largest middle class and therefore a particularly large service sector, from servants to restaurants.[24]

On the part of politicians, reform encompassed an attempt to woo, as well as redefine, the expanding urban electorate. On 3 July 1852, the leader in the *Western Times*, a free trade paper, declared:

'The Exeter Election is fixed for Wednesday and Thursday next. The crisis demands the earnest zeal and unabated exertions of every Reformer. The Enemy has been tampering with, and endeavouring to seduce the poorer votes by the usual profligate expenditure in intoxicating drinks. Many a poor family will lament the broken health of its Parent and Protector, ruined and debauched by the agents of the Protectionist faction – the protected friends of religion and order. The honest and independent portion of the electors must endeavour, by all lawful means, to defeat the corrupters, by watching over the weak, and warning them of the consequences of accepting the Tory bribes, whether in drink or coin.'

The Municipal Corporations Act of 1835 was followed by the Second and Third Reform Acts of 1867 and 1884, the 1885 Redistribution of Seats Act, and Local Government Acts in 1888 and 1894, which created county councils and county borough councils, and borough and district councils.[25] These bodies then launched many local Acts of Parliament, taking forward a long-established practice, in order to improve their localities.[26]

There were also major electoral consequences, which were both general to the country and also specific to particular constituencies. As a result of the 1867 Second Reform Act, about 60 per cent of adult males in boroughs had the vote. There was also a redistribution of seats, as a result of which less populous boroughs, such as Honiton, lost their seats, while the designation of new parliamentary boroughs, such as Darlington, Hartlepool and Stockton, reflected population growth. This could contribute to political transformation. Thus, in the election of 1868, the Marquess of Londonderry's son lost at Stockton to a Liberal.

Meanwhile, the 1870 Education Act provided the context of spreading literacy. Alongside the end of newspaper taxes and therefore falling costs, this was a background to the expansion of the press. Whereas, in 1868, fourteen of the largest English provincial towns, including Birmingham, Liverpool, Manchester, Sheffield, Newcastle, Bristol, Plymouth, Nottingham, North Shields and Bradford, had daily newspapers, by 1885 47 did. They sought to cater for particular local needs and to direct local opinion, while making profits and varying content. Thus, in Leeds, thanks to a newspaper focus on sport and other leisure items, there was success in creating a cross-class Conservative coalition, one that bridged the slums and the suburbs.[27]

The emphasis on the public that was increasingly common in political discussion from the late nineteenth century perforce focused on towns, as that was where the public was most numerous and active. Urban-based, the press also focused on towns, as in the issue of the Exeter-based *Western Times* of 30 August 1901 that mentioned 'the instincts of a democratic people' in a report on a substantial fall in the Conservative majority in a by-election at Andover. In that newspaper's issue of 29 January 1901, discussion of a change in political culture focused on the major towns:

> 'An effort is to be made in the forthcoming elections to Boards of Guardians to elect working men and women Guardians favourable to a liberal interpretation of the Local Government Board's Order respecting more outdoor relief for the aged poor, in preference to so often offering "the House" [workhouse]. The movement is, we hear, likely to be taken up in earnest in all the big towns and there seems to be no reason why it should not become general. Outdoor relief is humane and it has not been proved to be wasteful. It will be more economical than building and furnishing separate wings for aged couples who are permitted to live together in workhouses. At any rate the working classes are advised that they can now make an effective start in the direction of the old age pension so often promised them by voting only for such guardians as will promise liberal outdoor relief to the undisabled aged poor.'

In contrast to the agricultural depression in the countryside, the impact of food imports on prices greatly benefited the urban working class, providing the background for political disputes over free trade. Not only gaining the vote, affluent workers were a key support for the continual growth of consumerism. Low pay, casual work and underemployment ensured, however, that many in the working class could not share in these benefits. Moreover, the growing international competition that hit manufacturing affected many towns, leading to unemployment and encouraging emigration, which, alongside movement within the country was part of the 'churn' that characterised much of the urban population, and that affected urban life.

Towns, in turn, were policed, a process made obligatory by the County and Borough Police Act of 1856. This served not only to offer a protection from crime, but also sought by many of the poor for the regimentation of urban society, notably working-class immorality, which was much to the fore in towns as drinking, crime and illegal gambling were important leisure activities.[28] Practices judged unacceptable, such as public drunkenness, were subject to admonition, regulation and action. However, the complaints that focused on the Royal Commission on the Duties of the Metropolitan Police of 1906–8 revealed that low-level corruption, not least demanding money from prostitutes, was an aspect of this policing. A different form of action was provided by religious bodies such as the Salvation Army which was founded in London in 1865.[29]

The expanding middle class supported this transformation, with the new police encouraged to act. There was also the patronage of a great upsurge in art, poetry, and the performance or production of music.[30] Birmingham, Leeds, Liverpool, Manchester and Newcastle were prominent in a more general foundation of major art collections and musical institutions, such as the Hallé Orchestra in Manchester in 1857. Music halls and theatres were founded, and, thanks to railways, there were regular tours of theatrical groups and variety performers, which looked toward the later national patterning of culture seen with cinema.

In addition, civic educational bodies were created, building on the already buoyant practice of launching and joining learned societies. This was a case of the eighteenth century taken into the nineteenth and given a greater prominence and wider membership.[31] The foundation of universities was very much urban, and now located in major towns. Eventually part of the University of Birmingham established in 1900, Mason Science College was founded in 1880 by Sir Josiah Martin, a self-educated manufacturer of split-rings and steel pen-nibs who spent part of his fortune on local orphans as well as on his new foundation, which was designed to be especially useful for local industries. At the same time, it is important to offer in the account of progress, an understanding of the problems that arose along the way. Thus, Queen's College, Birmingham hit financial problems and in 1865 closed due to a lack of students.[32]

Men such as Martin set the tone of much of urban society, providing a tremendous stimulus to the process of improvement, civic and moral. There was a working-class equivalent in the form of co-operatives, friendly societies (mutual assistance sick and burial clubs), and schemes for improvement through education and temperance.[33]

Leisure developed to be an important feature of many towns. Sandwich, a medieval port of consequence, hit by the silting up of the harbour, the eventual failure of the cloth industry, the extent of disease, the poor water supply, and indifferent sanitation, languished for most of the eighteenth and nineteenth centuries, but, by the 1890s, was attracting visitors and new residents, notably as a leisure town with golf courses, and one that could be readily reached from London: rail services had begun in 1847 and improved in 1881.[34] This was an instance of the process by which national improvement and standardisation, especially through transport links and new governmental structures and implementation, also led to novel differences between towns.

At the same time, there were many inequalities. Women generally worked in low-pay occupations, and attempts to improve their condition met only partial success. As an aspect of a general process, trade unions co-operated with management in opposing the female woollen workers of Batley and Dewsbury from organising themselves in an 1875 dispute. Definitions of skills favoured men, and skilled women, such as the weavers of Preston and Bolton, were poorly recognised; although women in the pottery industry maintained status and pay despite male opposition. In 1907, women were given the vote in local elections. But, in national elections, this did not follow until 1918, when the male franchise was greatly expanded, and women did not gain a position of voting equality with men until 1928.

Social activities, moreover, focused on men. For the celebration of Queen Victoria's Golden Jubilee in 1887, the women and children of Ashby-de-la-Zouche sat down to a tea of sandwiches, bread and butter, and cake in the marketplace, while the men had earlier had a hearty meal of roast beef, mutton, potatoes, plum pudding and beer, which had been prepared by women.

The great increase in the urban population, from 8.99 million in England and Wales in 1851, 50.2 per cent of the population, to 28.16 million in 1911, 78.1 per cent, was in part a matter of people living in cramped housing, but there was also considerable expansion in the area covered by towns. This owed much to commuting by rail and other means. As a result, the green spaces between towns such as Oldham and Rochdale, South Shields and Jarrow, or Birmingham and Wolverhampton, became smaller or disappeared,[35] albeit leaving the legacy sometimes of parkland.

Tram systems were frequently run by town councils, in part to cater for the existing distribution of population, but, from the 1890s, councils subsidised fares in order to encourage people to move away from crowded town centres. In Bradford, Leeds and Sheffield, tramways were built into open country in order to encourage development. The fastest growing urban areas in 1891–1901 were suburban: Walthamstow and West Ham near London, King's Norton and Northfield near Birmingham. North of Newcastle, there was expansion in Jesmond and Gosforth, and I lived in 1983–96 in homes from this period. They were very well-built. In total, half a million acres of agricultural land was built over between 1893 and 1903.

To distinguish widespread urbanisation from other related changes of the period, notably industrialisation, politicisation, rapid communications, and the decline of hierarchy, deference and traditional social patterns, is mistaken. All had an effect. Nevertheless, new and newly-expanded towns created new living environments in which the rule and role of the old world were far less significant. The cumulative impact of change recast society.[36]

At the same time, the deadliness of towns due to disease and (far less) crime had an important consequence for their cultural representation. Urban violence in the form of juvenile gangs, such as the Sloggers in Birmingham, the prelude to the Peaky Blinders and then the Birmingham Boys, helped make major towns appear dangerous and created fear of a spread of inner-town criminality into the neighbouring suburbs.[37]

So also with the atmospheric pollution linked to industry, a pollution that rose to an unprecedented extent and provoked much discussion about the nature of the problem and the best solution. The benefit of activity and prosperity played a part in the debate, not least in Manchester which was termed the 'chimney of the world'.[38] Pollution helped produce fog as the modern indistinct, not the mist of a spectral landscape centred on medieval ruins, but a fog that sprang from the burning of coal. In 'The Truth, The Whole Truth, and Nothing But the Truth' (1873), the writer Rhoda Broughton referred to London as 'this great smoky beehive', while, in 1888, in *London and Paris Compared* Henry James praised the 'magnificent mystifications' of London fog, which:

'...flatters and superfuses, makes everything brown, rich, dim, vague, magnifies distances and minimises details, confirms the inference of vastness by suggesting that, as the great city makes everything, it makes its own system of weather and its own optical laws.'

Fog provided the cause, means and evidence of a visual lack of clarity that captured the slippage of sin, with evil and criminality exploiting the resulting possibilities. In Charles Dickens's unfinished novel *The Mystery of Edwin Drood* (1870), Cloisterham, which is modelled on Rochester, is a criminal setting, fog swirls, and the dark is feared:

'Ask the first hundred citizens of Cloisterham, met at random in the streets at noon, if they believed in Ghosts, they would tell you no; but put them to choose at night between these eerie precincts [of the cathedral] and the thoroughfare of shops, and you would find that ninety-nine declared for the longer round.'[39]

London might build an underground, but the underworld was deep in the urban as well as the rural psyche. In Bram Stoker's novel *Dracula* (1897), evil is on the attack in London, although the latter is also the counterpoise to the evil that takes place in church vaults: 'how humanising to see the red lighting of the sky beyond the hill, and to hear far away the muffled roar that marks the life of a great city.'[40]

The following year, there was a 'Hooligan' panic in London, one linked to concern about robbery, prostitution and disorder in South London. The imperial capital, indeed, troubled many. Today, the legacies of sewerage and transport systems which made London's rising population easier to service are a key element of continuation from the Victorians, one that throws light on the limitations of much subsequent governance. At the same time, the changes of the period were scarcely problem-free. Aside from the serious disruption of construction, there were disputes over costs, for example for water. Due to the ambitious nature of public policy, public spending levels in London were higher than elsewhere, at about £232 per 100 inhabitants in 1897–8, which was 50 per cent more than in the county boroughs. In particular, London expenditure on roads and police was greater due largely to the volume of services provided. Prefiguring the present, London's much higher rateable values, however, ensured that the resulting rates per head were lower.

There was scant sense of confident ease, but that feeling of unease was not specific to towns. Instead, there was a more widespread anxiety in the 1900s, one seen in an awareness of economic problems, not least in the face of American and German competition, as well as in concern about political extremism, social division and cultural decay. All of these elements had been present for decades, but became more so from the 1890s. These difficulties were not solely, or indeed particularly, a matter of towns. If there was an obvious relationship between these and working-class dissidence, notably trade union radicalism, especially in London and the North, much of the radicalism was 'rural', not in the sense of agrarian, but, for example, mining areas.

Yet, concern about the town became stronger. The causes were various, not least the degree to which immigration focused on towns, and notably Chinese and Jewish immigration in London. This created a sense of difference that fired anxieties. These extended to a widespread rejection of the inner-town that came to the fore in the 1900s, including in the urban variant of a garden city movement and of suburban villas.

In many towns, contrasts between poverty and prosperity were close, and even for London the detailed maps of 1898–9 of poverty and wealth by Charles Booth revealed the extent to which there was a close admixture of both. This, however, did not preclude there being both geographical tendencies and distinctive areas, for London and for other towns. Both tendencies and areas continued longstanding distributions, not least the degree to which industrial areas were often to the east of a town, with the prevailing westerly winds blowing the resulting pollution and smell away. Furthermore, detailed factors of topography and transport were important, including proximity to canals, railways, docks and coal supplies. These topographical features could be changed in their impact through the consequences of investment in transport; but they left a legacy on the landscape that affected residential preferences and, therefore, land prices that, in turn, sustained such preferences.

Yet, the twentieth century was to show that fashionable areas (and the converse) were far from fixed, as has been demonstrated by the rise of Islington and Notting Hill as fashionable areas in London over the last half-century. Urban regeneration was not, however, a major theme at this point other than in the form of slum clearance, as with the Kingsway scheme in London in 1902–4. The idea of improving existing residences was less to the fore; and certainly far less so than in the last decades of the twentieth century.

Slum clearance reflected the social politics of the 1890s and 1900s. There was an increasing working-class voice, notably but not only, through the new Labour Party, but the general approach toward those classified as social problems was to see them as lacking views that deserved attention and, indeed, as incapable of such processes. This was central to a harsh perspective however much it was eased by philanthropy and social ease.

But technology ensured that there was no possibility of statis. 'The Coming Force – Mr Punch's Dream', John Tenniel's *Punch* cartoon of 6 December 1882, satirised the enthusiasts for electricity, capturing their sense of excitement and anticipation of new frontiers as an earlier coal-based world of fog, chimney sweeps and coalmen succumbs; as, indeed, did happen within a century. The car was also to bring major change, the first in England, that built by Frederick William Bremer, making its first run on a public highway in December 1894. Cinema popularised new trends, as in fashion. Change was certainly increasingly to the fore.

Chapter 8

1900–1950

'Conflict in London streets
Baton Charge by Police on Big Unruly Crowd in Whitehall.'
Headlines in *Daily Mail*, 4 May 1926,
during the General Strike.

Poverty: A Study of Town Life (1901) by Benjamin Seebohm Rowntree (1871–1954), an account of his native York, sought to discover if poverty was the result of 'insufficiency of income' or 'improvidence' linked in particular to expenditure on drink. Determining that 27.8 per cent of the people there were living below the poverty line, he divided York between, 'The poorest districts of the city, comprising the slum areas. Some of the main streets in these districts are, however, of a better class'; secondly, 'Districts inhabited by the working classes, but comprising a few houses where servants are kept'; thirdly, 'The main business streets... Between these principal streets are many old and narrow lanes and courts'; and, lastly, 'Districts inhabited by the servant-keeping class'.

Rowntree found that poverty and ill-health were linked, and also argued that poverty was largely due to low wages; but, like many Liberal commentators, was critical of expenditure on drink. The lower frequency of pubs outside the centre of York owed much to the hostility of Justices of the Peace to the granting of licences. In the Southampton area of Shirley, the developers put a covenant on all properties preventing them from becoming licenced premises.

Pubs, however, were the centres of sociability, especially for singing, gambling and prostitution for the poor, who had few alternative places, as well as offering well-lit, warm and dry premises and a group privacy protected by frosted glass. Rowntree observed:

'Many of the songs are characterised by maudlin sentimentality; others again are unreservedly vulgar. Throughout the whole assembly there is an air of jollity and an absence of irksome restraint which must prove very attractive after a day's confinement in factory or shop.'

Where the wealthy lived in York, there were very few pubs because they were not part of the society of that social group. Upper- and middle-class clubs and associations, for example golf clubs and Masonic halls, did not earn the ire of temperance reformers. The same point could be made from the 'Drink Map of Oxford' produced in 1883 by the Oxford Committee of the Oxfordshire Band of Hope and Temperance Union.[1] Across the country, in 1904, nearly a quarter of the urban working households were in poverty, but, alongside high levels of vitamin and mineral deficiency among the very poorest, the unskilled working-class generally received a sufficient diet.[2]

In 1936, during the Depression, Rowntree published *Poverty and Progress*, in which he demonstrated a fall in the rate of absolute poverty in York since the previous survey, but also a switch in cause from low wages to the high unemployment that had followed the Slump that had begun in 1929. In his third study of York, *Poverty and the Welfare State* (1951), Rountree found an expanding economy and social welfare greatly improving the situation.

In 1901, the left-wing journalist John Hobson claimed that 'the neurotic temperament generated by town life seeks natural relief in stormy sensational appeals, and the crowded life of the streets, or other public gatherings, gives the best medium for communicating them.'[3] In hot weather, the sweltering urban population was more volatile and strike-prone, as in 1911–12.

The portrayal of London's East End could be far more lurid. The accounts of the Jack the Ripper murders in 1888 drew on and sustained this portrayal, one that affected the East End but, more generally, the poor areas of all major cities. In *The People of the Abyss* (1903), the American writer Jack London was critical of London:

'For here, in the East End, the obscenities and brute vulgarities of life are rampant. There is no privacy. The bad corrupts the good and all fester together. Innocent childhood is sweet and beautiful; but in East London innocence is a fleeting thing, and you must catch them before they crawl out of the cradle; or you will find the very babies as unholily wise as you.'

The following year, in the Arthur Conan Doyle short-story 'The Six Napoleons', Sherlock Holmes and Dr Watson go to Dockland, 'where the tenement houses swelter and reek with the outcasts of Europe'. This was an area that was to be covered in Thomas Burke's novel *Limehouse Nights* (1916),[4] with the additional idea, also seen with the Fu-Manchu novels, that sinister Chinamen were to be found in Docklands. The idea of London, the centre of population and a population growth which owed much to immigration, as a source of evil was satirised by Agatha Christie in her novel *One, Two, Buckle My Shoe* (1940), with Inspector Japp sceptical about Poirot's idea that a missing body has been weighted and was in the Thames: 'From a cellar in Limehouse, I suppose! You're talking like a thriller by a lady novelist.'

By 1901, three-quarters of the population of England and Wales lived in urban areas, while 45 per cent lived in towns of 50,000 or more. Subsequently, population growth was most pronounced in the London area, not least because it did not suffer the economic problems of the major Northern manufacturing centres. This was not just a matter of the contiguous London area, where, for example, the Metropolitan Railway Country Estates Limited developed railway-owned land into estates, notably at Wembley Park, Harrow Garden Village and in Pinner. Growth was no less rapid in nearby towns such as Woking, Brentwood, Watford and Maidenhead, which increased the significance of commuting into London. Meanwhile, industrial centres that expanded focused in the Midlands and South East, and included Birmingham, Coventry, Letchworth, Luton, Oxford, Slough and Welwyn.

'Londoners, like all English people, prefer to live in a house.' The poet John Betjeman, speaking on radio on 2 January 1939, attacked the slum-clearance schemes of the London County Council because, in building flats, they did not lead to the house-living that was in practice a key element in the expansion of suburbia. This expansion was not solely functional but had a cultural dimension. Building on an earlier literary support for suburbia that challenged previous and continuing critical stereotypes,[5] suburbia was linked by many commentators not just to a commitment to houses, but also to a ruralism seen in the vogue for gardens, and the non-Modernist tradition in art, music, literature and architecture. In his very popular *In Search of England* (1927), the Birmingham-born journalist H.V. Morton, claimed:

> 'The squares of London, those sacred little patches of the countryside preserved, perhaps by the Anglo-Saxon instinct for grass and trees, hold ... some part of the magic of spring ... the village that symbolises England sleeps in the subconsciousness of many a townsman. A little factory hand whom I met during the war ... visualised the England he was fighting for ... as Epping Forest, the green place where he had spent Bank Holidays. And I think most of us did. The village and the English countryside are the germs of all we have become: our manufacturing cities belong to the last century and a half; our villages stand with their roots in the Heptarchy [Anglo-Saxon period].'

Later in the book, Morton counterpoises a 'little hamlet', which is presented in a positive light as a place of faith, with, on the other hand, 'the pain of cities, the complexities'. Another image, that of the village cricket match, is memorably funny, in A.G. McDonnell's novel *England, Their England* (1933), and, drawing on Charles Dickens' *Pickwick Papers*, such a match appeared on the £10 note introduced in 1993; rather than his more characteristic urban scenes. The cult of the outdoors was mediated through, and in, the suburban garden, which greatly attracted the middle class, and in the parks of new suburbs. I grew up in outer London, in a 'Parkside Drive', built in the 1930s, alongside a new suburban park taken from farmland.

Urban community was more to the fore in J.B. Priestley's *English Journey* (1934), but again a sense of place took priority over cosmopolitanism, and the sense of place was identified with Englishness. An aspect was provided by a communal emphasis on civic identity that significantly, and on a longstanding basis, sought to keep both individualism and class division at bay. In this, urban societies, town pageants,[6] suburban urban ruralism, and a sense of civic commitment, were all parts of the equation and a progressive civic Liberalism remained potent, one that looked back to past movements for improvement. Thus, for example, in Norwich, until the Depression, the middle-class there, notably the Dissenting middle class, maintained a strong commitment to the town, a commitment underlined by residence there, by a religious subculture, and by their desire as employers for an effective environment.[7]

Although town centres did not change as greatly as they were to do in and from the 1940s, urban England altered greatly in this period, with the motor car a cause and enabler of lower-density housing. The tightly packed terraces characteristic of Victorian towns, for the middle as well as the working class, with parking now an issue for some, were supplemented (rather than replaced) by miles of 'semis'. These were semi-detached houses with mock-Tudor elevations, red-tiled roofs, and walls of red-brick or pebble-dash, with a small front and larger back garden, each with a small drive and a garage. These houses, in one of which I grew up, were built in large numbers, not only around London, but also on routes leaving all major towns, especially in areas of prosperity, such as much of southern England, but not only there. As a result, George Orwell was mistaken in his 1941 essay 'The Lion and the Unicorn' (which he reworked as *The English People*, 1947), in describing 'English civilisation' in terms of 'smoky towns and winding roads, green fields...'. He left out suburbia. The last was a matter not only of distinct suburbs, but also, for smaller settlements, of a scattering of new houses in the new style built on the outskirts.

Suburbs had spread greatly in the late nineteenth century with the railways, but development, especially dense development, then had generally not moved far from the stations. In contrast, car transport permitted less intensive growth. In advertisements, cars were pictured against backdrops of mock-Tudor suburban houses. Most of the new homes were for owner-occupier commuters. Building on new sites away from city centres ensured that cheap land was used, which helped reduce the cost of housing, but ate up land. Yet, this land was available, for the end of World War One saw the wartime protectionism enforced by German submarines ended and the resumption of large-scale food imports. Taxation and wartime casualties helped cause many estate sales, and thus land was both readily available and relatively cheap. This was a repetition of the impact, on land availability and cost, of the agricultural depression of the last quarter of the nineteenth century, and its benefit for rail-linked suburbia. As ever, urban development can not be separated from other branches of national history.

The idea of the Garden City Movement founded by Ebenezer Howard (1850–1928) reflected a desire to unify town and country in order to create a new form of civilisation, a theme outlined in his *Tomorrow: A Peaceful Path to Real Reform* (1898).[8] Building density was balanced with the preservation of open spaces and the natural environment, first for Letchworth Garden Suburb in 1903, and then, in London, with Hampstead Garden Suburb, begun in 1906 and expanded north of the A1 in the 1930s. These were models in the discussion of new towns and suburbia, although both were generally more pinched in the space available than Letchworth or Hampstead Garden Suburb. In part, this reflected the determination after World War Two to use new towns to address housing shortages rather than to provide quality of life.

Alongside undoubted interwar (and earlier) demand for suburban housing, there was criticism of the results. Suburbia, indeed, a term first used in English in the 1870s, came into use as a pejorative noun in the 1890s. There was an unwelcome sense of sameness. This extended to the gardens, for, although they provided a degree of individuality, they generally had similar plantings. The garden cities also allowed only a very narrow diversity. In 1926, in 'The Adventure of the Three Gables,' Sherlock Holmes visits Harrow Weald, a suburb in north London:

'A short railway journey, and a shorter drive, brought us to the house, a brick and timber villa, standing in its own acre of undeveloped grassland. Three small projections above the upper windows made a feeble attempt to justify its name. Behind was a grove of melancholy, half-grown pines, and the whole aspect of the place was poor and depressing.'

As so often, writers were rude about the lifestyle of others. The novelist D.H. Lawrence, in his 1929 piece 'Nottingham and the Mining Countryside,' criticised 'little red rat-traps'. Betjeman described Swindon's houses as 'brick-built breeding boxes of new souls'. Aside from aesthetic reflections, there were also those of planners. Semis were to be criticised as lacking in individuality, being wasteful of space and for being cause and consequence of dependence on the car. Separately, the Restriction of Ribbon Development Act of 1935, which attempted to prevent unsightly and uncontrolled development along new or improved roads, such as those leading from London, was an admission of a serious problem.

In fact, the sameness of suburbia was deliberate. A predictability of product helped make new houses sell, while mass production with standardised components, such as prefabricated doors and windows, reduced costs. Brick was dominant as a building material, and brick-making was very much by the Fletton process using the Jurassic clays of the East Midlands, whose high carbon content cut the cost of firing. The new transport system permitted mass production and absorbed the costs of long-range distribution because lorries could move housing materials from central manufacturing sites, including large brickworks, as near Whittlesey and at Fletton in Peterborough, and from factories making prefabricated parts. In 1935, the London Brick Company which had a major presence in Fletton made over one and a half billion bricks, postwar output then rising to 1.75 billion.

There was also the mass production of the necessary finance. In the mid-1920s, new houses cost between £400 and £1,000 and the ability to borrow at low rates of interest from building societies in order to buy houses on mortgages was very important to the housing market. Speculative builders such as Richard Costain and John Laing were key entrepreneurs. Costain (1839–1902), the founder, in 1865, of Costain Group, launched a company that in the interwar period developed housing estates in Liverpool, Croydon and around London, particularly at South Hornchurch, where development on a site for 7,500 houses began in 1934. John William Laing (1879–1978), who inherited his father's business, played a major role in North London.

As with the car and the cinema, the 'semi' expressed freedom. In part, this was a freedom to escape the constraints of living in close proximity to others and, instead, to enjoy space. 'Semis' were not the suburban villas of the wealthier members of the middle class, but they captured the aspirations of millions, and offered them a decent living environment, one served by fairly-standard mock-Tudor 'parades' of shops, with accommodation above. There were also pubs in Brewer's Tudor style.

There was also the building of much public housing, in part as a result of slum clearing. Treasury loans for local authority building had been available from 1866, but most local authorities had been reluctant to incur debts, although the powers and responsibilities behind local authority housing schemes were expanded with legislation in 1903 and 1909. Town-planning was advocated as a goal, notably by John Burns, the President of the Local Government Board, in supporting the Housing, Town Planning Act of 1909, a measure that favoured zoning.

From 1918, as a consequence of the Housing, Town Planning Act of 1919, also known as the Addison Act after Christopher Addison, the relevant Minister, grants replaced loans and council-house building expanded with the aim of financing the construction of half a million houses within three years. This was designed to give bricks and mortar to David Lloyd George's promise of 'Homes fit for Heroes' for veterans at the end of World War One. Following many of the recommendations made in the Tudor Walters Report of 1918, the Act sought to provide such fit homes, not least in the shape of lower-density housing for the working class, while minimum room sizes were specified, as was the inclusion of internal bathrooms. Large new estates built as a consequence included Longbridge near Birmingham, Wythenshawe near Manchester, and Speke near Liverpool. Municipal housing was proportionately more significant in the North than in the South, although it was also significant there, notably in the London County Council area.

Building standards were eased in the 1930s to make housing more affordable for both buyers (both middle and working class) and council tenants, but the Tudor Walters emphasis on three bedrooms, a kitchen, a bathroom and a garden was maintained. Private houses also had a garage. These houses required furniture and other facilities.[9] There was also slum clearance, and neighbourhoods were destroyed as a result. Thus, the Rope Walk slum in Ipswich was demolished in 1937.

New housing required decoration, design, services and financing. These involved both the new and the inherited, with both shaped by pattern and custom, not least in the spaces that had to be filled, and through marketing, credit, advertising and regulations. Alongside Modernism, not least in the shape of Art Deco, came the 'Tudobethan' (Tudor Revival) exteriors and mock-Jacobean panelling that made wood and tradition appear foremost; both were earlier in development but became more influential in this period.

Effective house management was regarded as both goal and means to living well.[10] However, in many senses, it was the houseowners who were managed through aggressive marketing, and the shared profit-taking of builders and building societies, the latter of whom retained part of the mortgage advance made to the builder until the mortgage had been appreciably reduced.

Council housing was increasingly important as an alternative to the purchase that most could not afford, because the private rental market declined. In part this was because private landlordship had become less profitable and there was therefore less private investment in the building of new properties for rent. Council housing, indeed, was an aspect of an increasingly mixed welfare provision, one with old and new, local and national, characteristics.[11] Much of the private rental market was slum housing, and many people, as a result, continued to face harsh conditions in deprived areas.

There was also, however, private renting in the shape of urban building and conversions, often for single people. H.C. Bailey, in his short story 'The Broken Toad' (1934), referred to the conversion of houses by the forces of progress into modern ugliness as 'blocks of flats offering modern comfort to those who do without babies.'

Agatha Christie, who was particularly familiar with Devon, meanwhile, depicted left-behind towns, fictional testimony to bypassed market centres. In her novel *Dumb Witness* (1937), there is:

> 'the little town of Market Basing. Originally on the main road, a modern by-pass now left it some three miles to the north of the main stream of traffic, and in consequence it had kept an air of old-fashioned dignity and quietude about it. Its one wide street and ample market square seemed to say, "I was a place of importance once, and to any person of sense and breeding I am still the same. Let this modern speeding world dash along their new-fangled road; I was built to endure in a day when solidarity and beauty went hand in hand."'

In *The Moving Finger* (1943), Christie again wrote about a fictional town:

> 'somewhere in seventeen hundred and something, the tide of progress swept Lymstock into a backwater. The castle crumbled. Neither railways nor main roads came near Lymstock. It turned into a little provincial

market town, unimportant and forgotten, with a sweep of moorland rising behind it, and placid farms and fields ringing it round.'

At the same time, the economic fate of towns varied greatly, while, linked to this, rivalry between towns continued. Nearby towns were frequently rivals as well as often having elements of economic co-operation as with Manchester and Liverpool, or Leeds and Sheffield. Finished in 1914, Hull's King George V Dock competed with the Great Central Railway's Immingham Dock on the other side of the Humber, finished in 1912, a dock that involved the construction of three new short connecting rail lines. Coal exports, as well as iron ore deposits in Lincolnshire to the south of the Humber, were important to the development of rail capacity there, but Immingham could not rival the trade of Yorkshire, notably coal exports, as represented in the use of Hull's docks.

During the Slump of the 1930s, unemployment in Sunderland rose to 75 per cent of shipbuilders and half of the working population, and was associated with hardship and higher rates of ill-health. Jarrow, another shipbuilding town, also had unemployment levels of over 70 per cent and its MP Ellen Wilkinson helped organise the Jarrow March to draw attention to this, and wrote *The Town that was Murdered* (1939).[12] Yet, in depressed areas, more generally across the North, but including towns such as Sunderland, there was still, for the many in work, good housing, a higher quality of life than hitherto, and more consumer choice. Moreover, compared to serious problems in shipbuilding towns and those on or near coalfields, there was growth and dynamism in some Northern areas, for example Manchester and Liverpool, with urban planning directed to that end.[13]

People, nevertheless, moved from many Northern towns to areas of greater economic opportunity, mostly in the Midlands and South-East, although there was much poverty also in these areas. The poverty of many people was captured in Christie's *ABC Murders* (1934) with the murder in Andover of:

> 'an old woman who kept a little tobacco shop... A couple of old worn blankets on the bed – a little stock of well-darned underwear in a drawer – cookery recipes in another – a paper-backed novel entitled *The Green Oasis* – a pair of new stockings – pathetic in their cheap

shininess – a couple of china ornaments – a Dresden shepherd much broken, and a blue and yellow spotted dog – a black raincoat and a woolly jumper hanging on pegs – such were the worldly possessions of the late Alice Ascher.'

Alongside movement between and within urban areas, there was also movement from country to towns. W.H. Auden was biting about social change in his *The Dog Beneath the Skin* (1935), writing of migration from countryside to towns:

'Their children have entered the service of the suburban areas; they have become typists, mannequins and factory operatives.'

Yet, the countryside benefited from towns. There was agricultural production for which imports were no substitute, notably with milk, market gardening and fruit. Moreover, rural, especially coastal, areas could benefit from tourism. Tourism grew in Cornwall in the 1930s, bringing prosperity to Bude and Newquay, both of which were Conservative strongholds. Across the country, for both urban and rural, working-class diets showed more energy provision and nutrient content for households headed by those in work, by about 20 per cent in energy. Children benefited from school meals and milk,[14] neither of which had been present a century earlier.

Whatever their prosperity, towns were the centre of an electricity revolution, electricity seen as clean and convenient and made available by the new National Grid. Power, heat and light in towns were increasingly dependent on electricity, as was refrigeration. In his novel *Invisible Weapons* (1938), John Rhode wrote of: 'all the latest gadgets – tiled bathroom, latest type of gas cooker, electric refrigerator, coke boiler for constant hot water … a labour-saving house.' By 1938, 65.4 per cent of homes were wired for electricity, and electric cookers, irons, fridges, water heaters and vacuum cleaners were plentiful. These contributed to a standard of living also seen for many with bathrooms, reasonably-sized gardens, and the provision of telephones. Moreover, these facilities provided the background to a more private and domestic pattern of family life. Town life, proportionately, was less on the street and more in the home than in the nineteenth century, and this was a major transformation in urban life, although one that very much varied by social group.

Towns were a centre of political agitation in England, although not the only sphere, as mining areas were also important. Moreover, the pattern of behaviour varied greatly. In 1919, a police strike that gained significant support in Liverpool led to looting and the restoration of order by troops.[15] Yet, most towns in England did not see comparable problems. Support for the General Strike of 1926 was strong in London, Birmingham, Liverpool, Hull, Norwich and Plymouth; although far weaker in Portsmouth and Southampton, and mixed in Bristol and Manchester. However, in 1935, the Conservative-dominated National Government, on 53.3 per cent of the vote (Labour gained 37.9 per cent), won 429 seats including all of those from such industrial towns as Blackburn, Bolton, Derby, Leicester, Newcastle, Oldham, Plymouth, Salford and Sunderland. Most of urban England supported the National Government.

Politics was very much demonstrated in the 1940s, most dramatically by German air (from 1940) and missile (from 1944) attacks. The remains of Old Coventry Cathedral are a continuing testimony to the devastation of the war. Much of the housing stock was destroyed or damaged. Yet, there were marked variations between and within cities, reflecting both German targeting and operational vagaries, not least because the bombs and rockets were 'dumb' munitions, and not 'smart' guided ones. There were particularly strong attacks on the docks through which food was imported and where the navy could operate, notably Liverpool, London, Plymouth, Southampton and Weymouth; as well as on industrial centres, for example Coventry and Manchester. Opportunity also encouraged attacks on settlements on or close to the South Coast, such as Plymouth, Southampton and Exeter. Many were killed. For the week of 21 April 1941 alone, 590 Plymouth civilians were killed and 1144 injured.

In E.C.R. Lorac's novel *Checkmate to Murder* (1944), wartime London has food shortages, blackout, gloom, irritation, and an officious and somewhat sinister Special Constable trying to buy up bomb-damaged property. For Christie, it is the bombing that is to the fore, and one that leaves a lasting impression of a society under assault, as in *After the Funeral* (1953): 'A brick or something hit her as she was walking down Tottenham Court Road – it was during fly bomb [V1-rockets, 1944–5] time … collapsed in a train to Liverpool twelve hours later.' In John Brandon's effective novel *A Scream in Soho* (1940), German spies readily go about their murderous business in London.

The war, which also brought the greatest movement of the urban population hitherto for the evacuation of children and others, was accompanied by the removal of many men through conscription and through the movement of jobs and workers to war work. Wartime surveys, on for example the evacuation of children, suggested that existing health and welfare services were inadequate, contributing to the idea that social amelioration through state policy had to be expanded and that poor conditions in towns, for example of sanitation, were the central problem.[16] There was also the impact of wartime employment on employment and wages, and money for an expansion of leisure activity such as the cinema which remained very popular including during the air raids.

Social mores were greatly affected by the war. There was more freedom for women, because far more were employed while there was a general absence of partners, as well as different attitudes. In June 1943, the Mass-Observation Survey, reporting on female behaviour in some pubs, found 'a free and easy atmosphere in which it was very easy and usual to pick up with a member of the opposite sex'. Illegitimate births increased.

Aside from changes resulting directly from the conflict, such as the presence of large numbers of the military, aspects of life as diverse as crime and religion, work and the arts, were all greatly affected by the war. Religious observance declined markedly. London was less closed down than it was to be during the (very different) Covid pandemic of 2020–2. The varied impact of the war included an attempt to disguise the city not only with the blackout, which was far more comprehensive than during German air raids in World War One, but also, for example, with the security restrictions that affected the *A-Z Atlas and Guide*.

The extent to which the war led to a consensual society is unclear. There was certainly a language of inclusiveness and sharing, and a stress on the 'Home Front', which made social distinctions seem unacceptable. Yet, there was also resistance to government policy, not least with the insistent 'black market', which proved a way to evade rationing and extended the makeshift economy to include much of society. Nevertheless, the overwhelming reality measured up to the public reputation: the population, including those in towns that were the focus of air attack, displayed tremendous fortitude and individual and collective self-reliance and mutual assistance, in the face of a sustained and deadly assault.

Wartime damage helped bring to fruition earlier discussion of planned urban reconstruction,[17] although planners designing for the post-war era often envisaged a rebuilding that was to break with the patterns of the past; providing, instead, a new future for a new society. In practice, their achievements often failed to match up to the hopes raised. Men like Patrick Abercrombie for London and Plymouth, and Thomas Sharp for Exeter, felt they had been presented with a blank slate on which to build, and this was broadened because of the many historic buildings also demolished after the war, as in Exeter. This slate apparently offered an opportunity to realise their pre-war inclinations for slum removal and 'improvement' through modern, progressive urban architecture, progress understood in their terms. In their view, it was not an option to rebuild cities as before, notably given the constraints posed by a shortage of resources and funds, and a pressure for speed. Instead, they sought a rapid embrace of change. In this, Abercrombie and other planners sought to separate residential, commercial and industrial areas into distinctive precincts. These measures were seen as likely to enhance efficiency and the quality of life, but they were ones that hit communities as well as damaging the workshop-based employment that had been so important in towns with industry and housing closely linked.

In practice, the new town centres also proved of limited visual appeal. Although Abercrombie's work appreciated the nature of community, there was an excessive willingness to remould the street pattern for the sake of motorists. In Plymouth, there was a failure to assess the consequences of opening up the town for exposure to wind and wind-driven rain, and notably so in the shape of the prevailing Atlantic westerlies.

The control of the state over towns was shown anew from the late 1940s, under the Labour governments of 1945–51, with New Towns designed to complement Green Belts, and to replace suburbia by providing new settlements that did not rely on providing commuters. London was to be contained with a Green Belt, so that the town did not leap forward, for example from Edgware to Elstree. The New Towns, made possible by the New Towns Act of 1946 and the Town and Country Planning Act of 1947, were to be built beyond this Green Belt. The first, Stevenage, was chosen in 1946.

V.F. Soothill, the Medical Officer for Norwich, wrote in 1935 that the spread of suburbia was a 'quiet social revolution'. Yet, by the late 1940s a different social revolution was at hand, one that looked toward greater state control and was in accordance with the more general social norms, policy prescriptions, and cultural and intellectual emphases of the Labour governments. Already, the Housing, Town Planning Act of 1909 had been the first piece of legislation to use the term 'town planning'. John Burns, the President of the Local Government Board, a radical Liberal, introduced the legislation in 1908 by telling Parliament that it set out 'to provide a domestic condition for the people in which their physical health, their morals, their character and their whole social condition can be improved ... to secure the home healthy'. The results, however, were to be mixed, as the reforms of the late 1940s were to show.

Chapter 9

1950–2000

'It was rather like a slow motion picture. That was the fog of course. Nothing could really move in a fog like this. The buses would be stopped – and the cars – and the people who were abroad would crawl like beetles and wish to be home again – and the watches and clocks would all slow down.'

The nightmarish quality of a smog, the acme of atmospheric pollution, was captured in the description of London in Patricia Wentworth's *Ladies' Bane* (1954). Smogs were a key element in the collective imagination of town life in the beginning of the period, not least in London, but one that was to disappear by its close. Indeed, environmental change was a major factor in urban life. The first smokeless zone legislation was introduced in the Manchester Corporation Act of 1946, a smokeless zone established in Coventry in 1951, and controls spread rapidly from the mid-1950s, with a Clean Air Act in 1956 followed by another in 1968. Central heating replaced coal fires, and, from the 1960s, gas came in pipelines from the natural gas fields in the North Sea, and was no longer made from coal, ensuring that 'the gasworks' became a part of town lost to memory as it was redeveloped. The palls of smoke that used to hang above towns went.

So also as a major factor in urban life was ethnic change, which very much altered many (but not all) towns socially. Ethnic change was overwhelmingly urban and particularly pronounced in London, the Midlands,[1] Lancashire and Yorkshire, but far less so in the towns of the North-East and South-West, for example Sunderland and Plymouth. From the 1950s, there was large-scale immigration from the New Commonwealth, especially the West Indies and South Asia, although many of the immigrants intended only a limited stay. A temporary labour shortage in unattractive spheres of employment, such as transport, especially the buses, and nursing, led to an active sponsorship of immigration that accorded with the Commonwealth idealism of the period.

Black people encountered severe discrimination in the housing market, as well as much personal hostility, a theme explored in the film *Pool of London* (1951), where a Jamaican merchant seaman is a key character. Many immigrants found landlords unwilling to accept them as tenants. The cooking smells of West Indians and Indians were criticised, while the former were condemned for loud parties and sexual immorality. Racism played a role in neighbourhoods and workplaces; and 'White flight' came to be involved in the housing pattern, an under-reported theme that has continued to the present.

Notting Hill in 1958 witnessed a race-riot with White thugs attacking recently-settled Blacks. In response, the Notting Hill Carnival was started the following year, while Oswald Mosley failed in his attempt to exploit the immigration issue during the 1959 electoral campaign. At the same time, the limited incorporation of West Indians into the community was shown in that election: of the 7,000 West Indians entitled to vote in North Kensington, only 1,000 did so.

Much of the initial New Commonwealth immigration was from the West Indies, but South Asia, both India and Pakistan, subsequently became more important. Areas such as Southall came to seem 'Little Indias' to other Londoners, and the railway station has Indian signs. Due to immigration, there were significant variations in settlement patterns across London and many other towns. For example, whereas over ten per cent of the population of six London boroughs, Hounslow, Ealing, Brent, Harrow, Redbridge and Newham, were of Indian background in 1991, thirteen other boroughs had a percentage smaller than 2.5. The concentration in the case of Bangladeshis was more pronounced, with over 10 per cent in Tower Hamlets (replacing the Jews who had moved out, mostly to North-West London), over five per cent in Newnham and Camden, and fewer than one per cent in most other boroughs. From the late 1990s, Tower Hamlets promoted the Brick Lane area as 'London's Curry Capital' and Banglatown, an idea originating in the late 1980s and reflecting the approximately 80,000 British citizens of Bangladeshi heritage living there. Brick Lane became the stereotypical cultural centre for successive waves of immigrants: Huguenots, Jews, Bangladeshis.

Additional immigrant flows into London included Vietnamese to Hackney in the 1980s, and Iraqis to north-west London in the 1990s and 2000s. In an immigration that began in the 1970s, over 10,000 South Koreans live in the 'Koreatown' in New Malden, which includes restaurants, food markets and travel agencies. Yemenis congregate near Warwick Avenue. These are examples of the range of new Londoners, with their distinctive experiences. People not born in Britain have become the majority of Londoners, while about 5 per cent of London's population allegedly are illegal immigrants. Many flee hardship to find broken expectations.

London faced the major social burden of coping with half the net international immigration affecting the United Kingdom. Partly as a result of this immigration, London's population which had risen to about 8.7 million by 1938, before falling to 8.2 million in 1951 and 6.7 million in 1988, as large numbers moved to new housing in the Outer Metropolitan Area, rose to 9.3 million in 2020. These were very significant changes, in individual, aggregate and percentage terms, changes that helped contextualise, if not characterise, the experience of being a Londoner or a member of a London-linked network.

Novelists presented London as a central site for a change in racial composition. In Agatha Christie's novel *Hickory Dickory Dock* (1955), Miss Lemon's sensible sister, Mrs Hubbard, becomes warden of a London student hostel, Lemon commenting:

> "'these students at the hostel are of all nationalities … some of them actually *black*."
>
> "Naturally," said Hercule Poirot.
>
> "Half the nurses in our hospitals seem to be black nowadays," said Miss Lemon doubtfully, "and I understand much pleasanter and more attentive than the English ones.'"

In his novel *The Worm of Death* (1961), 'Nicholas Blake' (Cecil Day-Lewis) presented Nelly, a perceptive former Docklands prostitute who takes in lodgers:

"'They're nice boys, most of them – don't give any trouble – particularly the spades."

"I'm glad you don't have a colour-ban."

"Not me." She chuckled comfortably. "Nelly the Ever-Open Door – that's me. We're all the same underneath the skin, I always say.'"

More generally, change to urban life came at a greater pace in the late twentieth century, in part because towns became multi-ethnic and in part due to the need to respond to population growth which owed much to immigration, and the resulting demand for new housing. Existing towns increased in size, some greatly so, for example Bristol which, after London, was the major English town with the highest rate of increase. Smaller towns could also expand greatly, for example Exmouth.

There was also the establishment of New Towns, albeit not always successfully and with scant interest in the views of residents. While Milton Keynes, the fastest-growing economy outside London between 1997 and 2011, was economically a success as were Harlow and Stevenage, others, such as Peterlee, translated old social problems to new, poorly-planned sites.

The low density model of 'garden cities' that had been the basis for New Towns, of which fourteen were designated by the 1945–51 Labour governments, was replaced from the 1950s, first in a Conservative reaction that owed much to wariness about the costs and political impact of more New Towns and then, from the 1960s, due to a 'Modernist' emphasis on greater housing densities. New Town development corporations were chopped in the 1980s; only for the idea to be revived in the early twenty-first century, in part due to support from Charles, Prince of Wales (now Charles III), but also, from the 2010s, due to pressure to address housing provision.[2] Elected in 2024, Labour pledged to introduce more New Towns.

This was a different model of provision to the new towns of the medieval period which had largely been the creation of local landowners. Instead, the situation was more similar to that under the Romans.

Old or new, town parking became far more significant as an issue, for both individuals and communities. Multi-storey carparks disfigured many townscapes. Pressures for by-passes grew and the towns that gained them, such as Honiton in 1966, became more attractive places to live, although

Newbury was not alone in having a by-pass that was too close to the town centre so that it was absorbed into the road network and did not help reduce traffic there. Ring-roads within towns were far less attractive. Carlisle's, opened in 1974, cut the castle off from the city, and was followed by the replacement of a long-established area by a shopping centre. That in Wolverhampton was comparably damaging. Inner-city motorways brought great, albeit localised, destruction, for example in London and Newcastle, but there were not marshalling yards or large stations comparable to those for trains.

In contrast, the cuts under *The Reshaping of British Railways* (1963), a report better known as the Beeching Report, led many towns to lose their rail links, including Bideford, Buckingham, and Ilfracombe, while former junctions instead found themselves served only by a single line.

In contrast, there was a supplementing, on a longstanding pattern, of rail links in the London area. This was most pronounced as a result of the tube being added to the rail system. Thus, Ealing, on the Great Western Railway line to Paddington, acquired a District Line service in 1880, the Central in 1920, and then the Piccadilly. The London Underground stations at Ealing Broadway merged with the Great Western Railway station in the 1960s. There was also a dedicated line to Heathrow.

The closure of rail services essentially hit small town and rural England, and, introduced by the Conservatives and backed by Labour, engaged relatively little political interest. In contrast, the ownership of houses became a significant political issue, and indeed a major aspect of the Thatcherite 'revolution' of the 1980s. Following the 1915 Rent and Mortgage Interest (War Restrictions) Act, which owed something to concern about rent strikes, private landownership became less profitable, tenants' rights more secure, and renting from local authorities, 'council housing', more important. Partly due to the 'fair rent' system, which allowed rent officers to fix rents below the market level, supposedly to protect tenants from rapacious landlords, the private rental sector fell greatly, from the majority at mid-century, to less than 10 per cent by 1988, which greatly lessened the flexibility of the property market, helping to stoke up demand for owner-occupation.

Meanwhile, the 'Greenwood' Housing Act of 1930 gave local authorities power to clear or improve slum (crowded and substandard housing) areas, and, after 1945, slums were swept aside and their inhabitants moved into new publicly-owned housing estates. These were reflections of the priority given to rehouse people and to create an acceptable living environment, although many of the available resources had initially instead to be devoted to repairing the war-damaged housing stock. Prefabricated methods of construction ensured that new housing, including multi-storey blocks of flats, could be built rapidly, and local councils, such as Gateshead and Newcastle in the 1960s, took pride in their number, size and visibility.

Moreover, municipal housing policies helped in the consolidation of Labour's electoral base. Set in the Potteries, Mary Kelly's novel *The Spoil Kill* (1961) captured the changes:

> 'new colleges, factories, offices, thrusting sheer above surrounding waves of low slate roofs that dipped and sagged with age. Progress and consciousness were gradually but ineluctably sponging down the past. An improvement, of course; but it was impossible not to murmur occasionally, from the deep forgetful rosy well of sentiment, a sad farewell to the old bottle ovens and the soot.'

Extolled at the time, and illustrated alongside castles and cathedrals in guidebooks of the 1960s, municipal multi-storey flats were subsequently attacked as ugly, out of keeping with the existing urban fabric, of poor quality, as lacking in community feeling, and as breeders of alienation and crime.

Urban culture, in the sense of attitudes to urban living (and by whom?), is often difficult to recover. Thus, the attitudes of the 1950s towards modern dense housing schemes have been affected by subsequent perceptions. In practice, many of the buildings of the 1950s were relatively generous with space, certainly compared with earlier slum housing, the sole experience on offer, and often provided people with their first bathrooms and inside toilets. The problems of poorly-built estates were more apparent from the 1960s, whereas earlier examples were frequently better-built and more popular.

From the 1960s, there was also more concern about the dispiriting character of the new urban environment, although the issue of housing provision was affected by poverty. Moreover, the failure of many tower-block estates, designed as communities with elevated walkways called 'streets in the sky', may have owed more to an absence of social cohesion rather than to poor planning. Coherent and longlasting neighbourhoods had been swept away. Thus, Little Italy in Manchester was broken up by slum clearance in the early 1960s. In contrast, the high-rise new towns built in the New Territories of Hong Kong from the 1970s, such as Sha Ting, avoided many of the social problems seen in England in schemes of this kind.

At the same time, even the most vexed schemes were integrated into wider networks with the provision of electricity, gas and telephone, while many new council houses were low-rise suburban estates, built to 'Parker Morris' standards, for example the Middlefield Lane estate in Gainsborough.[3] Meanwhile, the continuing housing crisis was seen with the number of young single adults and young couples still living with parents, and this acted as a prompt to new building, as did political promises.

There were constants across towns in the shape of government policy and national regulations, but housing was also affected by specific 'civic cultures'; although in practice that meant the views of councillors and planners rather than those of tenants or potential tenants. Indeed, both the latter groups were patronised and their opinions ignored. At the level of individual towns, there were also the major variations caused by land availability, financial muscle, and the support or opposition of neighbouring councils, whether urban or not. Thus, Manchester, which saw flats as 'un-English' and had in the interwar years pursued a garden suburbs policy, as at Wythenshawe, was obliged, due to the opposition of other, neighbouring, local authorities, both Conservative and Labour, and the cost and shortage of land, to build up, in part reflecting a new culture of modernity which led to estates, notably at Hulme, which rapidly faced major structural and social problems.[4] The Hulme Crescents estate, constructed in 1972, was subsequently abandoned in 1984 and demolished in 1993–4, before being replaced by low-rise and medium-rise housing.

Moreover, alongside the municipal housing, there was also a brutal, Modernist, rebuilding of many town centres, as in Birmingham, Manchester and Newcastle, with both political parties supporting the process.[5] Already, in 1951, W.H. Auden referred in his poem 'The Chimeras' to 'Absence of heart – as in public buildings'. Anxiety about the destruction of past townscapes led to the foundation of the Victorian Society in 1958, but much was torn down in the 1960s. Losses in Manchester included the Milne Building and Cavendish Street Independent Chapel, while in Newcastle most of Eldon Square made way for a shopping centre. Modernist functionalism drove the pace of architectural development, as with Richard Seifert's uncompromising slab-like Centre Point (1967) skyscraper in central London. Erno Goldfinger, after whom Ian Fleming named a Bond villain, was responsible for Modernist horrors including Trellick Tower, also in London. This Modernism was seen in hospitals, schools and other buildings, as well as in housing. Ironically, it was often far from functional, not least due to a misguided preference for flat roofs, a mistaken design in a rainy climate. Concrete cladding also frequently proved a problem.

The combination of developers, planners and town councils often produced a trashy rebuilding. In Christie's *Third Girl* (1966), 'the old-fashioned market town' is assailed by 'Progress' in the shape of a new supermarket. In the twentieth and twenty-first centuries, there was a much-repeated complaint about the growing sameness of town centres, with architectural trends and the decline of independent shops both presented as key causes of a development that owed much to a reliance on private capital.[6]

There were also allegations of corruption or favouritism in the granting of planning permission. The economic downturn that followed the 1973 oil price hike provided more protection for the townscape than legislation such as the Town and Country Planning Act of 1969. At any rate, Modernism as a strategy, culture and process was increasingly discarded.[7] In May 1984, the future Charles III, speaking at a gala evening of the Royal Institute of British Architects, complained that his audience had 'consistently ignored the feelings and wishes of the mass of ordinary people in this country', and left the towns with 'concrete stumps' and 'glass towers'. In addition, there were more numerous segments of society hostile toward the central process of governmentally-driven urban change.[8]

In pursuit of a 'property-owning democracy', the Conservative governments of the 1950s fostered owner-occupation and restricted rent control. In turn, the 'right to buy' Housing Act of 1980, also passed by a Conservative government, introduced the sale of council housing to tenants which expanded home ownership but also depleted the stock of public housing. Whereas, in 1914, 10 per cent of the housing stock was owner-occupied, by 2000 the percentage, and of a far larger stock, was 70. Furthermore, the 'fair rent' system was abolished, which encouraged a revival in private-renting.

	Types of Housing Tenure in England and Wales (To nearest percentage)		
	Owner-occupiers	Rented from local authority	Rented from private landlords
1914	10	1	80
1939	31	14	23
1966	47	26	15
1977	54	32	8
1985	62	27	8
1990	67	24	7

Meanwhile, alongside the 'urban renewal' of town-centre 'rebuilding', the 1960s saw a cultural pulse toward the North, not least with the 'Mersey beat'. The key change was the response to the Beatles, a Northern popular group who, with their debut single 'Love Me Do', released in October 1962, set the 'Mersey beat' (Liverpool, their home city, was on the River Mersey), and who offered working-class experiences both prominence and sound.[9] Pop music challenged the 'received pronunciation' of the English language, providing a regional difference that was taken up by the BBC where the importance of conformity in diction, style and tone declined from the 1960s. The film director Guy Hamilton later noted:

> 'The combination of angry young men, Michael Caine and the Beatles killed the leading men who all spoke with Oxford accents... Unless you had a Brummy [Birmingham] accent, forget it. I think the Beatles and the pop scene in general had a major influence on the cinema at this time.'[10]

Other groups and performers also came from Liverpool including Cilla Black. Indeed, popular music lent itself to female as well as male performers. If the bands, with their emphasis on electric guitars, were very much male preserves, many singers were women. This was very different to the alternative Liverpool cult, football. Interest in Liverpool was also shown by the popularity of *The Liver Birds*, a television sitcom set there that began in 1969. This was a North very different to the urban working-class one depicted by L.S. Lowry as in his football painting *Going to the Match* (1953) and his *Lancashire League Cricket Match* (1964–9).

In practice, in the context of 'Beatlemania' in 1963–4, the Beatles went south, to London, and became a global as well as a national product. It set the sound of the Sixties. Their broadcast of 'All You Need Is Love' in 1967, transmitted to 26 countries, was seen by about 400 million people. Thanks largely to the Beatles, popular music became a British industry, replacing the American 'rock and roll' of the 1950s.

The Beatles contributed powerfully to the idea of a 'New Britain', an idea that was very powerful in the mid-1960s. This idea was linked to the policies advocated by the Labour Party, which governed the country from 1964 to 1970 and which entitled its 1964 general election manifesto 'The New Britain'. Labour introduced a range of social legislation. This idea was related to a variety of cultural and product developments, all urban, including the new clothes fashions pioneered in Carnaby Street in London, and the modern design themes often related to new technology, such as the supersonic Concorde aircraft and the Post Office Tower in London (1964). Harold Wilson, who cultivated his image as a northerner, and also went south, ensured that the Beatles were given honours.

The mid-1960s saw a cycle of 'Swinging London' films, including *Darling* (1965) and *Blow-Up* (1965), both of which examined the morals and mores of a permissive society in which the roles of family values and of the churches were largely redundant. For 'Alfie', in the 1966 film of that name set in London, women, clothes and cars were commodities that proved one could get on in the world without the privileges of birth and education. On a national scale, supermarkets provided new, anonymous, shopping experiences and spaces, and at this stage were mostly within towns rather than outside them.

This new world was to be hit hard by financial and economic crises from 1967 on, while a rising degree of disturbance in towns was increasingly apparent in the 1960s. Thus, the *Daily Telegraph* of 21 July 1969 reported from St Ives, where a petition had called 'for tighter vagrancy laws to rid the town of beatniks…' and 'a group of people tried to break into a derelict building occupied by beatniks' and, separately, that 'more than 300 angry people staged a sit-down protest outside Leigh Park Gardens, Havant, Hants, yesterday over the gaoling of six parents who a week ago demonstrated against a proposed 6d increase in admission charges to the park, which belonged to Portsmouth Council. The town as a troubling environment containing lawless groups was scarcely new, but the idea was readily transposed onto anxieties about new cultural and social trends, while also being revived by them. In an urban society, however, this attitude was focused on sections of towns rather than the town itself. Nevertheless, urban rioting was small-scale prior to 1981.

Linked to this, major changes in urban society were more generally national. These included the decline in the number of (living-in) servants in the first two thirds of the century, followed by a rise, as living-out servants expanded greatly from cleaners and gardeners to include carers, while an increase in jobs for full-time professional women in turn led to the employment of more help.[11] The more widespread expansion of the service economy focused on towns and provided more employment for women.

Within that more general context, the success of individual towns varied greatly, depending on their economy and on the economy of the surrounding regions. Thus, the Mersey Docks and Harbour Board hit serious problems in the early 1970s. Such factors were also pertinent within towns, with the appeal of housing stock and the associations of neighbourhoods both particularly important. In 1987, rates of unemployment in the Newcastle wards ranged from 8.9 per cent in Westerhope to 36 per cent in West City, an area affected by deindustrialisation.

These issues, problems and changes encouraged a very varied depiction of urban life. It included responses that scarcely matched homilies, whether those of Victoriana, municipal Liberalism, Welfare State Socialism, or Thatcherite effort. *Till Death Us Do Part* (1965–75), an unsentimental account of the London East End, was followed by *Bread*, a television series that ran for more than 70 episodes from 1986, and whose audience grew to over 20 million. This sympathetically depicted a Liverpool family whose younger members were mostly unemployed and ready to cheat the Social Security system. It was to be followed by *The Royle Family*, a sitcom about a television-fixated family living in a Manchester council house, which ran for three series. The television police series *The Sweeney* (1975–8) brought to an abrupt end the cozy image of the kind-hearted London policeman seen in *Dixon of Dock Green* (1955–76), a comforting series much at variance with the far darker reality of crime and policing, notably corruption.

At the same time, there was much regional, local and social variation. In 1976, Johnny Rotten and the Sex Pistols, a radical band, made their first appearance outside London, playing in a nightclub in Northallerton, a small, quiet Yorkshire town. The noise and lyrics did not go down well, and much of the audience promptly left.

Many towns that had been part of the Workshop of the World were now in grave difficulties, in part urban wastelands, such as that Mrs Thatcher was photographed visiting on Teesside in September 1987. It was not only that unemployment was highest in traditional mining and heavy industrial areas, but also that the highest expenditure per head on income support, and the greatest percentage of households with a low weekly income were highest in these areas. Urban support for Thatcher reflected socio-economic factors, not least in divisions within the working-class. Thus, in 1987, the Conservatives won key marginal seats in the Midlands unlike in the North-East with its highly unionised heavy industry.

The Full Monty (1997), a comedy film set in Sheffield, had, as its bleak background, unemployment and urban decay, and Sheffield was indeed affected by international competition in its traditional metallurgy. From the perspective of a more mobile society, American viewers expressed surprise that the unemployed did not move to areas of greater opportunity, although the nature of the housing market makes that more difficult in England than in America. For the English, *The Full Monty* was another version of the 'Grim Up North' approach, prevalent from the nineteenth century, and, more especially, 1930s, as well as the focus on neighbourhood that was significant to the view of urban living.

Across the country, but especially in the North, there were low levels of both gross domestic product per head and economic growth, in traditional manufacturing areas such as Cleveland where iron and steel were hit, and some earlier areas of growth such as Teesside where chemicals were in trouble. More generally, alongside the decline of heavy industry, such as steel and shipbuilding, in England as a whole, there was also decline in more recent spheres of growth, such as the chemical and car industries.

International competition was important, while labour relations were a significant factor. Long-established ports with militant dockers, especially Hull, Liverpool, London and Southampton, lost business to those where a more flexible workforce welcomed container loads, for example Dover, Felixstowe and Harwich.

Liverpool was hit hard not just by a degree of economic pressure and social strain that put a harsh light on the aftermath of the Beatles, but also by political division. Run by a revolutionary internal group, Militant Tendency, the Labour Party in Liverpool sought to cause a class war by setting an illegal council budget, bankrupting the town and leading to the redundancy of all the council staff. This was described in 1985 in the Labour Party Conference by Neil Kinnock, the party leader, as 'the grotesque chaos of a Labour council – a *Labour* council – hiring taxis to scuttle round a city handing out redundancy notices to its own workers.' Urban radicalism was also seen in London, leading to Thatcher abolishing the Greater London Council.

Separately, the impact of business consolidation, generally to the benefit of national companies run from London, was that of a lack of urban autonomy, and then often activity. Thus, Whitbreads took over the Portsmouth breweries of Brickwoods, Gales and Strong, brewed in the town and then in 1983 ceased doing so, bringing brewing there to an end.[12] This was an example of a very common pattern in the consolidation of ownership and production. Under the Local Government Act of 1972, the reorganisation of local boundaries included the creation of new urban-based counties, notably Avon, Cleveland, Humberside and Tyne and Wear. This affected traditional town identities.

At the national level, there were shifts in economic activity and a major rise in the service sector. Management, research and development jobs were increasingly separate from production tasks, and concentrated in the South-East, notably in the M4 corridor west of London and near Cambridge. Thanks in large part to the decline of employment in the car industry, the percentage of the working population in Oxford engaged in engineering manufacturing fell from 28 in 1971 to 7 in 1991, while that in professional occupations rose from 24 to 30.

These areas represented opportunities for the political parties. The electoral geography of England changed with Labour becoming far from a party only of the old industrial areas. In the 1966 election, it won many seats never held before, including Brighton, Cambridge, Exeter, Lancaster, Oxford and York.

In contrast to prosperity and growth in the South-East, there was (and is) also much poverty there, not only in London, but also along the Thames estuary, in the Medway towns, notably Chatham, in coastal towns such as Margate, and in Crawley. So also for other regions.

There were also important local variations in work and housing. Council house sales in the 1980s were widespread but skewed. The better housing in the wealthier areas sold, while the public sector increasingly became 'sink housing', rented by those suffering relative deprivation. In desperation, local authorities increasingly, from the mid-1990s, demolished such housing, as on a large scale in west Newcastle. Looked at differently, this was an aspect of the way in which, from the Victorian period, areas judged squalid and criminous were demolished in town planning in which social judgment and discrimination were to the fore, as with the building of St. Pancras and Kingsway in London on cleared slums, and, later, the rebuilding of St. Ebbe's in Oxford.[13]

Much of the current urban fabric derives from the twentieth century, as therefore do the accumulated memories of life. Greater longevity ensures that more people can interact with their grandparents, and this further helps ensure the focus on the twentieth-century town and, increasingly, the late twentieth-century town. And so also with television programmes focusing on the genealogies of people, houses and streets; and with the literary focus on a here-and-now of experience and memory that encompasses lifespans that include much of the late twentieth century. The idea of the 1960s as a transformative generation and period remains important, although it is likely to fade.

Confidence in the present in towns and much else is at the moment very tempered, and this lack of confidence extends to insufficient and often poorly-constructed recent housing, as well as to an urban fabric and culture that is seen as under great pressure. These concerns encourage a degree of re-examination of previous ideas about the redundancy of past conditions. The twentieth-century will be an important site for this re-examination.

Chapter 10

Towns Today

'The senseless wickedness, the ignorant prophaneness' of Newcastle's poor troubled John Wesley in 1745 as he feared it would endanger divine support at the time of the threatening Jacobite rebellion.[1] Towns have always challenged control and order, indeed posed moral panic. They are usually seen as the setting for criminality and for the lawless 'mob,' as well as for the dissolution of norms thanks to ready money.

Towns have also been centres for contention over identity, both their own and more generally, and this situation continues. The *Evening Standard* of 10 October 2017 published the results of a poll revealing that 46 per cent of the Londoners surveyed named 'Londoner' as their primary identity, while the remaining 54 per cent divided between European, British and English. These results were qualified by the question of how strongly they felt each of these identities on a scale of zero to ten: Londoner came top with 7.7. In this case, town identity was top in that of multiple identities.

As so often, tensions involving London both interacted with pressures and divisions within it, and crossed with other differences in the country, for example between the North and the South. Alongside these differences came internal migration, with London being the destination of about a third of new graduates in 2021, a year in which, in addition, as part of a 'churn' linked to age-related movement, 3.1 per cent of London's population moved to other parts of Britain, mostly southern England.

Between 2008 and 2018, moreover, alongside large-scale immigration, 550,000 more Britons left London than moved to it. In part, this was a matter of seeking more affordable and larger properties from which to commute into the city, and, linked to that, the demographic 'churn' of generational change. Yet, there was also a degree of 'white flight', or, more correctly, movement that in part reflected what was revealed by successive well-being assessments by the Office of National Statistics: many individuals found London too expensive and were worried about crime, while companies moved jobs to less expensive locations outside London.

Attacks on London's role were incessant. Seen as London-centric, the BBC was a focus of criticism from across the political spectrum about 'metropolitan bias'. In May 2021, Andy Burnham, re-elected as the mayor of Manchester, argued that Labour had to end its 'London-centric' focus. Radio programmes from outside London frequently carried criticism, as with the claims in *Any Questions* on 29 May 2021, an episode from Bridlington in Yorkshire, about transport expenditure being lavished on London. In his speech in October 2023 dramatically curtailing the planned High Speed 2 rail network, the Prime Minister, Rishi Sunak, claimed:

> '…a false consensus has taken root that all that matters are links between our big conurbations. This consensus said that our national economic regeneration should be driven by cities, at the exclusion of everywhere else. It said that the most important connections those cities could have was to London and not anywhere else. And it said that the only links that mattered were north to south, not east to west.'

Instead, Sunak proposed more investment in regional rail and road links, notably in northern England. At the same time, London 'brands' successfully spread into the provinces. By 2020, Winchester had a Hoxton Steam Bakery, only for it to be a Covid casualty. Exeter, Oxford and Winchester gained Ivy restaurants.

For many, their town was in part the identity offered by particular institutions and facilities, such as the bank or the library. Many such faculties, however, have closed in recent years. 'I spend therefore I am,' but the abandonment by much of the public not only of small independent shopkeepers but also of traditional high-street shopping in favour of chains and/or out-of-town stores has also changed the image as well as prosperity of many towns. This became an issue that was national as well as local, as when, with reference to Malton, the *Daily Telegraph*, on 20 February 2016, carried a feature on 'How we saved our historic high street.' In practice, the closure of the local branch banks and post offices, and of facilities such as local newspapers, helped challenge a sense of urban identity. In 2015–24, over 6,000 bank branches closed.

These changes in part were a response as out-of-town shopping grew in scale and was seen in closed high street department stores, as in Bristol, Exeter, Nuneaton, Taunton and many other towns. At the same time, towns encompassed recent stand-alone centres, such as Brent Cross in north London, Lakeside in Thurrock, the Glades in Bromley, Meadowhall in Sheffield and the Metro Centre in Gateshead, and these brought changes to urban areas including to transport patterns. More recently, shopping online has been a major problem for established shops, restaurants and bank branches. Indeed, in place of concerns about the sameness of town centres, came the challenge to their very existence posed by out-of-town shopping and online shopping, culture and sociability. Given the significance of all these for urban life, and of markets in particular for the life of countryside towns, this challenge is of more than short-term modern concern. Thus, the growth of restaurant culture in the late twentieth century was challenged in the 2020s by the major expansion in online ordering and home delivery.

Despite general economic growth in the early and mid 2000s, many towns were hit hard as a result of economic and commercial transformation. A major change in urban society in all respects, as well as in function, has resulted from the number of towns that have lost their manufacturing, as well as their marketing and processing roles for local agriculture. Transformation was accentuated as fiscal and economic problems increased from 2007, while government austerity became a more significant factor in the 2010s. Thus, Birmingham, which had been an industrial powerhouse, faced growing problems and, by the 2010s, had relatively low rates of business start-ups and economic output per head. Very poor financial stewardship led Birmingham Council to have to introduce major cuts in 2024. Similar poor stewardship led to particular problems for a number of other towns, including Croydon.

Liverpool had offered much in popular music and sport, invigorating working-class experiences of life, but this impression could not be sustained, and both London and Manchester came to provide more potent images. Liverpool did poorly on the Barclays Prosperity Map, which calculates scores based on median household wealth, gross domestic product per head, the unemployment rate, average household expenditure, house prices, working hours, and charitable giving. Of the ten largest urban regions in Britain, Liverpool had the lowest growth in population in 2011–15, at 1.2 per cent, London and Bristol being the two highest. Urban regeneration has much to tackle in Liverpool.

More generally, the Local Government Association reported in 2014 that underemployment and underachievement were particularly acute in Northern towns, notably Sheffield, Leeds, Newcastle and Manchester, and local authorities that were the worst performing by GCSE exam results in both 2005 and 2021 included authorities in South Yorkshire, Teesside, Liverpool and Manchester.

'Ten Years of Tax: How Cities Contribute to the National Exchequer,' a July 2016 report by the Centre for Cities, noted that London generated as much tax as the next 37 largest UK towns combined, with a percentage rise of 24.8 per cent from 2004–5 to 2014–15. Most of the other nine fast-rising tax-paying towns were in the South-East, including Cambridge, Oxford, and Ipswich. Manchester's tax rose by 1 per cent, but it fell in many industrial towns, including Birmingham, Bradford, Huddersfield, Leeds and Preston. This contrast reflected not only wages, but also house prices in the shape of inheritance, land and property taxes.

This report was an instance of the plentiful amount of information available about towns, not least in relative terms. In part, this information provided a quantifiable index of the impressions held by townspeople. Most, for example, would not have been surprised in 2024 by the information that Newcastle saw far more going out than Plymouth, the two towns on the opposite sides of the scale. Nevertheless, reports revealed the scale of the differences that contributed so greatly to local identities.

At a more local level, there are striking variations within counties and often between nearby towns. In Cornwall, Truro is far more prosperous than St Austell; in South Devon, Dartmouth and Totnes than Dawlish and Paignton. The relationship between towns and the military could continue, with for example Aldershot and Catterick for the army. Carterton has become a significant Oxfordshire town in large part as a result of Brize Norton becoming the leading RAF base. Despite tourism abroad, coastal towns essentially catering for British tourists also continued to attract large numbers, both for stays or as day-trippers, notably Scarborough, Blackpool, Skegness, Torbay, Brighton and Margate.

There was, however, a general sense of decline in the urban space, in part due to a failure to compensate for the inroads and disrepair of time. The apparent lack of governmental commitment in many municipal areas reflected the agglomeration of local government authorities and the resulting lack of interest by now-distant local government officials. In part, this situation was seen in public concern about the urban loss of individuality, notably with the plight of high streets.

Malaise about the rate of change, not least through immigration, may have played a role in the majority for Brexit in the 2016 referendum on continued membership of the European Union. There were marked differences between towns. London, in particular, and university towns tended to vote Remain, but majorities could be slight: Newcastle voting 50.4 per cent and Leeds 50.3 per cent. Towns with a strong working-class composition tended to go for Brexit: 70 per cent in Hartlepool, 68.3 per cent in Barnsley, 62 per cent in South Tyneside, 61.3 per cent in Sunderland, and 57.5 per cent in Durham; although, alongside social and council tenants, a majority of homeowners who had no mortgage voted for Brexit.

There were also claims of a 'democracy deficit' in towns without local newspapers, not least due to less scrutiny of local officials and politicians. In Exeter, the *Express and Echo* went from being a daily to a biweekly. In 2018, Peter Luff, a former MP for Worcester and then Mid-Worcestershire, observed:

> 'Local papers still have a role, but it is diminishing fast, overtaken by local blogs and other social media. The challenge now is how to communicate with local voters… Nowadays people know the very local (their village, street etc) and have some awareness of their wider region, but often don't know what is going on in the neighbouring town. We have become simultaneously better informed about the world and less well-informed about our near communities.'[2]

The potential importance of the press to urban identity, however, was seen with the *Bristol Post* which managed to maintain a campaigning stance and local coverage. Thus, on 12 August 2015, the newspaper focused on a 'six-hour wait before dying of meningitis', which was both the leading news item and the topic of the editorial. The paper also drew on reader contributions, as in the 'Your Say' section and provided an opportunity to query content. The *Sheffield Telegraph* provided good coverage in 2018 of the controversy about the City Council removing many streetside trees.

Plymouth followed suit in 2024. There was a more general public ugliness, Simon Brett observing in 2000 in a novel set in a town on the South coast, the region in which he lived:

> 'The architect who'd designed the new supermarket (assuming such a person existed and the plans hadn't been scribbled on the back of an envelope by a builder who'd once seen a shoebox) had placed two wide roof-supporting pillars just in front of the main tills. Whether he'd done this out of vindictiveness or ... incompetence was unknowable.'[3]

Problems with the urban space were in large part a matter of difficulties for those who lived there. Pollution was particularly important as a challenge as quantities of waste, human and non-human, were both significant and rising. Wipes became major rubbish obstacles, in both sewage pipes and rivers, notably the Thames. Noise pollution, light pollution, and atmospheric pollution were most acute in towns. These helped drive pressure for policy and regulatory changes, and also encouraged Green politics. Many urban issues are longstanding, notably pollution. Car fumes greatly focus that problem today but, earlier, the impact of coal on the air had been noted, as by John Evelyn in the seventeenth century for London, and by Daniel Defoe (as also for Newcastle) in the eighteenth. In Defoe's novel *Roxana*, she refuses to live in London, pretending 'that it would choke me up; that I wanted breath when I was in London'. In 1716, an ill Robert Walpole left London and gained 'so great a benefit from the air that I gather strength daily'.[4]

Levels of mono-nitrogen oxides routinely break guidelines on what constitutes a safe maximum exposure. Measured in micrograms per cubic metre of air ($\mu g/m^3$), the World Health Organisation guideline was 10, and the 2021 figures were 52 for the Greater Manchester Urban Area, 50 for Greater London, 49 for the West Midlands Urban Area, 45 for Sheffield, 44 for Nottingham, 43 for West Yorkshire, Liverpool and Bristol, 39 for

Leicester and the Potteries, 38 for Portsmouth and Southampton, 37 for Teesside, Coventry and Hull and 34 for Tyneside. And those figures were greatly affected by the decline in activity due to Covid. 2023 rankings by Smart Air of the most polluted towns included Brighton, Portsmouth, Nottingham, Bradford, Bristol, London, Southampton and Manchester in the top ten. Rankings varied, those for the least polluted towns included in 2024 Leeds.

Pollution worried many, but housing remains a key issue. The 1988 Housing Act allowed Housing Associations to borrow privately (as opposed to relying on government loans), which led to a rapid expansion of Housing Association Provision, with over £70 billion in borrowing to the present. Unfortunately, there was an even greater fall in Local Authority provision. Local authorities saw their housing stock decline over a thirty-year period from a peak of 4.99 million units to 1.73 million in 2012. In contrast, Housing Association numbers of units increased from 281,000 to 2.4 million during the same period. Particular housing shortages developed for poor families, not least as inner-city regeneration and new inner-city housing focused on flats for single people, for childless couples, or for students, rather than for families. New housing provision remained inadequate in the 1990s, 2000s and 2010s, and, despite the promises of politicians, there is no sign of this situation changing.

Alongside inadequacy, there was the issue of cost. In 1986, the average first-time buyer paid just under £30,000 for a new home, whereas, in 2015, the figure was over £150,000 for England, and £330,000 in London. According to Nationwide, the average UK house price had risen to £196,930 by February 2016, a 60 per cent increase in 13 years, and one that encouraged investment in housing which drove up their cost, as investment for renting out or for Airbnbs put up purchase prices. The combined impact was a fall in homeownership. Research by the Resolution Foundation, published in August 2016, indicated that homeownership in England, having peaked at 70.9 per cent in October 2004, fell steadily, for example to 63.8 per cent for 2015. This was the same level as in 1986 (63.5% then), although then the number of owner-occupiers was lower as the population was lower, while the 1986 percentage was a rapid increase on that in 1980 when it had been closer to 57.

The housing crisis was not only seen in London, the place that overly dominates the news and political debate as it has long done. Outer London had a drop of 13.5 per cent in homeownership, from a peak of 71.4 in October 2000 to 57.8 in February 2016. The same trend was also the case elsewhere. In Greater Manchester, homeownership peaked in 2003 at 72.4 per cent, but has since fallen to 57.9 per cent, the biggest drop in the UK. The percentage falls in the West Midlands was 11.2, in West Yorkshire 10.6, and in Merseyside 9.1. There were sharp falls in Leeds and Sheffield. The mismatch of high house price increases, well above those in incomes, was crucial as it made the large deposits required to purchase a new home increasingly unaffordable, and that despite government efforts to help. As a result, renting came to the fore, but very high rents in the private sector made it impossible for many to save for a deposit. The percentage renting privately in England rose from 11 in 2003 to 19 in 2015, with that in Greater Manchester rising from 6 to 20, and both Outer London and West Yorkshire also seeing the percentage rise by more than 10 per cent.

A long-term rise in the price of housing led, in the early twenty-first century, to an increase in intergenerational living, which was part of a global trend. A 2016 report by Aviva forecast that, by 2025, there would be about 3.8 million 20 to 34 year olds living with their parents, about 31 per cent of this cohort; compared to 1.9 million in 2000, and to 2.8 million, just under a quarter, in 2015. Financial necessity was a key element in this situation, including saving to buy houses, as well as the common reasons of inability to afford rent and the need for help with childcare. The 2021 census revealed that in England and Wales, 77.9 per cent of households lived in a house, 21.7 per cent in flats and 0.4% in caravans. In 2021, 62.5 per cent owned the accommodation they lived in.

Pressure on housing was used as a reason not only for higher-density housing but also for building upwards, affecting longstanding vistas and shadowing neighbouring buildings, including houses, as in Exeter. By 2024, 107 of the 129 British buildings taller than St Paul's Cathedral were in London, with many more approved. Manchester followed, not least with the plan for a 241 metre high residential tower block, the tallest in Western Europe, as did Leeds. A letter published in the *Times* on 15 May 2024, included:

'Manchester is a prime example of near-identical tall buildings built like dominoes that are stacked so close together that they suffocate the city. They have tiny balconies all overlooking each other and resemble human versions of bird perches. Even worse, every piece of greenery has been removed: it has become a cement city in the sky.'[5]

The 'residences' in question are generally designed, and notably so in London, for foreign investors. Thus, of the 68 high-rise residential projects built in London in 2000–23, 6 per cent of the 22,000 housing units were 'affordable' and less than one per cent 'social housing' for the poor.[6]

In June 2024, Labour's Deputy Leader, Angela Rayner, set out indicative designs for new towns, 'the towns for the future', including Edwardian-style mansion blocks and 'tree-lined streets of townhouses', rather than '*identikit homes*' and 'dingy shoeboxes', and claimed that the 1.5 million homes to be built over five years would include 'only exemplary design with real character'. Labour also offered a government mortgage-guarantee scheme to provide loans of up to 95 per cent of a property's value for first-time buyers. In contrast, in 2023, only 158,000 houses were completed.

As a separate issue of urban strain, an increase in criminality, especially in contrast to the 1950s, was related to a widespread breakdown in the socialisation of the young, especially of young males. The numbers and percentage of young men with criminal records rose, and there was also an increase for young women. Although crime was not limited to these areas, crime hit most in run-down neighbourhoods, further de-socialising life there, and encouraging outward movement by those who could afford it. This situation led to a greater measure of social segregation, and was linked to the appeal of the suburbs.

Although blamed by many commentators on Conservative governments between 1979 and 1997, and their economic policies, crime had, in fact, increased from the 1950s and, for much of the period, unemployment rates were low and the standard of living of the poor in fact rose. Indeed, robberies in London rose by 105 per cent between 1991 and 2002, a period of falling unemployment. Many commentators, however, found it easier to blame Thatcher, the Conservatives, 'the system', or alleged racism.

Similarly, in 2011 and 2016, rioting and looting in London took place in a city with very high rates of employment. In 2011, anger with the police and looting for consumer goods both played a role. The number of rioters was relatively low, but a delayed response exacerbated the situation, and the rioters made good use of social media in order to organise and to thwart the police. Moreover, violence spread to Birmingham, and then to Manchester, Merseyside and Nottingham. Five people were killed in the riots, and over 3,000 people arrested. To cope with the situation, it was thought necessary to move police from elsewhere in the country, leaving many other towns poorly policed for a while. More generally, there was a sense that policing was inadequate in many towns, notably small ones threatened by 'county line' gangs, for example Marlborough, as well as in some major ones where policing was criticised, for example Nottingham.

Drug-use as assessed by the Crime Survey for England and Wales, a government survey, reveals that low income itself is not the cause of crime. Figures published in July 2016 for 2015–16 indicated that 3 per cent of people aged between 16 and 59 in households with an annual income of at least £50,000 said they had taken cocaine that year, and 2.2 per cent Ecstasy, up from 2.2% and 1.5% the previous year, whereas the lower-income drug usage was stable or falling. One in five people aged between 16 and 25 had taken a drug in the past year, compared with one in four a decade earlier: cannabis being the most common drug. This usage contributed to the profitability of crime. One novelist observed of Southampton in 2024: 'Organised Crime Group. One of the most common reasons for crime in the city. Drugs. Money. Gambling.'[7]

In practice, an explanation of rising crime, in London and elsewhere, in terms of unemployment, appears less pertinent than one that focuses on social dislocation, especially family breakdown. In addition, detailed variations chronologically owed much to changing age profiles, in the shape of the number of adolescent males, a group that was more likely to commit crime. Knife crime became more prominent in London in the 2000s, in part because large numbers of young men began to carry knives in order to give themselves a sense of protection. The resulting killings led to a change in the age profile of violent death among males.

However, the murder rate was low by global standards, and certainly compared to America; and that despite the fact that the country was relatively crowded, while imprisonment was less common than in America. The low rate of gun ownership, and notably of the legal ownership of guns, was an important factor in keeping the murder rate low; although there were notable issues in specific communities, and 'black-on-black' killings among young men in London, often with guns, caused concern. As so often, the weather played a role. In 2016, disturbances in London occurred on the hottest day of the year up to then, with temperatures peaking at 33.5°C. Conversely, when temperatures rose even more later that summer, there were no riots. There were also issues about the wider reporting of crime and of low conviction rates. Reporting issues led to dissension about real crime rates, notably for robbery. In particular, it was claimed that downward trends in police figures for many crimes were misleading. Low conviction rates were especially the case for rape.

There were major moral panics in some urban areas, especially about paedophilia in the 2000s and 2010s, and about the large-scale exploitation of girls, particularly girls in local authority care, in the 2010s. The term moral panic is frequently employed by academics as a distancing one that implies that the situation has been exaggerated in order to make moral or political points. In practice, both paedophilia and the 'grooming' of children for sexual exploitation were later revealed as major problems. In part, they were linked to new technology, in the shape of child pornography on the Internet.

Ethnic tension also played a major role, with young white girls in care in certain Northern towns, notably Rotherham, but also elsewhere in the country, for example Derby, Oxford and Rochdale, being exploited, and mostly by Asian Muslim men who used intimidation, 'grooming', rape, and getting young women addicted to drugs. Gang-rape was part of the process. Trial testimony suggested that the accused regarded white women as inherently sluttish and therefore ripe for brutal exploitation. For long, commentators would not refer to these issues, for fear of being labelled racist, and the same factor appears to have affected the police. As a result, the scandal when the stories broke in the 2010s, and many towns were revealed to have such gangs, reflected on the major problems England faced in looking at the nature of its society. The official report on Rotherham suggested that

14,000 girls had been exploited there, an astonishing number. Failures to act on the part of local authorities and the police caused justified outrage, although, possibly, not the level of public anger and action that would have been seen in some countries.

There was less of a sustained panic about the deadly suicide bomb attacks on the London Tube and bus system by Islamic extremists in 2005. A febrile atmosphere, which was exacerbated by the hunt for other would-be bombers, highlighted worries that a traditional tolerance, and especially the openness to immigrants and multiculturalism, might be sowing the seeds for sustained problems; but that anxiety was not allowed to capture the public mood.

Concern about crime in towns played a role in movement from those areas perceived as dangerous. In part, there was an urban flight to the countryside, what in America is called white flight, one that was especially marked in the early 2020s, in response both to the Covid epidemic of 2020–2 and to being able to work away from the office. As a result, after the Covid epidemic ended, urban offices, notably in London, became emptier, especially on Mondays and Fridays, with an impact on expenditure on commuting and meals. In 2023–4, there was a partial reaction, in part in response to train strikes (yet another reminder of the impact of external factors on urban fortunes), and there was a return to London by some who had left it. Nevertheless, there had been a significant impact and this in part a matter of a variant on a more general concern and resentment about large towns and a resulting move to smaller settlements elsewhere, whether suburban or not. Furthermore, there is still only a partial return to working in the office on Mondays and Fridays, and this alters the relationship between place of work and place of residence. Both are generally part of 'urban space' but in differing ways.

Alongside crime, as a reminder of the varied types of discontent, and in theory in response to it, the massive spread of CCTV (closed-circuit television) in towns ensured that life was literally under supervision as well as being more regulated, for poor and wealthy alike. Greater regulation left less space for autonomy or independence, unless permitted by government or, indeed, criminal activity. There was particular concern about restrictions on urban driving.

Meanwhile, uneasiness about the past was shown in 2020 when the statue of Edward Colston (1636–1721) was publicly thrown into the harbour in Bristol by a large crowd and without police intervention. This launched a more general criticism of sculptures, and even attacks on them. A Bristol-born, London-based, participant in the slave trade, although principally in Mediterranean trade, Colston was a major philanthropist; but, in 2020, St Mary Redcliffe Church in Bristol also removed a stained-glass church window dedicated to him. Liverpool had made a public apology in 1994 for its role in the slave trade, and the International Slavery Museum in Liverpool is very candid about its involvement in slavery.

The town as the centre for cultural iconography as well as action was differently seen in 2024 when the London Overground was renamed, with Lioness, Mildmay, Windrush, Weaver, Suffragette and Liberty lines. The line names were deliberately not geographical, as in North London line. However, those chosen did not necessarily resonate widely: the Mildmay Line was named after a hospital about which little was known, and the Liberty line celebrates the Royal Liberty of Havering, the old name for the borough of Havering. The lines had no reference to railway history, such as the navvies who built the railways, railway works or marshalling yards.

Far more significance can be attached to the attempt by the 2016 Conservative government to have elected mayors introduced across all regions of England as part of a new structure of local government that included powers for economic planning. In practice, this measure offered the basis for urban-focused regional government, but has so far created scant public support for regional government.

England's towns remain critical to economic growth and social development as essential and accessible meeting places. This necessity, which has become even more relevant post-Covid, has influenced their design, layout, and content as well as their management and governance. Get it right, and it hums; get it wrong, and no one wants to go there.

Humans are not sociable and, of late, there has been the transformation of many town centres and car parks (often replacing industrial workshops where no-one lived, to more mixed-use, high amenity, low-carbon neighbourhood clusters, anchored by civil or cultural buildings and public spaces, better served by public transport.

Public-private partnerships have played a key part in recent as well as more enlightened town planning, although lower dependence on cars does not suit all inhabitants, government needs epically to join up its housing and planning thinking with its economic planning, not least as counterweights to London for jobs within growth sectors.

'Decline in the urban space' meanwhile, was claimed by many who said they would prefer to live in the countryside. However, such a situation is relative chronologically, geographically and thematically. Indeed, what can displease one generation can be regarded as worthy of saving in another, as with the fictional Coburg Square near St Paul's, London described by Arthur Conan Doyle in 'The Red-Headed League' (1891):

> 'a pokey, little, shabby-genteel place, where four lines of dingy two-storied brick houses looked out into a small railed-in enclosure, where a lawn of weedy grass and a few clumps of faded laurel bushes make a hard fight against a smoke-laden and uncongenial atmosphere.'

Now, it would be a 'Des Res' and cost a lot of money.

List of Abbreviations

Add	Additional Manuscripts
Beinecke	Beinecke Library, New Haven, Connecticut
BL	British Library, Department of Manuscripts
Bod	Bodleian Library, Oxford
CRO	County Record Office
FO	Foreign Office Papers
HL	Huntington Library, San Marino, California
MO	Montagu Papers
NA	National Archives, London

Notes

Preface
1. Queen Victoria reigned from 1837 to 1901.
2. P. Colman, *The Baker's Diary. Life in Georgian England from the Book of George Sloper, Wiltshire Baker, 1753–1810* (Trowbridge, 1991). See also, for a shopkeeper, D. Vaisey (ed.), *Diary of Thomas Turner, 1754–1765* (East Hoathly, 1994).
3. J. Black, *Charting the Past. The Historical Worlds of Eighteenth-Century England* (Bloomington, Ind., 2019).

Introduction
1. Evelyn Papers, vol. 49 f. 25–6.
2. BL. Add. 58213 f. 216.
3. H. Summerson, 'The Criminal Underworld of Medieval England,' *Journal of Legal History*, 17 (1996), pp. 197–224.
4. E. Moss, *Night Raiders: Burglary and the Making of Modern Urban Life in London, 1860–1968* (Oxford, 2019).
5. A. Bayman, *Thomas Dekker and the Culture of Pamphleteering in Early Modern London* (Farnham, 2014).
6. R. Williams, 'Stolen Goods and the Economy of Makeshifts in Eighteenth-Century Exeter,' *Archives*, 31 (2005), pp. 85–96; H. Shore, *London's Criminal Underworlds, c.1720–c.1930: A Social and Cultural History* (Basingstoke, 2015).
7. A.J. Standley, 'The Staffordshire House of Correction,' *Staffordshire History*, 15 (1992), pp. 5–8.
8. Egmont to Daniel Dering, 27 Mar. 1722, BL. Add. 47029 f. 110.
9. Wharton to William, 1st Earl Cowper, 9 Aug. 1721, Hertford, Hertfordshire CRO, D/EP F57 f. 79.
10. M. Hallett and J. Rendall (eds), *Eighteenth-Century York: Culture, Space and Society* (York, 2003).
11. Reynolds to Lord Grantham, 20 July 1773, Bedford, Bedfordshire CRO, L30/14/326/2.
12. A.R. Bridbury, 'English Provincial Towns in the Later Middle Ages,' *Economic History Review*, 2nd ser., 34 (1981), pp. 1–24, quote p. 1; but see also, R. Tittler, 'Late Medieval Urban Prosperity,' *Ibid.*, 37 (1984), pp. 551–4.
13. T. Hitchcock and R. Shoemaker, *London Lives: Poverty, Crime, and the Making of a Modern City, 1690–1800* (Cambridge, 2015).
14. I. Ferris, P. Leach and S. Litherland, 'A Survey of Bridge Street and Mill Lane, Banbury,' *Cake and Cockhorse*, 12, 3 (summer 1992), pp. 54–65.
15. *'The Counties of Britain': a Tudor Atlas by John Speed* (London, 1988).
16. J. Szegö, *Mapping Hidden Dimensions of the Urban Scene: Modelling the Cartographic Anatomy and Internal Dynamics of Growing Towns and Cities for Application in Urban and Regional Planning and in Environmental Analysis* (Stockholm, 1994).

17. H. French, 'The Search for the "middle sort of people" in England, 1600–1800,' *Historical Journal*, 43 (2000), pp. 277–93.
18. M. Pitts and D. Perring, 'The Making of Britain's First Urban Landscapes: The Case of Late Iron Age and Roman Essex,' *Britannia*, 37 (2006), p. 189.
19. J. Blair, *The Church in Anglo-Saxon Society* (Oxford, 2005).
20. M. Bonney, *Lordship and the Urban Community: Durham and its Overlords, 1250–1540* (Cambridge, 1990).
21. C. Dyer, *Making a Living in the Middle Ages: The People of Britain, 850–1520* (London, 2003), p. 62.
22. J. Beckett, *City Status in the British Isles, 1830–2002* (Aldershot, 2005).
23. M. Beresford, *New Towns of the Middle Ages* (2nd edn, London, 1988).
24. J. Boulton, *Neighbourhood and Society: A London Suburb in the Seventeenth Century* (Cambridge, 1987).
25. C. Barron, 'Searching for the "small people" of medieval London,' *Local Historian*, 38 (2008), pp. 83–94.
26. R. Hall, 'The vanishing unemployed, hidden disabled, and embezzling master: researching Coventry Workhouse registers,' *Ibid.*, pp. 111–21.
27. E.A. Wrigley, 'Urban Growth in Early Modern England: Food, Fuel and Transport,' *Past and Present*, 225 (2014), pp. 79–112.

Chapter 1
1. I. Fay, *Health and the City: Disease, Environment and Government in Norwich, 1200–1575* (Woodbridge, 2015).
2. D. Walker et al, *A Bioarchaeological Study of Medieval Burials on the Site of St Mary Spital* (London, 2012).
3. C. Taylor, *Village and Farmstead: A History of Rural Settlement in England* (London, 1983).
4. M. Pitts and D. Perring, 'The Making of Britain's First Urban Landscapes: The Case of Late Iron Age and Roman Essex,' *Britannia*, 37 (2006), pp. 189–212; M. Pitts, 'Reconsidering Britain's first urban communities,' *Journal of Roman Archaeology* (2014).
5. J. Creighton, *Coins and Power in Late Iron Age Britain* (Cambridge, 2000); M. Pitts, 'Rethinking the southern British oppida: networks, kingdoms and material culture,' *European Journal of Archaeology*, 13 (2010), pp. 32–63.
6. M. Pitts and D. Perring, 'The Making of Britain's First Urban Landscapes: The Case of Late Iron Age and Roman Essex,' *Britannia*, 37 (2006), pp. 189–212; Pitt's 'Reconsidering Britain's first urban communities,' *Journal of Roman Archaeology*, 27 (2014), pp. 133–73.
7. H. Mattingly (ed.), *Tacitus on Britain and Germany* (London, 1948), p. 72.
8. H. Rayer, 'Are "Small Towns" Always Towns? A Classification of Roman Civil Settlements in Northern Britain,' in *International Journal of Student Research in Archaeology*, 1 (2016).
9. R. Reece, 'Town and Country: the end of Roman Britain,' *World Archaeology*, 12 (1980), pp. 77–92.
10. J. Gerrard, *The Ruin of Roman Britain: An Archaeological Perspective* (Cambridge, 2013). For a different view, R. Fleming, *Britain After Rome: The Fall and Rise, 400–1070* (London, 2010).
11. R. Fleming, *The Material Fall of Roman Britain, 300–525 CE* (Philadelphia, Penn., 2021).
12. Fleming, *Britain After Rome: The Fall and Rise, 400–1070* (London, 2010).
13. S.T. Loseby, 'Power and Towns in late Roman Britain and early Anglo-Saxon England,' in G. Ripoll and J.M. Gurt (eds), *Sedes Regiae, ann. 400–800* (Barcelona, 2000), 319–70, esp. 362–3.

14. J. Blair, *The Church in Anglo-Saxon England* (Oxford, 2005) and *Building Anglo-Saxon England* (Princeton, NJ, 2018), pp. 350–3.
15. A. Rumble, *Property and Piety in Early Medieval Winchester. Documents relating to the Topography of the Anglo-Saxon and Norman City and its Ministers* (Oxford, 2002).
16. D. Keene, *Survey of Medieval Winchester* (Oxford, 1985); A. Simms and H.E. Clarke (eds), *Lords and Towns in Medieval Europe: The European Historic Towns Atlas Project* (Farnham, 2015).
17. M. Camacho and others, 'Recovering parasites from mummies and coprolites,' *Parasites and Vectors*, 11 (2018), p. 248.
18. B. Yorke, 'Dorchester and the Early Shire Centres of Wessex,' *Proceedings of the Dorset Natural History and Archaeological Society*, 134 (2013), pp. 106–12.
19. Blair, *Building*, pp. 164–74, 254–6.
20. C. Scull, 'Urban centres in pre-Viking England,' in J. Hines (ed.), *The Anglo-Saxons from the Migration Period to the Eighth Century* (Woodbridge, 1997), pp. 269–310, and 'The Buttermarket Cemetery and the Origins of Ipswich in the Seventh Century AD,' *Proceedings of the Suffolk Institute of Archaeology and History*, 43 (2013), pp. 1–9; Fleming, *Britain After Rome*, pp. 31–8.
21. P. Sawyer, *The Wealth of Anglo-Saxon England* (Oxford, 2013).
22. R. Naismith, *Money and Power in Anglo-Saxon England: The Southern English Kingdoms, 757–865* (Cambridge, 2012).
23. S. Bassett, 'Divide and Rule: The Military Infrastructure of Eighth- and Ninth-Century Mercia,' *Early Medieval Europe*, 15 (2007), pp. 53–85.
24. D. Hill and A. Rumble (eds), *The Defence of Wessex. The Burghal Hidage and Anglo-Saxon Fortifications* (Manchester, 1996); J. Baker and S. Brookes, *Beyond the Burghal Hidage: Anglo-Saxon Civil Defence in the Viking Age* (Leiden, 2013).
25. J. Blair, *Building Anglo-Saxon England* (Princeton, NJ, 2018).
26. Blair, *Building*, pp. 243–6; A. Hood, with contributions from J. Blair and P. Blinkhorn, 'Excavations at St Georges Road, Wallingford: Evidence for a Complex Sequence of Defences near to the West Gate of the Late Anglo-Saxon Burh,' *Oxoniensia*, 88 (2023), pp. 323–42, at p. 336.
27. S. Bassett, 'The Middle and Late Anglo-Saxon Defences of West Mercian Towns,' *Anglo-Saxon Studies in Archaeology and History*, 15 (2008), pp. 180–239.
28. M. Biddle and D. Hill, 'Late Saxon Planned Towns,' *Antiquaries Journal*, 51 (1971), pp. 70–85.
29. F. Barlow, *Edward the Confessor* (London, 1970), pp. 54–7.
30. J. Paletta, 'English Towns and Urban Society after the Norman Conquest,' *Anglo-Norman Studies*, 38 (2016), pp. 125–40; D. Palliser, *Domesday York* (1990).
31. J. Munby, 'The Domesday Boroughs Revised,' *Anglo-Norman Studies*, 33 (2010), pp. 127–50.
32. H.L. Turner, *Town Defences in England and Wales. An Architectural and Documentary Study, AD 900–1500* (London, 1971), pp. 104–9.
33. D. Rollason et al (eds), *Anglo-Norman Durham: 1093–1193* (Woodbridge, 1994); R. Eales and R. Sharpe (eds), *Canterbury and the Norman Conquest: Churches, Saints and Scholars, 1066–1109* (London, 1995).
34. R. Pinter, *The Cult of St Edmund in Medieval East Anglia* (Woodbridge, 2015).
35. P. Nightingale, *A Medieval Mercantile Community: The Grocers' Company and the Politics and Trade of London, 1000–1485* (New Haven, Conn., 1995).

36. G. Rosser, *The Art of Solidarity in the Middle Ages: Guilds in England 1250–1550* (2015).
37. J.S. Bothwell, 'Making the Lancastrian Capital at Leicester: The Battle of Boroughbridge, Civic Diplomacy and Seigneurial Building Projects in Fourteenth-Century England,' *Journal of Medieval History*, 38 (2012), pp. 335–57.
38. S.R. Jones, *York: The Making of a City, 1068–1350* (Oxford, 2013).
39. C. West, 'Urban Populations and Associations,' in J. Crick and E. van Houts (eds), *A Social History of England, 900–1200* (Cambridge, 2011), pp. 198–207; H. Summerson, *Stamford and Magna Carta: The Start of the road to Runnymede* (Stamford, 2015).
40. C. Barron, *London in the Later Middle Ages: Government and People 1200–1500* (Oxford, 2004), pp. 298–9.
41. B. Hanawalt, *Ceremony and Civility: Civic Culture in Late Medieval London* (Oxford, 2017), 'Reading the Lives of the Illiterate: London's Poor,' *Speculum*, 80 (2005), pp. 1067–86, *The Wealth of Wives: Women, Law and Economy in Late Medieval London* (Oxford, 2007), and *Growing up in Medieval London: The Experience of Childhood in History* (Oxford, 1995).
42. Barron, *London*, pp. 148–51.
43. H. Summerson, 'Jews and felony in English communities and courts, 1190–1290,' *Jewish Historical Studies*, 52 (2021), pp. 70–117.
44. D. Butcher, *Medieval Lowestoft: The Origins and Growth of a Suffolk Coastal Community* (Woodbridge, 2016).
45. E. Rutledge, 'New Buckenham: The history of a market town,' lecture given to Norfolk Archaeological and Historical Research Group, 2018.
46. W. Smith, 'Wells 1201–2001: Eight Hundred Years of Royal Charters,' *Archives*, 26 (2001), pp. 149–71.
47. D. Defoe, *Tour*, 6.
48. M.R.G. Conzen, *Alnwick, Northumberland: A Study in Town Plan Analysis* (London, 1960).
49. J. Colson, 'Local Communities in fifteenth century London: Craft, parish and neighbourhood,' *Economic History Review*, 69 (2016), pp. 104–30.
50. P. Goodfellow, 'Medieval Markets in Northamptonshire,' *Northamptonshire Past and Present*, 7 (1987–8), p. 318; Summerson, 'Calamity and Commerce: The burning of Buxton Fair in 1288,' in Barron and A. Sutton (eds), 'The Medieval Merchant,' *Harlaxton Medieval Studies*, 24 (2014), pp. 146–65, at 148.
51. NA. King's Bench 27/18 rot. 12. I owe this reference to Henry Summerson.
52. M. Kowaleski, *Local Markets and Regional Trade in Medieval Exeter* (Cambridge, 1995).
53. Summerson, '"Most renowned of Merchants": The Life and Occupations of Laurence of Ludlow,' *Midland History*, 30 (2005), pp. 20–36.
54. R. Goddard, *Lordship and Medieval Urbanisation: Coventry, 1043–1355* (Woodbridge, 2004).
55. C. Hammer, 'Complaints of the lesser commune, oligarchic rule and baronial reform in thirteenth-century Oxford,' *Historical Research*, 85 (2012), pp. 353–71.
56. E. Hartrich, 'Urban Identity and Political Rebellion: London and Henry of Lancaster's Revolt, 1328–29,' *Fourteenth Century England*, 7 (2012), pp. 89–105.
57. J.R. Maddicott, *The Origins of the English Parliament, 924–1327* (Oxford, 2010).
58. Palliser, 'Thirteenth-century York – England's Second City?,' *York Historian*, 14 (1997).
59. E. Hartrich, *Politics and the Urban Sector in Fifteenth-Century England, 1413–1471* (Oxford, 2019).

60. R. Holt and G. Rosser (eds), *The Medieval Town: A Reader in English Urban History, 1200–1540* (London, 1990).
61. J. Wilson, 'The South Humberside Area Archive Office,' *Archives*, 22 (1997), p. 15.
62. C. Liddy, *Contesting the City: The Politics of Citizenship in English Towns, 1250–1530* (Oxford, 2017) and '"Sir ye be not king": Citizenship and Speech in Late Medieval and Early Modern England,' *Historical Journal*, 60 (2017), pp. 571–96.
63. Palliser (ed.), *The Cambridge Urban History of Britain, I, 600–1340* (Cambridge, 2000).
64. C. and M. Casson, 'Property rents in medieval English towns: Hull in the fourteenth century,' *Urban History*, 46, 3 (Sept. 2018), pp. 1–24.
65. A. Butcher, 'English Urban Society and the Revolt of 1381,' in R. Hilton and T. Alton (eds), *The English Rising of 1381* (Cambridge, 1987), pp. 84–111; S. Cohn, *Popular Protest in Late Medieval English Towns* (Cambridge, 2012); C. Barron, *Revolt in London 11th to 15th June 1381* (London, 1981).
66. C. Phythian-Adams, *Desolation of a City: Coventry and the Urban Crisis of the Later Middle Ages* (Cambridge, 1979); A. Kissane, *Civic Community in Late Medieval Lincoln: Urban Society and Economy in the Age of the Black Death, 1289–1409* (Woodbridge, 2017).
67. H.S. Cobb (ed.), *The Overseas Trade of London. Exchequer Customs Accounts, 1480–1* (London, 1990).
68. M. Forrest, 'Patterns of Economic Change in the South-West during the fifteenth century,' *Economic History Review*, 70 (2016), pp. 423–51.
69. For a different emphasis, G. Harriss, *Shaping the Nation: England 1360–1461* (Oxford, 2005), pp. 262–3.
70. J. Langton, 'Late medieval Gloucester: some data from a rental of 1455,' *Transactions of the Institute of British Geographers*, 2 (1977), pp. 259–77.
71. M. Kowaleski and P. Goldberg (eds), *Medieval Domesticity: Home, Housing and Household in Medieval England* (Cambridge, 2008).
72. J. Kermode, *Medieval Merchants: York, Beverley and Hull in the Later Middle Ages* (Cambridge, 1998); Palliser, *Medieval York: 600–1540* (Oxford, 2014).
73. S. Rose, *Southampton and the Navy in the Age of Henry V* (Winchester, 1998).
74. S.J. Drake, '"The Gallaunts of Fawey": A Case Study of Fowey during the Hundred Years' War, c.1337–1399,' *Historical Research*, 90 (2017), pp. 296–317.
75. J. Laughton, *Life in a Late Medieval City: Chester, 1275–1520* (Oxford, 2008).
76. R. Hilton, *Bond Men Made Free* (London, 1973), pp. 195–8; W.M. Ormrod, B. Lambert and J. Mackman, *Immigrant England, 1300–1550* (Manchester, 2019).
77. J. Thompson (ed.), *Towns and Townspeople in the Fifteenth Century* (Gloucester, 1998); E. Rutledge, 'An Urban Environment: Norwich in the Fifteenth Century,' *The Fifteenth Century*, 22 (2013), pp. 79–100.
78. D. Harry, *Constructing a Civic Community in Late Medieval London: The Common Profit, Charity and Commemoration* (Woodbridge, 2019).
79. C. Liddy, 'Urban Enclosure Riots. Risings of the Commons in English Towns, 1480–1525,' *Past and Present*, 226 (2015), pp. 41–77; P. Maddern, *Violence and Social Order: East Anglia, 1422–1442* (Oxford, 1992), pp. 175–205.
80. M.F. Stevens and R. Czaja (eds), *Towns on the Edge in Medieval Europe: The Social and Political Order of Peripheral Urban Communities from the Twelfth to Sixteenth Centuries* (Oxford, 2022).
81. M. Stoyle, *Water in the City. The Aqueducts and Underground Passages of Exeter* (Exeter, 2014).

82. C. Rawcliffe, *Urban Bodies: Communal Health in Late Medieval English Towns and Cities* (Woodbridge, 2013).
83. M. Pilkinton (ed.), *Bristol: Records of Early English Drama* (Toronto, 1997).
84. A. Watkins (ed.), *The Early Records of Coleshill: c.1120–1549* (Stratford-upon-Avon, 2018).
85. R.H. Hilton, *English and French Towns in Feudal Society: A Comparative Study* (Cambridge, 1995).
86. C. Liddy, *War, Politics and Finance in Late Medieval English Towns: Bristol, York and the Crown, 1350–1400* (Woodbridge, 2005).
87. P. Clark and L. Murfin, *The History of Maidstone. The Making of a Modern County Town* (Stroud, 1995); E. Hartrich, 'Charters and Inter-Urban Networks: England 1439–1449,' *English Historical Review*, 132 (2017), pp. 245, 248–9.
88. M.D. Lobel, 'The Value of Early Maps as Evidence for the Topography of English Towns,' *Imago Mundi*, 22 (1968), pp. 50–61.
89. L.T. Smith (ed.), *The Maire of Bristowe's Kalendar* by R. Ricart (London 1872).
90. E. Ralph, *Government of Bristol 1373–1973* (Bristol, 1973).
91. M. Macdonald (ed.), *The Register of the Guild of the Holy Cross, St Mary and St John the Baptist, Stratford-upon-Avon* (Stratford-upon-Avon, 2007).

Chapter 2
1. H.B. Wheatley and E.W. Ashbee (eds), *The Particular Description of England…*, by W. Smith (Hertford, 1879).
2. D. Smith, 'The Enduring Image of early British Townscapes,' *Cartographic Journal*, 28 (1991), pp. 163–75.
3. J.S. Lee, *Cambridge and its Economic Region, 1450–1560* (Hatfield, 2005).
4. J. Barry (ed.), *The Tudor and Stuart Town* (Harlow, 1990).
5. D. Palliser, *Tudor York* (Oxford, 1979).
6. R.O. Bucholz and J.P. Ward, *London: A Social and Cultural History, 1550–1750* (Cambridge, 2012).
7. C. Brett, 'Thomas Kytson and Somerset Clothmen, 1529–1539,' *Proceedings of the Somerset Archaeological and Natural History Society*, 143 (2001).
8. W.J. Petchey, *A Prospect of Maldon, 1500–1689* (Chelmsford, 1991).
9. H. Summerson, *Medieval Carlisle: The City and the Border from the late Eleventh to the Mid-Sixteenth Century* (2 vols, Kendal, 1993).
10. E. Roberts and K. Parker (eds), *Southampton Probate Inventories 1447–1575* (Southampton, 1992).
11. N. Holder, *The Friaries of Medieval London* (Woodbridge, 2017).
12. Palliser, *The Reformation in York, 1534–1553* (1971).
13. S.G. Doree (ed.), *The Early Churchwardens' Accounts of Bishops Stortford, 1431–1558* (Hertford, 1994).
14. C.J. Litzenberger (ed.), *Tewkesbury Churchwardens' Accounts, 1563–1624* (Gloucester, 1994).
15. J. Wilson, P. Howard and A. Hinckley, *Country and City: Wymondham, Norwich and Eaton in the 16th and 17th Centuries* (Norwich, 2006).
16. E. Phillips and I. Fay (eds), *Health and Hygiene in Early-Modern Norwich: Account Rolls of the Great Hospital, Norwich, 1549–50 and 1570–1* and *The Norwich River and Street Accounts, 1557–61 and 1570–80* (Norwich, 2013).
17. H. Turner, *The Corporate Commonwealth: Pluralism and Political Fictions in England, 1516–1651* (Chicago, Ill., 2016).

18. S. Brigden, *London and the Reformation* (Oxford, 1989); M. Stoyle, *A Murderous Midsummer. The Western Rising of 1549* (New Haven, Conn., 2022).
19. Barron, *London*, pp. 247–8.
20. J.E. Morgan, 'The Representation and Experience of English Urban Fire Disasters, c.1580–1640,' *Historical Research*, 89 (2016), pp. 268–93.
21. J. Lake, *The Great Fire of Nantwich* (Nantwich, 1983).
22. J. Barry and C. Brooks (eds), *The Middling Sort of People* (Basingstoke, 1994).
23. P. Clark and P. Slack (eds), *Crisis and Order in English Towns 1500–1700* (1972).
24. L. Fox (ed.), *Minutes and Accounts of the Corporation of Stratford-upon-Avon and Other Records* (Stratford-upon-Avon, 1990).
25. L.C. Orlin (ed.), *Material London, ca 1600* (Philadelphia, Penn., 2000), pp. 55–74, 193–225, 344–76.
26. J.F. Merritt, *The Social World of Early Modern Westminster: Abbey, Court and Community, 1525–1640* (Manchester, 20056).
27. D. Palliser, *The Age of Elizabeth: England under the Later Tudors, 1547–1603* (2nd edn, London, 1992), pp. 139–51; N. Goose, 'The Rise and Decline of Philanthropy in Early Modern Colchester: The unacceptable face of mercantilism,' *Social History*, 31 (2006), pp. 469–87.
28. C. Berry, *the Margins of Late Medieval London, 1430–1540* (London, 2022).
29. J. Webb (ed.), *The Town Finances of Elizabethan Ipswich. Select Treasurers' and Chamberlains' Accounts* (Bury St Edmunds, 1996).
30. I. Archer, 'Politics and Government 1540–1700,' in P. Clark (ed.), *The Cambridge Urban History of Britain II, 1540–1840* (Cambridge, 2000).

Chapter 3

1. Vernon to William Blathwayt, 4 May 1693, Beinecke, Osborn Shelves, Blathwayt Box 19.
2. D. Underdown, *Fire From Heaven: Life in an English Town in the Seventeenth Century* (1992).
3. Underdown, '"But the shows of their street": Civic pageantry and charivari in a Somerset town, 1607,' *Journal of British Studies*, 50 (2011), pp. 4–23.
4. C. Patterson, *Urban Government and the Early Stuart State: Provincial Towns, Corporate Liberties, and Royal Authority in England, 1603–1640* (Woodbridge, 2022).
5. C.D. Gilbert, 'Kidderminster at the Outbreak of the English Civil War,' *Transactions of the Worcestershire Archaeological Society*, 3rd ser. 11 (1988).
6. M. Atkin and W. Laughlin, *Gloucester and the Civil War* (Stroud, 1992); L. Haycock, *Devizes in the Civil War* (Devizes, 2000); P. Tennant, *The People's War in the South Midlands 1642–1645* (Stroud, 1992); R. Sherwood, *The Civil War in the Midlands, 1642–1651* (Stroud, 1992).
7. J. Topazio, 'The Impact of the Civil War on Reading,' *Southern History*, 36 (2014), pp. 1–28.
8. J. Barlow (ed.), *A Calendar of the Registers of Apprentices of the City of Gloucester 1595–1700* (Gloucester, 2001).
9. P. Knowlden, 'A Kent Market Town and the Great Rebellion: Bromley 1642–1660,' *Local Historian*, 38 (2008), pp. 122–31.
10. A. Hooper, '"The Great Blow" and the Politics of Popular Royalism in Civil War Norwich,' *English Historical Review*, 133 (2018), pp. 32–64.

11. J.F. Merritt, *Westminster, 1640–60: A Royal City in a Time of Revolution* (Manchester, 2013).
12. J. Barry, 'Civility and civic culture in early modern England: the meanings of urban freedom,' in A.P. Burke, B. Harrison and P. Slack (eds), *Civil Histories* (Oxford, 2000), pp. 181–96; J.B. Manterfield (ed.), *Borough Government in Newton's Grantham: The Hall Book of Grantham, 1649–1662* (Woodbridge, 2016).
13. W. Gibson, *Religion and the Enlightenment 1600–1800: Conflict and the Rise of Civic Humanism in Taunton* (Oxford, 2007).
14. T. Gray (ed.), *The Lost Chronicle of Barnstaple 1586–1611* (Exeter, 1998).
15. D. Smith, 'Inset town plans on large-scale maps of Great Britain,' *Cartographic Journal*, 29 (1992), pp. 118–36.
16. M. Thompson, *The Decline of the Castle* (Cambridge, 1987), pp. 179–85; R. Askew, 'Sheffield Castle and The Aftermath of the English Civil War,' *Northern History*, 52 (2017), pp. 189–210.
17. P. Drake, 'Captain John Chaffin of Sherborne,' *Notes and Queries for Somerset and Dorset*, 32, 325 (Mar. 1987), p. 578.
18. C. Stevenson, *The City and the King: Architecture and Politics in Restoration London* (New Haven, Conn., 2013).
19. M.J. Short, 'The Political Relationship between Central Government and the Local Administration in Yorkshire 1678–90' (DPhil., Leeds, 1999), p. 61.
20. I. Mason, 'The Government of Arundel, 1586–1677,' *Sussex Archaeological Collections*, 128 (1990).
21. W. Gibson, 'The Limits of the Confessional State: Electoral Religion in the Reign of Charles II,' *Historical Journal*, 51 (2008), pp. 27–47.
22. D. Roberts, 'Governing Winchester 1638–88: the politics of a seventeenth century corporation,' *Southern History*, 36 (2014), pp. 56–83.
23. J. Miller, 'Containing Division in Restoration Norwich,' *English Historical Review*, 121 (2006), pp. 1019–47.
24. G. Garrioch, '1666 and London's Fire History: A Re-Evaluation,' *Historical Journal*, 59 (2016), pp. 319–38.
25. M. Farr (ed.), *The Great Fire of Warwick, 1694* (Stratford-upon-Avon, 1992).
26. BL. Evelyn papers, vol. 49 f. 29.
27. J.H. Thomas, 'Devizes in the Eighteenth Century: The Evidence from Fire Insurance Records,' *Archives*, 30 (2005), p. 75–89.
28. S. Scott and C.J. Duncan, 'Smallpox epidemics at Penrith in the 17th and 18th centuries,' *Transactions of the Cumberland and Westmorland Antiquarian and Archaeological Society*, 93 (1993), p. 159.
29. A. Gooder, 'The population crisis of 1727–1730 in Warwickshire,' *Midland History*, 1 (1972), pp. 1–22.
30. A. Poole, *A Market Town and its Surrounding Villages: Cranbrook, Kent in the Later Seventeenth Century* (Chichester, 2005).
31. P. Borsay, *The English Urban Renaissance. Culture and Society in the Provincial Town, 1660–1770* (Oxford, 1991).
32. C. Davies, 'The Woolfes of Wine Street: Middling Culture and Community in Bristol, 1600–1620,' *English Historical Review*, 137 (2022), pp. 386–415.
33. F. Williamson, *Social Relations and Urban Space: Norwich 1600–1700* (Woodbridge, 2014).
34. S. Roberts (ed.), *Evesham Borough Records of the Seventeenth century, 1605–1687* (Worcester, 1994).

35. A. Wareham, 'The Unpopularity of the Hearth Tax and the Social Geography of London in 1666,' *Economic History Review*, 70 (2017), pp. 452–82.
36. R. Shoemaker, 'The London "Mob" in the Early Eighteenth Century,' *Journal of British Studies*, 26 (1987), p. 279.
37. J. Innes, *Inferior Politics: Social Problems and Social Policies in Eighteenth-Century Britain* (Oxford, 2009).
38. A. Leach, 'Being One Body: Everyday Institutional Culture in Canterbury and Maidstone Corporations, 1600–1660' (PhD., Kent, 2019).
39. J. Stobart and N. Raven (eds), *Towns, Regions and Industries: Urban and Industrial Change in the Midlands, c. 1700–1840* Cambridge, (2005).
40. D. Hey, *The Fiery Blades of Hallamshire, Sheffield and its Neighbourhood, 1660–1740* (Leicester, 1990).
41. J.W.F. Hill, *Tudor and Stuart Lincoln* (Cambridge, 1956). For a different perspective, J.A. Johnson (ed), *Probate Inventories of Lincoln Citizens 1661–1714* (Woodbridge, 1991).
42. G.A. Metters (ed.), *The King's Lynn Port Books, 1610–1614* (Norwich, 2009).
43. P. Nash, 'The Maritime Shipping Trade of Scarborough, 1550 to 1750,' *Northern History*, 49 (2012), pp. 202–22.
44. P. Lake and S. Pincus (eds), *The Politics of the Public Space in Early Modern England* (Manchester, 2007).
45. J. Smail, *The Origins of Middle-Class Culture: Halifax, Yorkshire, 1660–1780* (Ithaca, NY, 1994); J. Barry, 'Provincial Town Culture 1640–1780: urbane or civic?', in J.H. Pittock and A. Wear (eds), *Interpretation and Cultural History* (Basingstoke, 1991), pp. 198–234.
46. N. Smart, *The Royal Image and the English People* (Aldershot, 2001).
47. As argued by Alan Downie, *The Library*, 7th ser., 5 (2004), pp. 247–64.
48. Southwell to Michael Becher, 12 Feb. 1742, Bristol City Library, Southwell papers, vol. 7.
49. Mr Pye to Southwell, 14 Feb. 1742, *Ibid*.
50. Southwell to --, 15 Feb. 1742, *Ibid*.
51. John Tucker MP to his brother, Richard, Mayor of Weymouth, 10 Ap., and reply 12 Ap. 1742, Bod. MS. Don. c.105 f. 69, 72.
52. F. Grace, 'The governance of Ipswich c. 1550–1835,' in D. Allen, *Ipswich Borough Archives, 1255–1835: A Catalogue* (Woodbridge, 2000), pp. xxxx–xl.
53. Craggs to James, Viscount Stanhope, 27 Sept. 1720, NA. SP. 43/64.
54. P. Gauci, *The Politics of Trade: The Overseas Merchant in State and Society, 1660–1720* (Oxford, 2001).
55. P. Borsay and L. Proudfoot (eds), *Provincial Towns in Early Modern England and Ireland: Change, Convergence and Divergence* (Oxford, 2002).
56. BL. Evelyn papers, vol. 49 f. 36–7.
57. F. Poynter (ed.), *The Journal of James Yonge, Plymouth Surgeon* (London, 1963), p. 145.
58. Poynter (ed.), 'Extracts from Sussex Quarter Session Records, 1626–1800,' *Sussex History*, 32 (autumn 1991), pp. 38–41.
59. T. Hitchcock and H. Shore (eds), *The Streets of London: From the Great Fire to the Great Stink* (London, 2003).
60. S. Appleton and M. Macdonald (eds), *Stratford-upon-Avon Wills, 1348–1701* (Stratford-upon-Avon, 2020).
61. I. Warren, 'The English Landed Elite and the Social Environment of London c. 1580–1700: the Cradle of an Aristocratic Culture?,' *English Historical Review*, 126 (2011), pp. 44–74.

62. L. Davison et al (eds), *Stilling the Grumbling Hive. The Response to Social and Economic Problems in England, 1689–1750* (Stroud, 1992).
63. Borsay and Proudfoot (eds), *Provincial Towns*, p. 51.
64. S. Brown, '"A Just and Profitable Commerce": Moral Economy and the Middle Classes in Eighteenth-Century London,' *Journal of British Studies*, 32 (1993), p. 331.

Chapter 4
1. *London Chronicle*, 1 Jan. 1757.
2. R. Hyde, *A Prospect of Britain: The Town Panoramas of Samuel and Nathaniel Buck* (London, 1994).
3. M. Postlethwayt, *Universal Dictionary* (4th edn., 2 vols., London, 1774), I, i-ii.
4. W.A. Speck, *Literature and Society in Eighteenth-Century England. Ideology, Politics and Culture, 1680–1820* (1998).
5. Anon., *Reasons against building a bridge from Lambeth to Westminster* (London, 1722), p. 6.
6. N. Rogers, *Whigs and Cities. Popular Politics in the Age of Walpole and Pitt* (Oxford, 1989).
7. E. McKellar, *The Birth of Modern London. The Development and Design of the city 1660–1720* (Manchester, 1999).
8. P. Earle, *The Making of the English Middle Class: Business, Society and Family Life in London, 1660–1730* (London, 1989).
9. *Tour*, 9.
10. B. Trinder, *The Industrial Revolution in Shropshire* (3rd ed., Chichester, 2000), p. 27.
11. E. Saunders, *Joseph Pickford and Derby. A Georgian Architect* (Stroud, 1993).
12. P.D. Halliday, *Dismembering the Body Politic: Partisan Politics in England's Towns 1650–1730* (Cambridge, 1998).
13. Lincoln, Lincolnshire CRO., Massingberd Deposit, Mass/13/14; *Weekly Journal: or the British Gazetteer*, 31 Jan. 1730; BL. Add. 32689 f. 241.
14. D. Richardson and M.M. Schofield, 'Whitehaven and the Eighteenth-Century British Slave Trade,' *Transactions of the Cumberland and Westmorland Antiquarian and Archaeological Society*, 102 (1992), pp. 183–204, esp. 195.
15. M.D. Mitchell, 'Three English Cloth Towns and the Royal African Company,' *Journal of the Historical Society*, 13 (2013), pp. 447.
16. B. Purdue, 'Newcastle in the long eighteenth century,' *Northern History*, 50 (2013), pp. 272–84.
17. Browne to his father, 6 Aug. 1757, BL. RP. 3284.
18. L.D. Schwarz, *London in the Age of Industrialisation: Entrepreneurs, Labour Force and Living Conditions, 1700–1850* (Cambridge, 1992).
19. P. Borsay, *The English Urban Renaissance. Culture and Society in the Provincial Town, 1660–1770* (Oxford, 1991); J. Hinks and C. Armstrong (eds), *The English Urban Renaissance Revisited* (Cambridge, 2018).
20. Kendal, Westmorland CRO, WD/L.
21. J. Stobbart, 'Regional Structure and the Urban System: North West England, 1600–1760,' *Transactions of the Historic Society of Lancashire and Cheshire*, 145 (1996), pp. 45–73.
22. D. Hey, *The Fiery Blades of Hallamshire: Sheffield and Its Neighbourhood, 1660–1740* (Leicester, 1992).
23. Harley to Stepney, 10 Nov. 1704, BL. Add. 7059 f. 45.

24. B. Harris, 'Praising the middling sort? Social identity in eighteenth-century British newspapers,' in A. Kidd and D. Nicholls (eds), *The Making of the British Middle Class? Studies of Regional and Cultural Diversity* (Stroud, 1998), pp. 1–18; H. Wellenreuther, 'The political role of the Nobility in eighteenth-century England,' in J. Canning and Wellenreuther (eds), *Britain and Germany Compared: Nationality, Society and Nobility in the Eighteenth Century* (Göttingen, 2001), pp. 99–139.
25. P.J. Corfield, *The Impact of English Towns 1700–1800* (Oxford, 1982).
26. T.W. Perry, *Public Opinion, Propaganda, and Politics in Eighteenth-Century England: A Study of the Jew Bill of 1753* (Cambridge, Mass., 1962).
27. Lorimer to Sir Ludovick Grant, 11 May 1754, Edinburgh, Scottish Record Office, GD. 248/182/1/41.
28. C. Horner (ed.), *The Diary of Edmund Harrold, 1712–25* (Aldershot, 2008).
29. Hampden to George Grenville, 24 Aug. 1767, HL, Stowe Papers, STG. Box 22 (39).
30. Preston, Lancashire CRO., DDPR 131/7.
31. J. Fewster (ed.), *Morpeth Electoral Correspondence, 1766–1777* (Newcastle, 2017).
32. Bod. Ms. Don. B. 209 f. 5, 11.
33. William Buck to Thomas, Earl of Malton, 24 Jan. 1742, Sheffield City Archives, Wentworth Muniments, WWM/M1.
34. *Universal Spectator*, 6 Feb. 1742.
35. *Craftsman*, 8 July 1727.
36. N.E. Key, 'The Political Culture and Political Rhetoric of County Feasts and Feast Sermons, 1654–1714,' *Journal of British Studies*, 33 (1994), pp. 223–56.
37. J. Barry, 'Provincial Town Culture 1640–1780: Urbane or Civic,' in J. Pittock and A. Wear (eds), *Interpretation and Cultural History* (Basingstoke, 1991), pp. 198–235.
38. R. Sweet, *The Writing of Urban History in Eighteenth-Century England* (Oxford, 1997).
39. R. Tittler, *The Face of the City: Civic Portraiture and Civic Identity in Early Modern England* (Manchester, 2007).
40. P. Gauci, *Politics and Society in Great Yarmouth, 1660–1722* (Oxford, 1990).
41. Diary of Dudley Ryder, Sandon Park, papers of the Earls of Harrowby. I am most grateful to the last Earl of Harrowby for permission to consult these papers.

Chapter 5
1. T.A. Berg (eds), *R.R. Angerstein's Illustrated Travel Diary 1753–1755: Industry in England and Wales from a Swedish Perspective* (Stockholm, 2001); G. Gurtler, 'Impressionen einer Reise. Das England-Itineraire des Grafen Karl von Zinzendorf 1768,' *Mitteilungen des Instituts für Osterreichische Geschichtsforschung* (1985), pp. 33–69; N. Scarfe, *Innocent Espionage. The La Rochefoucauld Brothers Tour of England in 1785* (Woodbridge, 1995); A. Ableitinger and M. Brunner (eds), *Erzherzog Johann von Osterreich ... England-Reise* (Graz, 2010).
2. T. Pennant, *A Tour in Scotland, 1769* (4th edn, London, 1776), pp. 3, 7–8.
3. L. Haycock, '"In the Newest Manner": Social Life in Late Georgian Devizes,' *Wiltshire Archaeological and Natural History Magazine*, 97 (2004), pp. 1–14.
4. Shelburne to John Eardley Wilmot, 8 Aug. 1791, Beinecke, Osborn Shelves, Eardley-Wilmot Boxes.
5. C. Estabrook, *Urban and Rustic England: Cultural Ties and Social Spheres in the Provinces, 1660–1780* (Manchester, 1999).

6. P. Borsay and L. Proudfoot (eds), *Provincial Towns in Early Modern England and Ireland: Change, Convergence, and Divergence* (Oxford, 2002).
7. T. Gray (ed.), *The Exeter Cloth Dispatch Book* (Woodbridge, 2021).
8. J. Fiske, *The Oakes Diaries. I. Business, Politics and the Family in Bury St Edmunds, 1778–1800* (Woodbridge, 1990).
9. Richard Goodwin to William Fitzherbert, 20 Jan. 1750, Matlock, Derbyshire CRO. 239 M F 820.
10. S. Szreter and G. Mooney, 'Urbanization, mortality, and the standard of living debate: new estimates of the expectation of life at birth in nineteenth century British cities,' *Economic History Review*, 51 (1998), pp. 84–112; R.A. Bellingham, 'Dade Registers,' *Archives*, 27 (2002), pp. 134–47.
11. A. Levene, *The Childhood of the Poor: Welfare in Eighteenth-Century London* (Basingstoke, 2012).
12. S. Poole and N. Rogers, *Bristol from Below: Law, Authority and Protest in a Georgian City* (Woodbridge, 2017).
13. A. Tomkins, *The Experience of Urban Poverty, 1723–1782: Parish, Charity and Credit* (Manchester, 2006).
14. S. Avery-Quash and K. Retford (eds), *The Georgian London Town House: Building, Collecting and Display* (London, 2019).
15. Phelps to Thomas Horner, 6 Aug. 1775, *Notes and Queries For Somerset and Dorset*, 33 (1992), p. 113.
16. E. Saunders, *Joseph Pickford and Derby. A Georgian Architect* (Stroud, 1993); A. White, *The Buildings of Georgian Lancaster* (Lancaster, 1992).
17. *St James's Chronicle*, 23 Jan. 1766.
18. I. Mackintosh and G. Ashton (eds), *The Georgian Playhouse: Actors, Artists, Audiences and Architecture, 1730–1830* (London, 1975).
19. Named in honour of Queen Caroline, George II's wife.
20. R.S. Neal, *Bath: A Social History 1680–1850: Or a Valley of Pleasure, yet a Sink of Iniquity* (London, 1981).
21. P. Borsay, 'Image and counter-image in Georgian Bath,' *British Journal for Eighteenth-Century Studies*, 17 (1994), pp. 165–79.
22. Charles, Viscount Dungarvan to – Quick, 25 Jan. 1755, Exeter, Devon CRO. 64/12/29/1/121.
23. T. Fawcett, *Music in Eighteenth-Century Norwich and Norfolk* (Norwich, 1979).
24. E. Jaggard, 'James Boswell's Journey through Cornwall, August-September 1792,' *Journal of the Royal Institution of Cornwall* (2004), p. 29.
25. M. Burkett and D. Sloss, *Read's Point of View. Paintings of the Cumbrian Countryside* (Bowness, 1995); *Manchester Mercury*, 1 June 1756; N. Surry, 'Artistic Developments in Portsmouth and Plymouth, 1740–1830,' *Hatcher Review*, 40 (1995), p. 36 and 'Art and Opportunity: Artists and their Clients in Late Georgian Hampshire,' *Ibid.*, 37 (1994), p. 34.
26. J. Stovold, *Minute Book of the Pavement Commissioners for Southampton, 1770–1789* (Southampton, 1990).
27. P. Kaufman, *Libraries and Their Users* (London, 1969); M.K. Flavell, 'The Enlightened Reader and the New Industrial Towns: A Study of the Liverpool Library, 1758–1790,' *British Journal for Eighteenth-Century Studies*, 8 (1985), pp. 17–35; P. Sturges, 'The Place of Libraries in the English Urban Renaissance of the Eighteenth Century,' *Library and Culture*, 24 (1989), pp. 57–68.

28. J. Barry and G. Tatham, 'Robert Gadby, the *Sherborne Mercury* and the Urban Renaissance in South-West England,' in J. Hinks and C. Armstrong (eds), *The English Urban Renaissance Revisited* (Cambridge, 2018), pp. 57–95.
29. See also, eg. *Newark Journal*, 5 Oct. 1791.
30. See also, eg. *Salisbury and Winchester Journal*, 23 Feb. 1789.
31. C.Y. Ferdinand, *Benjamin Collins and the Provincial Newspaper Trade in the Eighteenth Century* (Oxford, 1997).
32. J.S. Holt, ed., *The Diary of Thomas Fenwick* (4 vols, London, 2011–12).
33. R.M. Wiles, *Freshest Advices: Early Provincial Newspapers in England* (Columbus, Ohio, 1969), pp. 29–30; G.A. Cranfield, *The Development of the Provincial Newspaper, 1700–1760* (Oxford, 1960); I. Maxted, 'Printing, the Book Trade and Newspapers c. 1500–1860,' in R. Kain and W. Ravenhill, eds, *Historical Atlas of South-West England* (Exeter, 1999), pp. 242–5; M.E. Knapp, 'Reading the *Salisbury Journal*, 1736–99,' *Yale University Journal*, 56, 3–4 (April 1982), p. 13. For the situation in France, J. Sgard, ed., *La Presse Provinciale au xviiie Siècle* (Grenoble, 1983); G. Feyel, 'La presse provincial au XVIIIe siècle: géographie d'un réseau,' *Revue Historique*, 272 (1984), pp. 353–74.
34. C.J. Griffin, 'Knowable geographies? The reporting of incendiarism in the eighteenth- and early nineteenth-century English provincial press,' *Journal of Historical Geography*, 32 (2006), pp. 38–56, and '"Cut down by some cowardly miscreants": Plant Maiming, or the Malicious Cutting of Flora, as an Act of Protest in Eighteenth- and Nineteenth-Century Rural England,' *Rural History*, 19 (2008), p. 47.
35. Anon., *Two Very Singular Addresses* (London, 1757), pp. 3–6.
36. J. Styles, 'Print and Policing. Crime Advertising in Eighteenth-Century Provincial England,' in D. Hay and F. Snyder, eds, *Policing and Prosecution in Britain 1750–1850* (Oxford, 1989), pp. 55–111.
37. S.E. Whyman, *The Useful Knowledge of William Hutton: Culture and Industry in Eighteenth-Century Birmingham* (Oxford, 2018).
38. G. Clark (ed.), *Correspondence of the Foundling Hospital Inspection in Berkshire 1757–68* (Reading, 1994).
39. J. Carré (ed.), *Journal d'Observations sur les Principaux Hôpitaux et sur quelques Prisons d'Angleterre, 1787* by J. Tenon (Clermont-Ferrand, 1992).
40. Elizabeth Montagu to George Lyttleton, 23 Sept. 1762, HL. MO. 1420.
41. Montagu to William, Earl of Bath, 23 Oct. 1762, HL. MO. 4592.
42. Lyttelton to Montagu, 14 May 1763, HL. MO. 1306.
43. S. Wright (ed.), *Parish, Church and People: Local Studies in Lay Religion 1350–1750* (London, 1988); H.T. Dickinson, 'Radicals and Reformers in the Age of Wilkes and Wyvill,' in J. Black (ed.), *British Politics and Society from Walpole to Pitt 1742–1789* (Basingstoke, 1990), pp. 123–4; J. Barry, 'The press and the politics of culture in Bristol, 1660–1775,' in J. Black and J. Gregory (eds), *Culture, Politics and Society in Britain, 1660–1800* (Manchester, 1991), pp. 49–81.
44. J.A. Phillips, 'From Municipal Matters to Parliamentary Principles: Eighteenth-Century Borough Politics in Maidstone,' *Journal of British Studies*, 27 (1988), pp. 327–51.
45. M. Fissell, *Patients, Power and the Poor in Eighteenth-Century Bristol* (Cambridge, 1992).
46. *Westminster Journal*, 19 June 1773, 9, 16 Ap. 1774.
47. D. Whitehead, 'The Georgian churches of Worcester,' *Transactions of the Worcestershire Archaeological Society*, 3rd ser., 13 (1992), p. 211.

48. P. Borsay, 'Gentry Papers: A Key Source for Urban Cultural History,' *Archives*, 19 (1991), pp. 376–7.
49. Francis, Marquess of Carmarthen, Foreign Secretary, to Keith, 26 Oct., 2 Nov. 1784, NA. FO. 7/9; Lansdowne to Keith, 24 June 1785, BL. Add. 35534 f. 245.
50. Eden to Carmarthen, 3 Oct. 1786, NA. FO. 27/20 f. 215.
51. Eden to Carmarthen, 3 Oct. 1786, 16 Dec. 1788, Yonge to Fraser, Under Secretary, 25 Jan. 1789, NA. FO. 27/20 f. 215, 72/13, 14.
52. I am most grateful to David Stewart for this information and for discussing the subject with me.
53. J. Smail, *The Origins of Middle-Class Culture: Halifax, Yorkshire, 1660–1780* (1994); A. Wilson, 'Conflict, Consensus and Charity: Politics and the Provincial Voluntary Hospitals in the Eighteenth Century,' *English Historical Review*, 111 (1996).

Chapter 6
1. E. Hopkins, *Birmingham: The First Manufacturing Town in the World, 1760–1840* (London, 1989); S. Whyman, *The Useful Knowledge of William Hutton: Culture and Industry in Eighteenth-Century Birmingham* (Oxford, 2018).
2. *Emma*, book 2, chapter 18.
3. H.I. Dutton and J.G. King, '"A Fallacy, A Delusion, and a Snare": arbitration and conciliation in the Preston strike, 1853–4,' *Transactions of the Historic Society of Lancashire and Cheshire*, 131 (1981), p. 65.
4. J. Taylor, '"Set Down in a Large Manufacturing Town." Sojourning Poor in Early Nineteenth Century Manchester,' *Manchester Region History Review*, 3, 2 (autumn/winter 1989–90), pp. 3–8.
5. D. Hey, 'The South Yorkshire steel industry and the Industrial Revolution,' *Northern History*, 42 (2005), pp. 91–6.
6. T. Koditschek, *Class Formation and Urban Industrial Society, Bradford 1750–1850* (Cambridge, 1990).
7. Addington to the Duke of Wellington, 21 Mar. 1820, Exeter, Devon CRO. 152 M/C 1820/OH 68.
8. *Mansfield Park*, book III, chapter 7.
9. M. Brown, 'From Foetid Air to Filth: The Cultural Transformation of British Epidemiological Thought, c.1780–1848,' *Bulletin of the History of Medicine*, 82 (2008), pp. 515–44.
10. H. Marland, *Medicine and Society in Wakefield and Huddersfield 1780–1870* (Cambridge, 1987), pp. 4–51.
11. *Durham 1849: Public Health Act, Report to the General Board of Health on Durham, 1849* (Durham, 1997); R. Woods and N. Shelton, *An Atlas of Victorian Mortality* (Liverpool, 1997).
12. J.V. Beckett, 'Politics and the Implementation of the New Poor Law: The Nottingham Workhouse Controversy, 1834–54,' *Midland History*, 41 (2016), pp. 201–23.
13. D. Fowler, 'Reading and Writing in Warwickshire, 1780s-1830s,' *Warwickshire History*, 16 (winter 1999–2000).
14. P. Brett, 'Early Nineteenth-Century Reform Newspapers in the Provinces: the *Newcastle Chronicle* and the *Bristol Mercury*,' in M. Harris and T. O'Malley (eds), *Studies in Newspaper and Periodical History, 1995 Annual* (Westport, Conn., 1997).

15. R. Gaunt, 'Nottinghamshire and the Great Peace: Reflections on the End of the Napoleonic Wars, 1814–1815,' *Midland History*, 41 (2016), pp. 20–36.
16. V. Gatrell, *Conspiracy on Cato Street: A Tale of Liberty and Revolution in Regency London* (Cambridge, 2022).
17. R. Gaunt, 'The Newcastle Diaries,' *Archives*, 28 (2003).
18. H. Barker and D. Vincent, *Language, Print and Electoral Politics, 1790–1832. Newcastle-Under-Lyme Broadsides* (Woodbridge, 2001).
19. E. Jaggard, *Cornwall Politics in the Age of Reform 1790–1885* (Woodbridge, 1999).
20. M. Goffin (ed.), *The Diaries of Absalom Watkin. A Manchester Man 1798–1861* (Stroud, 1993).
21. B.G. Awty, 'The Introduction of Gas-Lighting to Preston,' *Transactions of the Historical Society of Lancashire and Cheshire*, 125 (1975), pp. 82–118.
22. T. Koditschek, *Class Formation and Urban Industrial Society, Bradford 1750–1850* (Cambridge, 1990).
23. T.C.B. Timmins (ed.), *Suffolk Returns for the Census of Religious Worship in 1851* (Ipswich, 1997).
24. L. Darwen et al '"Unhappy and Wretched Creatures": Charity, Poor Relief and Pauper Removal in Britain and Ireland during the Great Famine,' *English Historical Review*, 134 (2019), pp. 620–45.

Chapter 7

1. A. Briggs, *Victorian Cities* (London, 1963).
2. S. Bunker, *Strawopolis: Luton Transformed 1840–1876* (Bedford, 1999).
3. J.E. Archer, *The Monster Evil: Policing and Violence in Victorian Liverpool* (Liverpool, 2011).
4. D. Cannadine, *Lords and Landlords: The Aristocracy and the Towns, 1774–1967* (Leicester, 1980).
5. Z. Samalin, *The Masses are Revolting: Victorian Culture and the Political Aesthetics of Disgust* (Ithaca, NY, 2021).
6. N. Williams and C. Galley, 'Urban-rural differentials in infant mortality in Victorian England,' *Population Studies* (1995), pp. 401–20.
7. D. Hughes, 'Liverpool Infant Mortality Rates, c.1865–1874: A City Maligned,' *Lancashire Local Historian*, 6 (1991), pp. 32–43; K. Davis, 'Maternal Mismanagement or Environmental Factors? High Rates of Infant Mortality in Middlesborough, 1890–1913,' *Cleveland History*, 62 (1992), pp. 40–60.
8. C. French, '"Death in Kingston Upon Thames": Analysis of the Bonner Hill Cemetery Burial Records, 1855–1911,' *Archives*, 28 (2003), p. 423.
9. D. Pam, *A History of Enfield, II, 1837 to 1914. A Victorian Suburb* (Enfield, 1992).
10. J.G. Williamson, *Coping with City Growth During the British Industrial Revolution* (Cambridge, 1990).
11. O. Betts, 'Working-Class Homes in three Urban Communities 1870–1914' (PhD., York, 2014); J. Harley, V. Holmes and L. Nevalainen, (eds.) *The Working Class at Home, 1790–1940* (Basingstoke, 2022).
12. V. Holmes, 'Accommodating the lodger: the domestic arrangements of lodgers in working-class dwellings in a Victorian provincial town,' *Journal of Victorian Culture*, 19 (2014), pp. 314–31.
13. J.A. Hargreaves, 'The Church of England in late-Victorian Halifax,' *Transactions of the Halifax Antiquarian Society* (1991), pp. 27–60.

14. J.A. Vickers, *The Religious Census of Sussex 1851* (Brighton, 1989).
15. R.L. Greenall, 'Ancient Church: Urban Parish, St Peter's Northampton in the nineteenth century,' *Northamptonshire Past and Present*, 9 (1997–8), pp. 377–83.
16. F. Grace, *Rags and Bones. A Social History of a Working-Class Community in Nineteenth-Century Ipswich* (2005).
17. G. Rimmington, 'Congregationalism and Society in Leicester, 1872–1914,' *Local Historian*, 37 (2007), pp. 29–44.
18. K. Butler, *Drink Maps in Victorian Britain* (Oxford, 2024).
19. A. Taylor, '"A melancholy odyssey among London public houses": radical club life and the unrespectable in mid-nineteenth-century London,' *Historical Research*, 78 (2005), pp. 74–95.
20. A.L. Beier, 'Identity, Language and Resistance in the Making of the Victorian "Criminal Class": Mayhew's Convict Revisited,' *Journal of British Studies*, 44 (2005), p 515.
21. BL. Add. 41410 f. 4.
22. A. Nofi, 'Profile-Defending London, 1858–1870,' *Al Nofi's Combat Information Center*, no. 342 (April 2011), https://www.strategypage.com/cic/docs/cic3426.asp.
23. R.W. Hoyle, 'The Enclosure of Preston Moor and the Creation of Moor Park in Preston,' *Northern History*, 49 (2012), pp. 281–302.
24. B. Assael, *The London Restaurant, 1840–1914* (Oxford, 2018).
25. D. Fraser, *Power and Authority in the Victorian City* (Oxford, 1979).
26. J. Sheil, 'Local Legislation: Its Scope and Context,' *Archives*, 30 (2005), pp. 36–50.
27. M. Roberts, 'Constructing a Tory World-View: Popular Politics and the Conservative Press in Late-Victorian Leeds,' *Historical Research*, 79 (2006).
28. M. Brodie, *Neighbours, District and the State: What the Poorer Working Class in Britain Felt about Government and Each Other, 1860s to 1930s* (Oxford, 2022), T. Kilburn, 'Drinking, Gambling, and Illegal Leisure Activities in late-Victorian West Bromwich,' *Staffordshire History*, 12 (autumn, 1990), pp. 34–51.
29. G.K. Horridge, '"Invading Manchester." Responses to the Salvation Army, 1878–1900,' *Manchester Region History Review*, 6 (1992), pp. 40–44.
30. S. Banfield, *Music in the West Country: Social and Cultural History Across an English Region* (Woodbridge, 2018).
31. W. Lubenow, *'Only Connect.' Learned Societies in Nineteenth-Century Britain* (Woodbridge, 2015).
32. W. Whyte, *Redbrick: A Social and Architectural History of Britain's Civic Universities* (Oxford, 2015), pp. 72, 96–7.
33. A. Rodrick, *Self-Help and Civic Culture: Citizenship in Victorian Birmingham* (2004).
34. T.L. Richardson, *Historic Sandwich and its Region, 1500–1900* (Sandwich, 2006).
35. J. Black and D. MacRaild (eds), *Nineteenth-Century Britain* (Basingstoke, 2003), p. 78.
36. F.M.L. Thompson (eds), *The Cambridge Social History of Britain 1750–1950* (Cambridge, 1992).
37. P. Gooderson, '"Noisy and Dangerous Boys": The Slogging Gang Phenomenon in Late Nineteenth-Century Birmingham,' *Midland History*, 38 (2013), pp. 58–79.
38. S. Mosley, *The Chimney of the World: A History of Smoke Pollution in Victorian and Edwardian Manchester* (Cambridge, 2001).
39. C. Dickens, *Edwin Drood*, chapter 12.
40. B. Stoker, *Dracula*, chapter 16.

Chapter 8

1. N. Millea, *Street Mapping: An A to Z of Urban Cartography* (Oxford, 2003), no. 24.
2. I. Gazeley and A. Newell, 'Urban working-class food consumption and nutrition in Britain in 1904,' *Economic History Review*, 68 (2015), pp. 101–22.
3. J. Hobson, *The Psychology of Jingoism* (London, 1901), p. 8.
4. A. Witchard, *Thomas Burke's Dark Chinoiserie* (Farnham, 2009).
5. S. Bilston, *The Promise of the Suburbs: A Victorian History in Literature and Culture* (New Haven, Conn., 2019).
6. M. Woods, 'Performing power: local politics and the Taunton pageant of 1928,' *Journal of Historical Geography*, 25 (1999), pp. 57–74; T. Hulme, '"A nation of town criers": civic publicity and historical pageantry in interwar Britain,' *Urban History*, 44 (2017), pp. 280–90.
7. B. Doyle, 'the structure of elite power in the early twentieth-century city: Norwich 1900–1935,' *Urban History*, 24 (1997), pp. 179–99, esp. 198.
8. F. Knight, *Ebenezer Howard: Inventor of the Garden City* (Oxford, 2023).
9. P. Scott, *The Making of the Modern British Home: The Suburban Semi and Family Life between the Wars* (Oxford, 2013).
10. P. Scott, *The Market Makers: Creating Mass Markets for Consumer Durables in Inter-war Britain* (Oxford, 2017); D.S. Ryan, *Ideal Homes, 1918–39: Domestic Design and Suburban Modernism* (Manchester, 2018).
11. N. Blacklaws, '"Old" and "New" Welfare: The Poor Law and Social Housing in Leicestershire, c.1925–1929,' *Midland History*, 43 (2018), pp. 82–96 and P. Broxholme, 'Back to the future? The Tory party, paternalism, and housing policy in Nottingham 1919–1932,' *Ibid.*, 38 (2013), pp. 99–118.
12. A.J. Arnold, 'Dependency, Debt and Shipbuilding in "Palmer's Town",' *Northern History*, 49 (2012), pp. 99–118.
13. C. Wildman, *Urban Redevelopment and Modernity in Liverpool and Manchester, 1918–1939* (London, 2016).
14. I. Gazeley and others, 'How hungry were the poor in late 1930s Britain?,' *Economic History Review*, 75 (29021), pp. 80–110.
15. R. Bean, 'Police Unrest, Unionisation and the 1919 Strike in Liverpool,' *Journal of Contemporary History*, 15 (1980), pp. 633–53.
16. J. Welshman, 'Evacuation, Hygiene, and Social Policy: The *Our Towns* Report of 1943,' *Historical Journal*, 42 (1999), pp. 781–807.
17. P. Larkham and K. Lilley, *Planning the 'City of Tomorrow': British Reconstruction Planning, 1939–1952: An Annotated Bibliography* (Pickering, 2001).

Chapter 9

1. P. Virdee, *Coming to Coventry: stories from the South Asian Pioneers* (Coventry, 2006).
2. S. Ward, *The Peaceful Path: Building Garden Cities and New Towns* (Hatfield, 2016).
3. I. Waites, 'Middlefield: The Development of a Provincial Post-World War Two Council Estate in Lincolnshire, 1960–1965,' *Midland History*, 40 (2015), pp. 264–85.
4. P. Shapely, *The Politics of Housing: Power, Consumers and Urban Culture* (Manchester, 2007).
5. O.S. Smith, 'Central Government and Town-Centre Redevelopment in Britain, 1959–1966,' *Historical Journal*, 58 (2015), pp. 217–44, and *Boom Cities: Architect Planners and the Politics of Radical Urban Renewal in 1960s Britain* (Oxford, 2019).

6. A. Fergusson, *The Sack of Bath: A Record and an Indictment* (Compton Chamberlayne, 1973), A Kefford, *The Life and Death of the Shopping City: Public Planning and Private Development in Britain Since 1945* (Cambridge, 2022).
7. O.S. Smith, 'The Inner City Crisis and the End of Urban Modernism in 1970s Britain,' *Twentieth Century British History*, 27 (2016), pp. 578–98.
8. J. Davis, *Waterloo Sunrise: London from the Sixties to Thatcher* (Princeton, NJ, 2022).
9. D. McKinney, *Magic Circles: The Beatles in Dream and History* (Cambridge, Mass., 2003); K. Gildart, *Images of England Through Popular Music* (Basingstoke, 2013).
10. A. Turner, *Goldfinger* (London, 1998): 89.
11. L. Delap, *Knowing Their Place: Domestic Service in Twentieth-Century Britain* (Oxford, 2011).
12. P. Eley, *Portsmouth Breweries since 1847* (Portsmouth, 1994).
13. J.S. Curl, *The Erosion of Oxford* (Oxford, 1971).

Chapter 10
1. Wesley to Matthew Ridley, 26 Oct. 1745, Ashington, Northumberland CRO., ZRI 27/5.
2. Luff to Black, 27 Aug. 2018, email.
3. S. Brett, *The Body on the Beach* (London, 2000), p. 58.
4. Robert to Horace Walpole, 11 May 1716, BL. Add. 63749.
5. Part of letter in *Times*, 15 May 2024.
6. I. Ijeh, *Tall Buildings: A Policy Framework for Responsible High-Rise and Better Density* (London, 2024).
7. L. Scarr, *Gallows Wood* (London, 2024), p. 157.

Index

Abbey of St John, Colchester, 35
Aberdeen
   Roman conquest, 1–2
Abergavenny
   newspapers, 101
Abingdon, 127
   Iron Age enclosures, 1
   monastic foundation, 36, 56
   riot, 15
Addington, Henry, 14
Agar town
   St Pancras, 129
Aire and Calder Navigation, 56
   see also Defoe, Daniel
Albert, Prince
   reform, visit to industrial towns, 122
   see also Birmingham (1843)
Alcester
   poor public health 1727–30, 53
Andover, 103, 118, 137, 153
Anglo-Saxon England, xviii, 6–7
   London, 7-8
   religious sites, xvi
Anne, Queen (r. 1702-14), vii, 2
   Bath visit (1702-3), 95
   'rage of party', 74
Anti-Corn Law League, 121
anti- Semitism, 84–5
   see also Edward I
Antwerp siege, 3
Appleby and Clifford, Sir Roger, 20
Arbury, 107
   see also Newdigate, Sir Roger
Archer, Thomas, 68
   see also London
Ashby de la Zouche, Queen Victoria's Jubilee 1887, 139
Assembly Rooms, 72-3
   see also Bath
   see also Stamford

Atheism, irreligion, 106, 133
Athelstan
   role of towns 12
Atherstone
   book club, 107
atmospheric pollution, 140, 179–80
   see also Broughton, Rhoda
   see also James, Henry
   see also mono-nitrogen oxide
Atterbury Plot(1721-2), 37
   see also Defoe, Daniel
Austen, Jane, *Mansfield Park* (1814)
   Price household, 116
Avon, and urban-based county,171
Axbridge, 33
   see also King John's Hunting Lodge

Bacon, Waller MP
   calico, woollen trade and East India Company, 83
Bailey, H. C.
   Broken Toad (1934), 152
Baines, Edward
   Leeds Mercury, 118
Baker, Robert
   map of Leeds, 117
Bangladesh, 160
Bank of England, 90
Barhaven, vi
   slaving port, 77
   see also Sykes, W Stanley
Barnet (1471), 32
Barnsley, 127
   Brexit, 177
Barnstaple, 114
   Civil War history, 47
   slaving port, 77
Barnwell (1792)
   brick crescent, 98
Barrett, William, 87

Barrow-in-Furness, iron industry and rail link, 126
Basingstoke, 103
Bath, 62, 70, 96, 101, 114, 129
   Circus (1754–64), 96
   display, 164–5
   Elder's Queen Square (1728–34), 96
   'fashionable city' and moral panic, 95–7
   King's Circus (1752), 96
   Palladianism, 96
   place of gallantry, 96
   Pulteney Bridge, 96
   Roman settlement, 11
   Royal Crescent (1767–74), 96
   walks and gardens, 97
   see also Defoe, Daniel and *Moll Flanders*
   see also Smith, William
   see also Wood, John the Elder
Battle (Sussex)
   health issues, 118
Baxter, Richard, Puritan preacher, 44
Beatles, the
   Liverpool depression, 171
   urban renewal, 167
   see also Liverpool
   see also pop music
beatniks, 168–9
   see also Havant
Beckford, slaving port, 77
Bedford
   control of electorate, 59
   see also Bedford, Duke of
Bedford, Duke of and Woburn
   urban development, xv
Berwick, 25
   defences and Civil War, 32
Betjeman, John,
   attacks slum clearance, 146–7
   Swindon housing, 149
Beverley, 24,
   economic problems, 25
Bideford, 77
Bills of Mortality, 52–3
   see also Defoe, Daniel
Birmingham, 76, 90, 106, 108, 112, 122, 126, 129, 138–40, 155, 146, 176, 182
   Albert, Prince and visit (1843), 122
   Austen, Jane, and *Emma, 111*

Birmingham Commercial Herald, 121–2
   city status, xviii
   economic problems, 175
   'gentrification', 97
   libraries (1799), 99, 101
   Murphy Riots (1867), 123
   Queen's College, 138
   St Philip's church, 97
   town description, *London Chronicle*, 103–4
   University of Birmingham, 138
   see also Bolton, James
Bishops Stortford
   English Language Bible, 35
   Marian period items, 35
Black, Cilla
   pop music, 167
Black Death (1348–9)
   rural population, 23
   urban history, 62
Blackbird Leys, xix
   see also Oxford
Blackfriars Bridge riot (1769), 67
Black Friars, Dominicans, 34
Blackpool,
   day trippers, 177
Boards of Guardians
   outdoor relief, 137
   see also workhouses
Boden, John and Derby Lace Works (1830), 113–14
Bodmin, 59
   see also Robartes of Lanhydrock
Bolton, Royalist town, 44
Bolton, Duke of
   control of boroughs, 59
Booth, Charles and poverty maps, 142–3
Boroughbridge, 48
Boston, 13th century fair, 20, 100
Boswell, James
   Falmouth, 98
Bosworth (1485), 32
Boudicca and Iceni, 2, 4
   see also Colchester, London and St Albans
Bournemouth, leisure town, 127
Bradfield, 98

Bradford, 130, 136, 179
  wool industry, 109–10
Bradford-on-Avon
  carding machines, attack, and new technology, 94
Bradford Sanitary Committee, 116
Brandon, John, *A Scream in Soho* (1940), 153
Brazil, 60
Brecon, 101
Bredon, 101
Bremmer, William, and the car 143
Brent Tor, 63
Brentwood
  London links, 3
  poll tax opposition, 14, 23
Brett, Simon, and new public building criticism, 178
Brewer's Tudor style, 150
Brexit (2016)
  towns, 177
Brick Tax (1850), 131
Bridgenorth
  booksellers, 101
Bridgeport
  French landing, 84
  see also French Revolution
Bridgewater, 100–101
Brighton and Hove, 172, 179
  city status, 2020, xviii
  Religious Census (1851), 132
  water pollution, 134
Brind, Richard, 70
Bristol, 19, 30, 57, 66, 91, 106, 115, 129, 136, 155
  Charter, xvii
  Defoe, Daniel, and free market system 19
  double population, 19
  Edward Colston (138-1721) statue, 184–5
  Feast of Corpus Christi, 27, 31, 57
  history, 87–8
  hot wells, 70
  key port and manufacturing centre, 55
  loss of department stores, 175
  maps, 55

merchants and London, 77
newspapers, 100
privateering losses, 77
Southwell, Edward MP, 58
Theatre Royal, 98
transatlantic and international trade, 92
  see also Defoe, Daniel
  see also Millard, James
  see also slavey and slave trade
Bristol, Earl of, 59
Britannia Inferior, 3
  see also York
Bromley,
  stand-alone stores, 175
Bronze Age (2000-800 BCE)
  nomadism and peasant farming, 1–2
Broughton, Rhoda, 'The Truth, the Whole Truth, and Nothing But the Truth' (1893)
  pollution, 140
Bruton, 36, 130
  Abbey Foundation, 30
  damp houses, 130
  silk production, 114
Browne, Lieutenant, Rochard, 79
Buck, brothers, 65
Buckingham, 101
Buck, William
  electoral violence, 85
Bude, 154
buildings and urban wealth, 55
Bungay
  newspapers, 100
Burghs, 10-12
  see also Alfred, king of Wessex (r. 871–99)
  see also Offa
Burlington, Lord, 67
Burgoyne, General Sir John
  fortifications, 134
Burnham, Andy, elected Mayor of Manchester (2012)
  London-centric focus, 174
Burns, John
  Housing Town Planning Act (1909), 151, 158

Burton-on-Trent,
  newspapers, 100
Bury St Edmunds, 15, 100
  by-passes and ring-roads, 162
  Dissolution of monasteries and
    Burghley House, 35
  Peasants' Revolt, (1381), 23
  printing and publishing, 81
  see also Bailey, T

Cadbury hill fort, xvi
Caister, 100
  bishopric post-Viking invasion, 10
Calvert, Sir William
  Jewish Bill, 84–5
Cambridge, ix, 23, 30–1, 101
  attack by mayor, 24
  city status, xviii
  industrial decline, 172
  Peasants' Revolt (1381), 23
  1966 election, 176
  see also King's College
Camden, William
  Bristol origins, 87
Canal building c.1000–1200, 18–19
Canterbury, 2, 8, 10, 23, 30
  Barbarian' conquests, 6
  church centre, 8
  mint and moneyers, 12
  oppida, 8
  prohibition of Christmas, 46
Carbonton
  RAF, 176
Carlisle, 2, 25, 32, 40, 64, 79, 115–16
  Cathedral 34
  cholera, 116–17
  cotton manufacture, 115
  handloom riots, 114
  Pilgrimage of Grace, 36
  siege, 32
  see also Howthaite, Sir Richard
Carlisle, Earl of, 85
Carlyle, Thomas, 108
Carmarthen 11, 107
Carr, Jonathan Dudgeon, 117
Catholic hierarchy reestablished, 123
Cato Street Conspiracy, 120
Catterick, and military rule, 176

Census (1851), 128
  see also Ireland
  see also immigration
Ceolwulf II (r. 874-9), 11
Chadwick, Edward, *Report on the Sanitary
  Conditions of the Laboring Population of
  Great Britain* (1839), 117
Channel Tunnel (1994), 170
Charles I in London and Lincoln
  (1642), 44
Charles II (r.1660-85), 48
  corporate government purse, 74
  Corporation Act, 49
  defeat, 47
  Proclamation xx
  urban planning, 49
Charles III
  support for New Towns, 162
Charles Prince of Wales
  Modernism, 162, 168
Chartist movement, 122
  founded (1848), 133
Chelmsford, as quasi-new town, 18–19
  John Walker map, 30
  rabies cure, 104–105
Chester, 2, 25, 36, 75
  Cathedral vandalised in Civil War, 5
  Roman fortress, 7
Chester, earls of, 15
Chesterfield, 67, 90, 100
  see also Pennant, Thomas,
Chester-Le-Street, 10

Chichester, 2
  former Roman settlement, 11
Chinese immigration, 142
  see also immigration
Chippenham, 94, 101
Christie, Agatha,
  After the Funeral, 155
  One, Two Buckle My Shoe (1940), 146
  The ABC Murders (1934), 153-4
  The ABC Murders (1936), x
  The Dumb Witness (19387),152–3
  The Moving Finger, (1943), 152–3
  The Third Girl (1966), and re-building
    critique, 166
church building, 67–8

Church role in medieval towns, 15
Civil Wars (1642-6), 43–50, 54, 62
   see also Archbishop Willam Laud
   see also Charles I
   see also town divisions
City Elections Act (1775), 68
Clarendon, first Earl, and Clarendon House (1664-70), 55
Clark, George Thomas
   Durham sanitation, 117
Clean Air Act (1938), 159
Cleveland, 171
Clifford, Richard
   urban-rural tension, 20
Cloisterham, 141
   see also Dickens, Charles
Clubman movement, 46
Cnut, king of Denmark, 12
coal as major fuel, 92–3
Coal-based industries and towns, 77–8
Cobbett, William
   Sheffield knives, 108
coinage and trade, 9-10, 12
Colchester
   Boudicca, 2
   Dutch textile merchants, 40
   oppida and Roman city, 2, 4
   Roman capital, 4
   textile production, 92
Colleton, 98
Compton, Spencer, 2nd Earl of Northampton, 45
'Condition of England', class and tastes, 125–6
Congleton, brick crescent(1792), 70
   iron works, 73
Connaught, Duke of and parks (1881), (1885), 135
Cook, Ian and Poundbury, ix
cooperation and rivalry of towns, 153
   see also Hull,
   see also Liverpool
   see also Leeds
   see also Sheffield
Congleton, 70
Contested election, 89
   see also Leicester
   see also Nottingham

Corfe, castle 'slighted', 47
Corporation Act, 49
   see also Charles II
corrupt court, 68
   see also South Sea Bubble
Coryat, Thomas, 72
Costain Richard (1839-1902), 150
council house building, 101–102
council housing and purchase, 152
County and Borough Police Act (1856), 137–8
Court of Burgesses (1585) 41
Courtneys, Earls of Devon, xvii
Coventry, 25, 33, 40, 45, 146
   Civil War siege, 45
   ribbon manufacture, 33, 90, 155
Covid epidemic (2020-2), 53, 62, 150, 174
   air-pollution (2023), 179
   partial return to workplaces, 184
   post-Covid and meetings, 185
Craftsman, the, 83
Cressy, Edward, 122–3
Crewe, 109
Crime Survey of England and Wales, 182
Cromwell, Elizabeth, 69
Cromwell, Thomas,
   Lewes Priory, 35
Crossley, Sir Francis MP and Peoples' Park, Halifax, 135
crowded towns and health, 116-8

Danegeld, 12–13
Darlington, Earl of, 129
   see also Bath
Darlington
   new Parliamentary borough, 136
Dartmouth, 77, 177
   see also slavery and slave trade
Dawlish ,176
   libraries, 114
Decker, Thomas (1522-1622), The *Bellman of London*, xi
Defoe, Daniel
   Aine and Calder Navigation, 56
   Alresford fire (1689), 51
   Atterbury Plot, 37
   Bread (from 1986), 169
   churches and cathedral, 67–8, 73

Index

Colonel Jack (1722), 55
Dixon of Dock Green (1955–76), 170
free market system, 19
greater ships, xx
Great Plague, 52-3
Ipswich, 66
Liverpool, 77
London trade, 66
Maidstone Assembles, 71
Moll Flanders (1722), 52,69
Nottingham Guildhall, 72
present state of towns, shipping and trade, xix, xx
religious toleration in towns, 74
Roman Catholics and Dissenters, 88
Roxana (1724), 69
'rotten boroughs', 48-9
Till Death Us Do Part (1965–70), 169
The Royle Family, 169
The Sweeney (1975-81), 169
wealth of Londoners, 73-4
Wilton House, 56
York Assembly criticism, 71
see also Pembroke, Earl of
see also South Sea Bubble
see also Mansion House
see also City Elections Act (1725)
see also slavery ports
diocesan system reorganisation, 15
Derby, 75,78
　ethnic cleansing and female exploitation, 183
　see also Gull, Sir John
Derby, Earl of
　political influence, 85
Devon and Exeter Hospital, 98
Devonshire Duke of
　Eastbourne, 129
Dewsbury
　female woollen workers, 139
Dickens, Charles, 11–13
　Hard Times (1854) 111-12
　Nicholas Nickleby (1838–9), 112–13
　Pickwick Papers, village life and cricket, 147
　The Old Curiosity Shop (1840–1), 112
Dick Whittington, 9
diphtheria and measles and the poor, 130

Domesday Book (1086), xvii
Dover and defence, 134
Droitwich, 101
Dullborough, 113
　see also Dickens, Charles
Dunwich
　North Sea storms, 25
　Viking invasions, 10
Durham, ix, 10, 92
　Brexit, 177
　new cathedral, (1004), 126
　Viking invasions 10
　see also Smollett, Tobias
Durham Report in London *Daily Post* (30 January1731), xii

Ealing, 163
Earl Gower, 59
Earl Robarts, 59
East Central Motorway, 177
Economic growth and population, 93–4
Eden, William, trade envoy, 108
　Nottingham stocking industry, 108
Edgar (r.957-75), 16
Edgware, 158
Edward I (r.1272–1307)
　New Winchelsea, 19
　revocation of London liberties, 32
　see also London
Edward IV (r.1461-70), 27
　see also London
Edward the Confessor (r. 1042–66), 12–13
　see also Wessex dynasty
Edward the Elder,11
elected mayors, 185
　see also Burnham Andy
Eliot, T. S., *The Waste Land* (1923), 110
Elizabeth I (r.1558-1603)
　and ecclesiastical settlement 37
　see also Mystery Plays
　see also Spanish Armada
Elstree, 157
　see also New Towns and Green Belt
Ely, 100
　city status, (2020), xviii
English Civil War and regional variations, 38
　see also Civil Wars

Enlightenment and faith, 106
  see also Wesley, John
  see also Methodism
ethnic change, 159–62
  see also immigration
ethnic tension and 'grooming', 183–4
  see also Rotherham
Evelyn, John, 60,
  fire at Truro and stone buildings, 51-2
  Frost Fair, (1683-4), 43
  praise for small towns (17–2), 60
  Stuart Restoration, 48
Evesham,
  urban environment, 54
Exeter, xv–xvi
  Civil War and for Parliament, 44–5
  crisis of Exeter Election and *Western Times* 3 July 1852, 135-6
  Devonshire Bank (1770),98
  Dissenters, 61
  Exeter Bank (1769), 98
  Exeter Council and latrines, 38
  fire damage, 61
  Labour hold, 172
  Law Courts (1773-5), 98
  Methodism,106
  new draperies, 32
  population, 31, 33
  prosperity, 24
  rebellion, 36–7
  Roman port, 2, 32, 45, 57, 64, 98, 155, 157, 172
  Roman settlement, 11
  siege, 45
  slaving port, 77,111
  The Devon and Exeter Hospital (1743), 98
Exeter Trust, 66
Exmouth
  libraries, 114
Eyres, John
  map (1765), 116

Falmouth
  trade with Portugal, 60
fashionable areas in twentieth century, 142–3
Feines, Celia, 55-6

Fenwick, Thomas, and newspapers, 101
Fielding, Henry, 85
  corrupt court, 68
financial and economic crisis, 168–9
fire danger in London and list of towns, 51
  as major issue, 82
  Great Fire of London, 52
First Civil War (1642-6)
  Church of England, 46
  large town backing Parliament, 44–7
  Parliamentary towns, 45–6
  reflection of town divisions 45-6
  Royalist towns, 44–6
  sieges, 45
  see also James Duke of Youk and James I
  see also Laud, Archbishop William
  see also Civil Wars
Flemming, Ian and Modernism, 166
  see also Trellick Tower
Frederick, Duke of York
  denunciation of sale of commissions in army,118
French Revolution, town responses, local paranoia, 108
Fulford (1066), 11,
Full Monty, the, (1997), 170

Gainsborough, iron works, 73
  Parker Morris Standards, 165
Garden City Movement, 149
  see also Howard, Ebenezer
Garnett, Jeremiah, 122
Gateshead, stand-alone Metro Centre, 175
Gay, John
  Beggars' Opera (1728), xi
General Strike (1926)
  Labour in support in industrial towns and Conservative provinces, National Government (1935),155
Gentleman's Magazine
  new rich system, 116
George I, 60
George II, 82
George III, 105
  Buckingham House, 67
  London critique, xiv
  loyalty to, xiv

observed by Josiah Reynolds, xiv
Portsmouth visit, xiv
Germany and Coventry, missile and air attack, 155
see also Coventry
Gillow, Richard, 95
Gissing, George, urban poverty and painting *Workers in the Dawn* (1880), 129
Glasgow, and radical violence, 115
Glastonbury, 36
Glastonbury Abbey, 35
Glastonbury tor, 55
'Glorious Revolution' (1688-9)
City of London, 50
parliamentary elections, 83
towns, xxi, 57
Gloucester, 36, 44–5
assessment of, 24
Civil War and fortifications, 45–6
Civil War siege, 23
colonia, 2, 14
communications with, 91
effect on towns, xxi
'Glorious Revolution' 57
new port, 3
Godalming, xiv
Gosforth, and urban growth, 140
Grafton, Duke of, Duke of Grafton's Servants, 98
see also Norwich Comedians
Grantham, 100
Great Agriculture Depression(1870s), 127–8
Great Casterton, 11
Great Fire of London, 52
Sun-Fire Office, 52
see also Defoe, Daniel, *Moll Flanders*, 52
see also fire danger
Great Frost Fair (1683–4), 43
'Great Hospital' Norwich, 36
see also Norwich
Great Plague (1555), 52
flight from London, 52–3
see also Defoe, Daniel
Great Irish Famine (1845-51), 123
see also immigration
see also Ireland

Great Yarmouth
brewer immigrants, 25
Dissent, 88
major regional port, 24
mercantile business, 59
see also Craggs, James
Greene, Maurice (c.1696-1755), organist, composer at Chapel Royal, Master of King's Music, 70
Greenwood Housing Act (1930),163–4
Grosvenor, Sir Richard, 67
Guildford
cathedral and city status, xviii
Gull, Sir John,
defeated Royalist in Derby, 45
see also Compton, Spencer, Second Earl of Northampton

Hadleigh and cloth production, 24
Atterbury Plot (1721-2), 37
Halifax
newspapers, 78
Halle Orchestra (1857), 138
Hamilton, Guy
pop music, 167
pronunciation, 167
Handel, G. F., 70
Hanse Merchants
Steelyard in London, 26
Hargreave, James
spinning jennies, 94
Harley, Edward Lord
salt panes in South Shields, 55
Harold Harefoot,
Viking assault, 12
Harris, Reverend, the
Darlington Horticulture Society and taste, 125
Harley, Edward Lord
salt panes in South Shields, 55
Harrison, Thomas, provincial architect, 95
Harthacanut (1016-42),
Viking assault, 12
Hartlepool
independent borough, 136
independent port 114
Harlow New Town, 162
see also New Towns

Harrow, Garden Village, 146
Havant, 169
   beatniks 168–9
   machine-made net and lace, 113
Heathcoat, John,
   machine- made lace and net and riot damage,113
Henry I
   London Bridge toll, 17
   see also London
Henry II, 27
   Exchequer to London, 13
   London, 22
Henry III, 14
   opposition, 22
Henry VI, 35
   loyalty to London, 27
   see also King's College, Cambridge
Henry VIII
   cathedral status, xviii
Hereford, 45
   Clubmen, 46
   bishopric, (680), 11
   burgh (893), 11
   poor communications, 91
Honiton, fires (1747,1765), 82
Hook, Andrew,
   newspaper proprietor and urban history, 87
'Hooligan' panic, 141–2
   see also London
Hopton Heath (1644), 4, 45
Horton, 101
House price increase, 1987–2016, 179
Housing
   costs and ownership, 80, 179
   improvement, 134, 164
   Thatcherite 'revolution', 163
   see also Resolution Foundation
Housing Act (1980), and right to buy, 106–107
Housing Act (1988), and Housing Associations, 179
Housing Association Provisions, 179–81
Housing Town Planning Act (1909), 158
Housing Working Classes Act (1890), 134
Hove, see Brighton and Hove

Howard, Ebenezer (1850-1928), *Tomorrow: A Peaceful Path to Real Reform* (1898), 149
   see also Garden City Movement
Howthwaite, Sir Richard, execution after Pilgrimage of Grace, 35–6
Huddersfield, 114, 176
   Luddites and woollen trade, 119
   see also Luddism
Huguenots, 60–1,160
   see also immigration
Hull, 25–6, 155, 171
   Civil War siege, 45
   fortified in Civil War, 32
   royalist town, 44
   see also Defoe, Daniel
Humberside, urban-based county, 171
Huntington, 100
Hutton, William, and history of Birmingham,104
   see also Birmingham

Ilfracombe, 163
'Improvement' as national policy, 122–3
Improvement Classes Act (1847), 134
Industrial Revolution precursors, 42
industrial towns importance, 76–7
Industry and towns, 110
inequalitarian society, 39–40
Interregnum (1649–60), 47, 49
   Parliament, 48
   see also Civil Wars
Ipswich, 23, 66, 123,176
   Anglican worship, 123
   leading port, 9
   see also Black Death
   see also Defoe, Daniel,
   see also Peasants' Revolt
   see also Taylor, Dr Rowland
Ireland, xxi
   Parliamentary union, xxi
   slaves,77
   woollen industry, 77
   see also Great Irish Famine 1843-51
   see also immigration
   see also Murphy Riots
Iron Age, 2
   oppido, 2
Islamic extremism, 184

Jacobite army at Carlisle and Derby, 64
Jacobite rebellion
   Wesley, John, 173
James II (r. 1685-8), 49, 57
James, Duke of York a failure as James II
   urban politics and destruction of
      meeting houses, 47, 55
James, Henry
   fog, *London and Paris Compared
      (1866)*, 140–1
Jarrow and March, 139
   see also Wilkinson, Ellen
Jefferson, Thomas
   Civil Wars victory at Worcester, 47
Jewish Community
   Expulsion, 18
   Jewish Naturalisation Act (1753)
      repeal, 85
   see also anti-Semitism,
   see also Edward I
John, Archduke of Austria, 90
John, King, 16
   see also London Collection
Justices of the Peace and influence, 39
Juvenile gangs, 140

Kendal
   immigration to towns, 21
Kenilworth, and 'slighted' castles, 47
   see also Civil War
King's College, Cambridge (1471)
   clearances for chapel site complete
      (1515), 35
   see also Henry VI
King's Lynn, and foreign brewers, 25–6
   Kett's Rebellion, 37
King's Sutton, major fire, 106–107
   see also fire damage

Labour governments (1945--57), 157–8
   see also New Towns
   see also Green Belts
Laing, John William (1879–1978), 150
Lamborne and branch line1864), 127
Lancaster, 172
   slave trade, 77
Langport and Clubmen, 46

Lansdowne, William, Marquess of, see
   Liverpool industrialization, 91
Laud, William, Archbishop
   Arminianism and theology, 44
Lavenham
   cloth production, 24
   Guild of Corpus Christi (1528–9), 33
Lawrence of Ludlow (c.1250-94) and wool
   trade, 21
Lawrence, D. H., 'Nottingham and the
   Mining Countryside', 149
Layer, Christopher, Jacobite and report of
   execution, 82
Ledington, and contrasting building
   styles, vi–vii
Leeds, 78, 106, 115, 120, 140, 176
   Conservative coalition, 136
   large parish of chapelries and
      curacies, 132
Leicester
   drink maps, 133
   election riots, 89,
   General Strike (1926), 155
   leisure and seaside resorts, 127
   'new draperies', 32
   stocking frames riots, 94
   Viking invasion,10–11
leisure and seaside resorts, 127
Levenson Gowers, 129
Lichfield 8
   Offa of Mercia, 8
   quasi new town, 18–19
Lincoln
   Charter, xvii
   Roman forte, 2
   Roman river port, 3
   Vikings, 11
Lindisfarne, and Viking invasion,10
Liverpool, 64, 115, 128, 133, 138, 156,
   172, 176
   Beatles, The, 167
   housebuilding and park suburbs, 128–9
   key port for North America and
      Caribbean, 91
   slave port, 91
   slave trade,77
   third most populous town (1801),116

Index   215

Livery Companies, 41
Lloyd George, David
    'Homes fit for Heroes', 151
Local Government Act (1894), 136
Local Government Act (1972), Avon,
    Cleveland and Humberside, 171
Local Government Association report
    (2014) and underachievement, 175
local news and economic value, 102–104
Lombe, Thomas
    Italian silk machines, 78
London, 2–3, 8, 11, 26, 28, 31, 38, 40, 57,
    70, 75, 80, 90, 114–16, 148, 166, 168,
    170, 173, 175
    Anglo-Saxon Kingdom, 7-8
    atheism and irreligion, 133
    A-Z, and street maps, xv
    Boudicca, 2
        after Boudicca's revolt, (60 CE), 4
    Building Act 1894, 134
    capital of state and crime, xi
        see also Gay, John
    citizenship, 17
    Common Council, 18
    Court of Aldermen, 18
    Court of Burgesses (185), 41
    Cultural community, 69–70
    Domesday Book (1089), xvii
    fortification in Civil War, 45
    'Glorious Revolution', 50
    Greater London Council abolished, 171
    Guilds and Livery Companies,
        16–17, 41
    Immigration from New
        Commonwealth, 159–161
    Lord Mayor's Show, 41
    Magna Carta (1215), 18
    Mary Spital and famine, 1
    Mayor and Corporation, 41
    Mayoral elections, 18
    militant dock workers, 171
    Jewish Community, 18
        see also Edward I
    Pope Gregory's Archiepiscopal, 8
        as moneyer, 12
        communal growth, 13
        Edward the Confessor and
            Westminster Abbey, 13
    population move, 173–4
    poverty maps, 142
        see also Booth, Charles
    prime residential property, 67
    rail and tube links, 163
    relationships to kings, Edward I,
        Edward II, John, Henry III, Henry
        VI, 22
    Re-building Acts, 51
    Roman establishment Thames, 3–4
    Roman London, 4-7
    Roman settlement, 5–6
    slum clearance, 142, 172
    smog, 159
        see also Wentworth, Patricia, Ladies'
            Bane (1954)
    squares, 64, 66, 69, 147
    Stationers' Company, 49
    tradesmen, 65–6
    Treasury, 13
    Tudor London and immigrants, 40
    underground building, 141
    underworld, 141
    under the Stuarts (1603–1714), 23
    William I and London, 13 check
        collection of laws and customs, 16
    wards, 18
    Westminster relationship, 40–1
    women's rights, 17–18
    see also Defoe, Daniel
    see also for literary comment, Christie,
        Agatha, Hickory, Dickory Dock (1955),
        Nicholas Blake (Cecil Day Louis) and
        The Worm of Death (1961)
    see also Greater London Council
    see also Great Fire, the
    see also Great Plague, the (1665)
    see also Nelson, George
    see also newspapers
    see also Harley, Sir Richard
    see also insurance, Sun Life Office
    see also Walpole, Sir Robert
London destination for graduates
    2021, 173
Londonderry, Marquess of, 120
Longbridge
    housing after Tudor Walters Report
        (1918) 151

Long Melford
  cloth production, 8 ,100
Lorac, A. C. R., *Checkmate to Murder*
  (1944), 155–6
Lorimer, William, 84–4
Louth
  St John's Abbey, Colchester, 35
Lowry, L. S.
  Going to the Match and *Lancashire
    League Cricket Match* (1953), and
    urban working class, 167–8
Lucas, Sir Thomas, 35
Luddism, 119–20
  see also Nottingham
Luff, Peter MP
  local newspapers, 177
Lundenwie, 7
Luton, 146
Luttrells, the of Dunster Castle
  control of Minehead
    'rotten borough',120
Lyme Regis, 45
  Civil War siege, 45
  'Reform Meeting Lyme Regis' 121
Lyne, Richard
  Cambridge map (1574), 30
Lyttelton, George
  fires, 105
  see also Montague Elizabeth

M4 corridor, 171
Macclesfield, 73, 90
Magna Carta (1215), 18, 22
  see also London
Maidenhead, 146
Maidstone, 23, 54, 71
  paper-making, 32
  see also Defoe, Daniel
Maister House, Hull, 95
Malling,
  declaration of war with Spain, *St James'
    Evening Post*, 20 December 1718, xx
Malton and historic high street, 174
*Mapping the Past - Wolverhampton
  1577-1986*, xvi
maps and mapping, xv-xvi
Margate, 127, 172

market development, 19–20
Manchester, 44, 48, 115, 116, 120, 121,
  133, 136, 138, 155, 176
  as 'chimney of the world' and
    pollution, 140
  incorporated (1835), xvii
  industrial dispute, 94
  Little Italy,166
  popular music, 175
  St Anne's Square, 64
  'un-English' flats, 165
  WHO guide lines for mono-nitrogen
    air pollution, 178
  see also Watkins, Absolum
Manchester Corporation Act (1946), 159
Manchester Small Weavers Society, 94
Marlborough, 101, 162
  parish church and Dissent, 105–106
markets and fairs growth, 20
  see also Boston
Marston Moor (1644), 45
Martin, Sir Josiah and Mason Science
  College (1880), 138
Mass Observation Survey (1943), 156
Mary I (r.1553-8), 37
  London support, 28
  see also Wyatt, Sir Thomas,
  see also Boston
McCulloch, John, and description of
  Manchester, 125
McDonald, A G, *England, Their England*
  (1933), village life and cricket, 147
Mearns, Andrew, *The Bitter Cry of Outcaste
  London* (1883), and urban poverty, 129
Members of Parliament, MPs, and
  towns, 75-6
'Mersey beat', 167-8
  see also Beatles 171
  see also pop music
Methodism, 108
  see also Wesley, John
Metropolitan Railway Country Estates
  Limited, 146
'middling sort' of town society, 98–9
Migration, 21
  from country to town, 128
  from Ireland, 128

poor relief, 41–2
see also Ireland
Mildenhall, 123
Millard, James, and maps of Bristol, 55
Milton Keynes and economic success, 162
Minehead, xx
see also Defoe, Daniel
Ministry of Health report on coal fire
   pollution (1920), 132
Mithras, 3
Mock-Tudor houses, 148
see also Orwell, George
Modernism and critics, 165–6
Mono-nitrogen oxide pollution, 178–9
Montague, Elizabeth, 105
Moor Park Preston (1867), 135
Moral panics 2000 -2010, 133, 183–4
Morcombe, 127
Morley, John, *Life of Gladstone* (1903)
   prostitution, xii
mortality rates and children, 130
Morton H V, and non-Modernist
   tradition, *In Search of England*
   (1927), 147
MPs and towns, 75
   see also Chester and items in
   Birmingham Journal 21 May 1730
   see also Thompson, Edward MP
Mosley, Oswald, failure (1959), 160
Municipal Corporations Act (1835), 6, 136
   police forces in London (1829),
      provincial towns, and upsurge in local
      politics, 120-1
murder rate low compared with USA, 183
Murphy Riots (1867), 123
   see also Birmingham
mystery plays, 27, 37–8
   see also Elizabeth I

Nantwich
   Elizabeth I, 39
   major fire (1583), 30
Nash, Richard, 'Beau', 96
   see also Bath
National Grid Power
   electricity revolution, 154
Newark, 100, 120
   see also Henr, Duke of Newcastle

New Buckingham
   Buckingham Castle household, 19
Newbury, 103
Newcastle, ix, 57, 78–9, 91, 97, 124, 128–9,
   136, 138, 155, 163, 176
   Assemblies, 72
   border town, 42
   coal, 54, 56
   fortress against Jacobites, 95
   defences in Civil War, 43–4
   post-Civil War, 54–5
   rooms, 95
   theatre, 95
   see also Foster, Mules, Birket
   see also Gissing, George
   see also Mearns, Andrew
   see also Scotland
   see also Scott, William Bell
Newcastle-under-Lyme
   social change and violent politics, 120
   see also Levenson Gower
New Commonwealth, 159
   see also immigration
Newdigate, Sir Roger, 107
'new geography' and canal-rail links, 115
new industrial development, 94
New Maldon and South Koreans, 161
Newquay, 127
newspapers and press, 78–9, 99–106, 109,
   119, 121–2, 136, 177–8
   see also Luff, Peter MP
new technology and towns, 113–14
New Territories and Hong Kong and
   high-rise towns, 165
New Towns Act (1946), 158
New Towns and Green Belts,
   157–8, 162–3
   Labour Government, 162
   see also New Towns check
New Winchelsea
   Edward I, 19
non-Modernist tradition, 146-7
   see also Morton, H. V.
Northallerton
   Whigs and Dissenters, 74
   see also Defoe, Daniel
Northampton, 11, 20, 45, 51, 101
North-Eastern Railway, 127

Northfield, 140
North Shields, 136
Norwich, 15, 23. 26, 31,30, 57,64, 71, 81, 93, 106 ,113, 133, 147
   Assemblies, (1754), 72–3
   fire damage, 39
   Flemmings immigration, 26
   'Great Hospital', 36
   middle-class Dissent, 147-8
   'motte and bailey' castle, 14
   Quaker Meeting House, 61
   regional capital, 70
   replaced by Bristol as England's second town, 53
   town loyalty, 50
   urban renewal, 54
Norwich Comedians, the, the Duke of Grafton's Servants, 98
Nottingham, 15, 89, 91, 120, 136, 182
   Luddism centre, 119-20
   new Guildhall, 72
   regional capital, 70
   stocking industry,78
   see also Defoe, Daniel
   see also Luddism
Notting Hill Carnival (1959), 160
Notting Hill race riots, 160
Nuneaton, 107, 175
   see also Newdigate, Sir Roger

Offa and London and Mercian towns, 8, 10
Orwell, George, 9, 148
   The English People (1947), 148
   'The Lion and the Unicorn' (1941), 148
Oxford, 78, 146
   as fast-rising tax paying town, 176
   burgh, 11
   ethnic tension and 'grooming', 183
   Labour hold, 1966, 172
   Oxford House mission, 133
   St Ebbs, 172

Paighton, 176
Parker Morris Standards, and low-rise council estates,165
parks, 134-5

park suburbs, 123
   see also Liverpool
Paycock's House, Coggeshall, 33
Peasants' Revolt, (1381), 23
Pembroke, Earl of, 56
   Wilton House, 56
   see also Defoe, Daniel
Pennant, Thomas, manufacturing dynamism, 90
   see also Chesterfield
   see also Macclesfield
Pershore, 101
Peterborough, 100
   Fletton bricks, 150
Peterloo New Town, 162
   see also New Towns
Peterloo Massacre (1819) ,120
Peter the Great, and London shipbuilding, 90
Phelps, Edward, 94-5
Pickford, Joseph, architect (1734-82), 73, 95
Pilgrimage of Grace, 36–7
Pinney, William, MP unseated at Lyme Regis for bribery, 121
Plymouth, 44, 98, 155, 157, 159
   Civil War siege, 45
   cholera (1832), 113
   Royalist in Civil War, 44
   slaving port, 77
   urban working class, 113
Police forces establishment, 121
   see also London, Metropolitan Police (1829)
political social, economic and cultural history, xii
Pontefract, 47
   political and religious conflict, 49
Poplar pastimes criticism, 105–106
Pool of London (1951), film and black discrimination, 160
Poole, 77, 102
   slaving port, 77
Poor Law Amendment Act 1834
   care and workhouses, 118
   poor relief, 93–3
Pope, Alexander
   An Essay on Criticism (1711), 69–70

Population density and suffering, 128–9
Porlock,
　harbour for greater ships, xx
　see also Defoe, Daniel
ports and rail links, 126–7
Portsmouth, 99
　defence, 134
　slaving port, 77
Postlethwayt, Malachy
　Universal Dictionary of Trade and Commerce (1766), 65,
Poundbury
　Cook, Ian, ix
poverty, ill-health and pubs, 144–5
Preston, 176
　city status 2002, xviii
Priestley, J. B.
　English Journey (1934), place and Englishness, 147
Priestly riots, 103
Primrose League, 123–4
Printing and urban national culture, 34
Provincial newspapers, 100–7
Public Health Act (1875), 134
　cellar dwellings, 131
　parks, 135
　see also Town Improvement Act

Ramsgate, 127
Rayner, Angela, 181
　see also New Towns
Read, Mathias, Lake District painter (1669-1749), 98
Reading
　biscuits, 116
　Royalist town, 44
　siege, 4
Recreation Grounds Act (1854), 135
Redbridge, and Indian origin population, 160
Redistribution of Seats Act (1888), 136
Reform Act (1832)
　towns, 120
　see also 'rotten boroughs'
Reform Acts, Second (1867) and Third (1894), 136
Reformation
　'modernity, 28

monastic suppression, 34–8
town crisis, 62
town Protestantism and Catholicism, 38
towns status, 28
religion and tension in towns, 85, 123
religion, social problems and poverty, 132–3
Religious Census, (1851), 132
　see also Brighton
Rent and Mortgage Interest (War Restrictions) Act (1915), 163
Resolution Foundation, 179
Restriction of Ribbon Development Act (1935), 149–50
Retford, 100
Reynolds, Josuah, xiv
Rhode, John
　gadgets, *The Invisible Weapons*, (1938), 154–5
Ricart, Robert, 28
Ricci, Marco
　Views of the Mall from St. James Park (c.1710), 69
Richborough,
　Kent port and Roman links, 3
ring roads, inter-city motor ways, 163
Rochdale, 139
　ethnic tension and 'grooming', 183
Rochester, 30
　bishopric, 8
　Cathedral, 34
　city status, xviii
　diocesan centre, 8
Roe, Charles, 92
Roman Britain ends 409–10 CE, 5–6
Rotherham
　ethnic tension and 'grooming', 183–4
Rotten, Johnny, 170
　see also Sex Pistols
Rowntree, Seebohm (1871-1954), 144–5
　Poverty: A Study of Town Life (1901), 144
　Poverty and Progress, 145
　Poverty and the Welfare State (1951), 145
Royal African Company
　control of slave trade, 77

Index 221

Royal Commission on Housing and
    Working Class, 1884–5, 134
Royal Commission on the Metropolitan
    Police (1906-8), 138
Rupert, Prince
    threat to four towns, 46
    see also Civil War
Ryder, Sir Dudley
    Jacobites in Derby, 88

Salisbury Corporation, 103, 118
    Frederick, Duke of York, 118
    see also George III
Salkeld, Lancelot, 36
Salvation Army (1856), 138
    see also Booth, Charles
Sandwich
    as leisure town, 139
Scarbrough
    day-trippers, 177
    displacement of elite, 24
    spa town, 70
Scotland
    border town fortifications, 41
    Parliamentary union, xxi
    see also Newcastle
Sefton, Earl of, and Sefton Park
    (1872), 135
Seifert, Richard, and Centre Point
    (1967), 166
service and manufacture, 73
Shaftesbury
    local and national politics, 121
    monastic foundations, 36
    Municipal Corporations Act,121
Shakespeare, William
    dialect, strangers and distance, 38
    'rabblement', in *Julius Caesar*, 38
Shakleton, Robert
    industrial pollution, *Touring Great
        Britain* (1914), 112
Shaw, George Bernard, *Widowers' Houses*
    (1892), 129
Sheffield, 47, 90, 106,120, 139
    major steel production for Europe, 114
Shepton Mallet, 94
Sherborne, 101

Shrewsbury, 70, 101
    burgh, 11
Sidmouth, 114
Silchester, 2
    oppida, 2
Skegness for day-trippers, 177
Skipton, 47
slave trade and slave ports, 77, 91
    see also Barnstaple, Bideford, Dartmouth,
        Exeter, Lancaster, Plymouth, Poole,
        Portsmouth, Topsham, Whitehaven
Slough, 146
Smith, William
    *Particular Description of England with
        the Portraits of Certain of the Chiefest
        Cites and Towns* (1568-88),30
smokeless zones, 159
Smollett, Tobias
    electoral corruption, 85
    Launcelot Greaves (1760-1), and clash of
        interest ad culture, 83
social system in towns, 80–1
Somerset, Duke of, 59
Soothill, W F, and 'quiet
    social revolution',158
Southend
    city status xvii-xviii
    leisure,127
Southhampton
    militant dockers,171
    naval base and Normandy invasion, 25
    organised crime(2024),182
    'rookeries', 117
    spa development, 99
    Thames bridge link, 11
South Hornchurch, 150
South Sea Bubble, 68
South Shields, 77
Southwell, ecclesiastical centre, 8
Spalding, 100
Spanish Armada (1588)
    anniversary of defeat, 1588, 38
    danger to English towns, 32
    see also Elizabeth I
Speed, John,
    town plans, 47
    see also Civil War

Speke, 151
Sport boom, 135
squares, 64, 66–7, 69
Stafford House of Correction, xii
Stamford, 11, 100
   burgh, 11
   Palladium Assembly Rooms, 95
Stamford Bourne Mill
   Lucus, Sir Thomas, 35
Stamford Bridge (1066), 11
Stephen (r.1135–54), 14
Stevenage New Town (1948), 158
Stockport, population, 91
Stockton, 114
Stoke, industrial centre. 90
St Albans
   Boadicca, 2
   monastic foundation, 15
   oppida, 2
St Austell, 176
St Cuthbert and Durham Cathedral, 14
St Germanus, Bishop of Auxerre, 5
St Ives, 100
   vagrancy, 168
St John the Baptist Warwick Hospital, 35
St Michael's Glastonbury Tor, 35
St Michael's, Honiton, 34
St Neots, 100
St Pancras, 172
St Paul's Cathedral (167597, 1711), 67–8
   Marco Ricci, 62
   see also Sir Christopher Wren (1675-97)
Stafford, 101
stand-alone shopping centres, 175,
Stephson, Robert and railway engines, 125
Stevenage New Town, 158, 162
Stoke and canal and link to canals and rail, 115
Stoker, Bram
   Dracula (1897), 141
Stourbridge, 101
Stratford-upon-Avon
   as ecclesiastical centre, 8
   wells, 140
Stow-on-the Wold, 101
Stuart rule (1603-1714), 28
Suburbs and literary support, 146–8

Sunak, Rische, and High Speed 2, 174
Sunderland, 90, 120, 155
   coal export, 177
   ethnic change, 159
   world ship-building, 126
Sun Life Office, 67
   see also Great Fire
Swaffham, 127
   see also Great Agricultural Depression
'Swinging London', 168
Sykes, W. Stanley (1894-1961)
   The Missing Money-Lender, (1931), vi

Tacitus, Roman historian and Britons, 3
tall buildings, 180-1
Taunton, 9
   Civil War, 46–7
   Royalist town, 44
Tavistock, 59
Taylor, John Edward, founder of
   Manchester Guardian, 122
Taylor, Dr Rowland (1555)
   Marian persecution, 37
   see also Defoe, Daniel
   see also Mary, Queen
Teignmouth, 114
Telford, Thomas
   Grand Union Canal, xii
   Monford Bridge, xiii
Tenniel, John
   Punch cartoon of dream of electricity, 143
Tenon, Jaques, 105
'Ten Years of Tax: How Cities Contribute to the National Exchequer' (2016), 176
Tewksbury (1471), 32
Thatcher, Margaret, and Conservative Governments (1979-1997)
   crime and living standards, 181
   government opposition, 27
   'Workshop of the World' decline, 170
Thompson, Edward, MP York, 75
Tiverton, 99, 113
   fire (1598), 38–9
Topsham, slave port, 77
Torbay
   day-trippers, 99

tower block estates concern, 164
town cooperation and rivalry, docks and rail, 153
town and consumer society, 80-3
Country Act (1947), 158
Town and Country Planning Act (1969), 166
town discontent at industrial development, 94
Town Improvement Classes Act (1847), 134
towns as investment centres, 107
towns and Parliament, 21–2
towns and the press, 78–9
  see also newspapers and press
towns urban renewal and industry, 54-5
Towton (1461), 32
traditional terraced housing, 131–2
  see also Public Health Act (1875)
Trent to Burton navigation and brewing (Act of 1699), 56
Trier, 4
Troubridge, 94
Tudor Walters Report (1918), 151
  see also Housing Town Planning Act (1919)
Tunbridge Wells, 70
  'display', 95
Truro
  prosperity, 176
Turner, William
  successful Whig candidate assaulted (1742), 86
  see also Buck, William
Turnham Green (1642), 45
Tyne and Wear, 171

ULEZ (Ultra-low emission zone), ix-x
Usk, Thomas and small towns, xix

Vagrancy Laws and beatniks, 168–9
  see also beatniks
Vanbrugh, John, *The Release* (1696),73
Vernon, James
  food riots, 43, 61
Vernon, John
  weather-related dearth (1693), 43

Victorian Society (1958), 165–6
Viking invasions, 11–12
  Five Boroughs and Danish *farldom* 11
  Stamford, 11
  see also Athlestan
  see also Cnut, King of Denmark and Norway
  see also Wessex, House of

Walker, John
  map of Chelmsford, 30
  matches 'Lucifers' and fire risk, 114
Wallingford, 47
Wallpaper Tax (1661), 131, 132
Walpole, Sir Robert
  criticism of ministry, *Daily Courant,* 86
  Norwich poll disturbances, 76
  replacement of (1742), 87
Walthamstow, 140
War of the Spanish Succession and unregulated press, 57
Warwick, 101
  lack of industrial base, 24
Warwick, Earl of
  leadership challenge at Northampton, (1796), 108
Watford, 146
Watkins, Absolum (1787-1861),121
  see also Municipal Corporations Act
Watling Street, 3–4
Wedgewood, Josiah, and Eturia, 73
Weldon, John (1676-1736), and music, 70
Welwyn, 146
Wembley Park, 146
Wentworth, Patricia and *Anna Where Are You* (1933), vi
West Ham, 139, 140
Wesley, John and Newcastle's poor (1845), 173
  see also Methodism
Westminster Bridge
  new route over Thames, 67
Westminster, distinct from London, xii, 40–1
West Riding
  domestic production of woollens, 93

Index 223

Whitacker, John
  The Charter of Manchester translated with Explanations and Remarks (1787), 87
'White flight' (2008–2018), 173–4
  see also migration (1830–7)
Whitehaven, 77
White, Thomas, and Nottingham Guildhall, 72
William I, 13
  castles and Tower of London, 14
William II and Carlile castle, 14
  Cumbria (1092), 108
William III (r. 1689–1702)
  'rage of party', 74
William IV (r. 1830–7), vii
Wilkinson, Ellen MP
  Jarrow March, 153
  The Town that was Murdered (1939), 153
Wilkinson, John
  mill at Birmingham, 90
  see also de La Rochefoucauld, Francois and Alexandre
Wilson, Harold
  support for Beatles, 168
Winchcombe, *burgh*, 11
Winchester, 4,8
  City Mill, 30
  'Glorious Revolution', 50
Winstanley, Hamlet (1694–1756), 98
Wise, Henry, Queen Anne's gardener
  the Mall,69
Woking, 146
Wolverhampton, xvi, 163, 90, 103, 112, 115, 117, 128, 135, 139
  city status(2000), xviii
Wood, John, the elder
  Bath and Palladianism, 96
Worcester
  Civil Wars major siege, 44
  low growth rate, 78

textile production, 92
Royalist and fortifications, 45
urban expansion, 31
Wordsworth House, Cockermouth, 95.
Workhouses, 118
  see also Poor Law Amendment Act (1834), 118
Workington (1862–74)
  iron and steel works, 126
'Workshop of the World' decline, 170
  see also Thatcher, Margaret
World War One (1914–18)
  A-Z Atlas and Guide, 156
  end of German submarine threat and food imports,148
  German air raids,153
World War Two (1939-45), 132

Yarm and Tees crossing, 91
Yonge, James, and 'rude and brutish' locals on Bent Tor, Dartmoor, 61
York, Lieutenant Colonel Joseph MP
  London size, x–xi
York
  archepiscopal status (725), 8
  Assemblies, 71
  Civil Wars siege, 45
  clubs for upper and middle classes, 144
  economic problems, 25, 31
  kingdom of Northumbria, 8
  Labor win in 1966 election, 172
  new port, 3
  Pilgrimage of Grace, 36
  Roman fort 2
  unhealthy life, 9, 31
  see also Defoe, Daniel
  see also *Britannia Inferior*
Youlgrave, 93